Managing the Presidency

Published by the University of Pittsburgh Press,

Pittsburgh, Pennsylvania 15260

Copyright © 1986, University of Pittsburgh Press

All rights reserved

Feffer and Simons, Inc., London

Manufactured in the United States of America

Library of Congress Cataloging-in-Publication Data

Campbell, Colin, 1943–
  Managing the presidency.

  (Pitt series in policy and institutional studies)
  Includes index.
    1. Presidents—United States.   2. United States—
Executive departments.   3. United States—Politics and
government—1977–1981.   4. United States—Politics and
government—1981–   .   I. Title.   II. Series.
JK518.C36 1986   353.03′1   86-4069
ISBN 0-8229-3537-6

To my fellow Jesuits

Frederick William [IV of Prussia] found himself in one of those situations he most enjoyed, so energetically assailed by conflicting advice from different quarters that he could bask in the sensation of decision-making while in fact simply allowing his advisers to cancel each other out.—Edward Crankshaw, *Bismarck*

I practiced this method [consultation of cabinet] because the harmony was so cordial among us all, that we never failed by a contribution of mutual views on the subject, to form an opinion acceptable to the whole.—Thomas Jefferson

Contents

Tables

Figures

Acknowledgments

This is my fourth book. As I look back over the last several years in which it took shape, I am reminded once again of the fact that a work such as this simply would not have reached this point without the assistance of a host of dear friends.

First among these is Donald Naulls—a graduate student of mine while I was at York University in Toronto. Naulls began on the project in 1980. At first, he concentrated on the task of preparing machine-readable files of interview data from the Carter administration. By 1982–83, he was working for me full-time. He involved himself in every dimension of the project, including verification of interview transcripts, coding of responses, making the Carter and Reagan data sets as compatible as possible and conducting most of the computer runs. We engaged in days of lively discussions about various aspects of the project. Ultimately, Naulls chose to use the data base for his dissertation and we have coauthored two chapters for edited collections that are spinoffs of this project. While the completion of this book marks my loss of a faithful research assistant, it celebrates the continuation of a deeply valued colleagueship. And Naulls's wife, Kathy, deserves a special note of thanks for her generosity and understanding throughout the project.

Gail Lyons—also formerly of York University—had acted in much the same capacity as Naulls when I was preparing the Carter data for use in my comparative book, namely, *Governments Under Stress: Political Executives and Key Bureaucrats in Washington, London and Ottawa*. I treasure all of her contributions that eventually found their way into this book. For example, her meticulously prepared codebook withstood superbly the intrusion of sixty Reaganites. Others from York who served as research assistants include Robin Esco, Margaret Evans, Lucinda Flavelle, Bruce McLeod, and Mark Sudnick. As well, Patricia Humenyk completed many of the interview transcripts for the Carter segment of the study.

Nothwithstanding the advent of the word processor, no project as large as this would get far without first-rate secretarial support. During the interview phases (1979 and 1982–83), I relied heavily upon the Work Place in Washington, D.C., for typing. There Jean Levin, Beverly Nadel, and Stephanie Haftel did most of the interview transcripts. When I joined the faculty at Georgetown, Stephanie Haftel became the first secretary for the "Martin Chair." She typed and corrected innumerable drafts of the manuscripts of this book. In summer 1985, Jenefer Ellingston became my secretary. Her stylistic criticism helped me smooth out the final drafts. And she prepared the index for the book.

Before I joined the faculty at Georgetown, the Brookings Institution provided a Washington base by granting me two separate guest scholarships. Several administrators at the institution made my stays there memorably pleasant. These include Bruce MacLaury, the president, Neil Cullen, Bernadette Toomey, and Dianne Hodges. As for the community of scholars at Brookings, I simply could not have found a better group of people for exchanging views on this project. However, I would like to give special thanks to Joel Aberbach, Martha Derthick, Stephen Hess, Robert Katzmann, Herbert Kaufman, Charles Levine, Paul Peterson, Paul Quirk, James Reichley, Bruce Smith, Gil Steiner, and James Sundquist.

I received my financial support for this research from several sources. At a critical stage in which I was coding the Carter data, York University gave me a Faculty of Arts Fellowship (1980–81). My York sabbatical and a Leave Fellowship from the Social Science and Humanities Research Council of Canada (SSHRC) permitted me to take 1982–83 off in order to conduct the Reagan interviews. Through numerous grants between 1979 and 1983, the SSHRC also provided abundantly for my secretarial and research assistance. Finally, my chair—established by the late Edward Martin—allowed me to write this book in two years. As well, it supplied all the necessary physical support for generating numerous drafts of each chapter. Meanwhile, my deans, Peter F. Krogh of the School of Foreign Service and Richard B. Schwartz of the Graduate School, have lent their enthusiasm for the scholarly component of the obligations associated with the Martin Chair.

Bert A. Rockman, the editor of the Pitt Series in Policy and Institutional Studies, played a crucial role in the development of this book through his unfailing encouragement, depth of scholarly insight, and incisive criticisms. As well, several other colleagues—not already mentioned in the Brookings litany—left their mark on the book through oral or written comments or simply a published work which has had a strong influence on my grasp of the presidency. Apologizing in advance for serious omissions, I should specifically mention: James Christoph, Fred Greenstein, Matthew Holden, Paul Light, B. Guy Peters, James Pfiffner, Nelson Polsby, Roger Porter, Richard Rose, George Szablowski, Norman C. Thomas, Richard Watson, Stephen Wayne and Margaret Wyszomirski. Jane Flanders helped immensely with her numerous queries for clarification as she guided this book through the various phases of production at the University of Pittsburgh Press. And Frederick A. Hetzel, director of the press, began enthusiastically to support the concept of the book as far back as 1980.

I deeply appreciate the help of the 192 officials who consented to be interviewed for this project. Although they must remain nameless, many, in fact, have become valued friends. No amount of praise would do justice to the unstinting way in which most public servants in Washington will contribute time to worthy scholarly research.

My final words go to the people to whom this book is dedicated. The unquestioning support of my fellow Jesuits has really served as the sustaining force behind my scholarship. By way of one very concrete example, my superiors allowed me a research year in 1978–79 which enabled me to take a leave from York and conduct the Carter interviews. As well, I was granted the Martin Chair largely through the persistence of James A. Devereux, S.J., the rector of the Jesuit Community at Georgetown, Timothy S. Healy, S.J., the president of the university, and J. Donald Freeze, S.J., the provost. In the course of this project, I have lived in four separate communities, all of which have provided ideal circumstances for the priest-scholar. These are Bellarmine Residence in Toronto, Carroll House, the Georgetown Jesuit Community, and the Woodstock Jesuit Community in Washington. Again, I hesitate to list names. However, the following Jesuits' dedication to our order's commitment to scholarship has strengthened me especially in the course of writing this book: Walter Burghart, Michael Fahey, Thomas Gannon, Joseph Gavin, John Langan, Richard McCormick, Jacques Monet, Leo O'Donovan, Brian Peckham, Thomas Reese, George Schner, Joseph Schner, and Jeffrey von Arx.

Managing the Presidency

1. The Presidency, Executive Harmony, and the State Apparatus

When we speak of the *president* we actually refer to three things. We have individual presidents, including their unique personalities and the peculiar clusters of issues and crises that they face. We have, as well, "administrations." This term evokes images of a president's style that take in an incumbent's adeptness at rallying and sustaining public support for his most cherished policies and goals. It also implies the skill with which he appoints and directs his coterie of partisan advisers and officials, both within the White House and in the departments and agencies. Finally, we have the "presidency." Beyond the character and times of individual presidents, and the vagaries and coherence of their appeal and advisory systems, there is the ongoing office. Each incumbent fleshes out the presidency in a different way. In the process, each contributes to, or detracts from, its legacy.

What do we mean by the legacy of the presidency? Clearly included here are the explicit and implicit prerogatives of the office. To be sure, individual presidents alter these by seeking and attaining congressional enactments, pressing and winning cases before the judiciary, issuing and implementing executive orders, and generally interpreting and safeguarding the Constitution. However, the presidency also denotes a gargantuan collection of disparate institutions.

Closest to the president, there exists the White House Office. Various incumbents organize this office differently. But few observers question the need for a large and specialized staff of loyal appointees dedicated to the task of balancing the president's personal goals, partisan commitments, public trust, and executive prerogatives.

One step removed, the Executive Office of the President (EOP) provides a polyglot resource centered mostly upon the president's relations with the formal governmental apparatus of the United States. Most of the partisan appointees in EOP work in a neo-baroque wedding cake next to the White House. The oarsmen largely base themselves in a ten-story, red brick monstrosity across Pennsylvania Avenue. And the oarsmen are overwhelmingly career civil servants. Thus, EOP comprises a polyglot for two reasons. It houses staffs concerned with such diverse matters as management and budget, economic advice, national security, domestic policy development, trade, environmental quality, and science and technology. It represents as well an amalgam—albeit loose and uneven—of the partisan responsiveness of appointees and the bureaucratic acumen of permanent officials.

The monumentally severe buildings that line Washington's triumphal avenues contain the operational side of the presidency. Everything that takes place in these structures occurs in the name of the president. A passenger about to land at National Airport can barely glimpse the corners of this vast imperial complex. One building—the Pentagon—could readily accommodate the entire central administration of all but a handful of nations. Yet the Constitution states emphatically that all authority exercised behind these oppressively bureaucratic facades emanates from the president. It matters little that most advanced democratic nations view executive powers as shared collectively by chief executives and their cabinet secretaries. Nor does it count that leading experts on the comparative study of executive leadership consider collegial government essential in modern, complex political systems.¹ Formally, the U.S. presidency incorporates the entire state apparatus.

It has become a truism that not every incumbent interacts well with these three concepts associated with his job. As incomprehensible as the thought might strike us, not every president remains in touch with his own character, including its limitations, or understands his times. In this respect, Jimmy Carter never adequately checked his penchant for detail while Ronald Reagan almost flaunts his ignorance of the world beyond the White House lawn. As well, presidents vary greatly in their execution of administrative style. Jimmy Carter frittered away his public support by failing to pare his agenda; he also selected his advisers poorly and let them run helter-skelter after their own projects. Ronald Reagan staked out simplified objectives; he also assured that his appointees satisfied loyalty tests and maintained a sense of teamwork.

With regard to the state apparatus, Jimmy Carter succumbed to a fascination with every nut and bolt. Ronald Reagan and his closest aides held much of official Washington in "contempt." Their attitude did not even spare permanent officials in such neutral-competence units as the Office of Management and Budget. Historically, these civil servants have associated themselves strongly with the long-term interests of the presidency.

For the most part, studies of U.S. presidents have focused their attention on matters of character and style. This has been to the detriment of thoroughgoing inquiries into the nature of incumbents' relationships to the presidency. In a sense, the conventional wisdom has assumed that incumbents can survive despite poor relations with the ongoing apparatus of the presidency. Assessments of fatal faults in character, such as Nixon's venality or Carter's compulsion for detail, thicken the presidential plot by showing how vulnerable the highest office in the land is to personal foibles. Likewise, the study of whether his times proved auspicious for an incumbent uncovers the element of luck in executive leadership. Evaluations of presidents' styles and the organization of their advisory systems tap the intriguing process whereby political resources are harnessed and utilized or, in many cases, squandered.

On the other hand, a focus on incumbents' relationships to the legacy of their office can appear to exist on a level of abstraction unnecessary for those trying to understand the presidency. Time and again, the question arises whether the degree to which individual presidents engage the apparatus of state makes much difference to their own and their administration's performance and record. This book argues strongly that no president or administration can be fully understood without thoroughly linking character and performance to the task of governance.

Take the instance of Jimmy Carter. He became mesmerized by the state apparatus because its intricacies intrigued him. Yet he lacked a countervailing sense of how to put *his* administration through its paces. On the other hand, Ronald Reagan has revealed excellent political timing and his administration has manifested exceptional internal discipline. However, his principal initiatives have either run roughshod over or ignored the positive craft of governance embodied in the standing resources of the executive branch.

The further we get into the Reagan years, the more this administration's failure to engage the state apparatus becomes clear. Tax simplification provides a clear instance. Only a pale reflection of the original plan will ever come to fruition under this president. Unlike across-the-board tax cuts, it requires more than snake-oil tours to pass through the bureaucratic labyrinth and Congress. Regarding the Pentagon, the administration has, if anything, weakened the preparedness of the services. No municipal police force would purchase a fleet of Cadillacs to improve service and reduce costs. Yet the Reagan administration has come perilously close to doing the military equivalent with this nation's national security establishment.

Many observers will note that some presidents can escape being held to account for their inattention to governance. After all, Ronald Reagan has maintained his popularity and renewed his mandate. His equivalent of Cadillac patrol cars has spruced up the neighborhood and renewed almost everyone's sense of national esteem. At the same time, many people believe implicitly that we all will crash one day into the appalling ineffectiveness and diseconomy of his approach. Yet we will have to wait until history renders its final judgement before we know for certain. In this respect, the case of Dwight Eisenhower proves instructive. As Fred Greenstein has noted, Eisenhower had lulled the nation into the belief that he was a do-nothing president. In retrospect, such accomplishments as ending the Korean war, exercising caution in the expansion of domestic welfare programs, controlling inflation, and restraining military expenditures stand up very well against the achievements of Eisenhower's more popular successors. They came from what Greenstein terms the "hidden-hand presidency." Perhaps Eisenhower engaged the apparatus of state selectively, but he did so effectively. Greenstein writes:

> As long as Eisenhower had established general guidelines within which departments were to operate he was prepared to leave many specifics to the department secretary. . . . Knowing that a president who attempted to do everything would wind up accomplishing nothing, Eisenhower made substantial delegations in some areas in order to have a maxium impact in others. Part of his style . . . was assessing who could be left to operate reasonably independently and who should be monitored or even supervised. Another part was to delegate without

abdicating by promulgating clear general guidelines and by fostering in colleagues a strong sense that they *should* pull together.[2]

Eisenhower thus struck an approach to office that optimized his strongest character traits. He did this by reducing public expectations for ebullient leadership and quietly carrying out the affairs of state. This book will not end up prescribing this approach for all presidents. It does, however, hope to serve as a caveat against the behavior exhibited by three types of incumbents: presidents who are in too great a hurry to learn how to utilize *all* of the resources of their office available for the implementation of their policy objectives; those who lack a sense of proportion about the utility of the various parts of the executive branch; and those who are so ahistorical that they fail to see that posterity rather than polls will judge an administration's contribution to the nation's tradition of executive leadership.

Expectations for Presidents and Underutilization of the State Apparatus

During the past twenty years, Americans have become acutely aware of the presidency's immense burdens. Since John F. Kennedy, every incumbent of this most powerful position in the West has left office politically broken. In assessing why recent presidents have tended ultimately to collapse under the pressures of office, we find almost too many causes. Post–World War II presidents lead a bloc as much as a nation. The immense pressures of the thankless task of giving some direction to the West grinds down presidents, especially as it becomes more difficult to persuade allies of the urgency of the "Soviet threat." At home, the American public has gone on an antigovernment binge. This has led to the ruin of many candidates with extensive Washington experience even very early in presidential races.

Ironically, the electorate's messianic expectations for presidential candidates conflicts with the lynch law of its judgments of presidential performance. High expectations are manifested in voters' obviously firm belief that an untried quantity will set things right simply because he seems to be a sincere and able leader who owes members of the Washington establishment relatively little. Lynch law sets in through the disillusionment that seizes even true believers when incumbents adapt to the folkways of Washington or, much worse, make one or two big mistakes.

One of the tasks of this book is to cut to the very heart of this irony. Is there not something fundamentally defective about the national state of mind whereby wonders are expected from presidents who are untainted by experience? If presidents must be *in* but not *of* Washington, and—above all—avoid errors in judgment, what can be done to give them a firmer grasp on the executive branch?

Much of the state of crisis surrounding the U.S. presidency stems from the notion that part of the president's job is to help avoid calamities. We should not view this as an illegitimate and, therefore, dangerous expectation. To the contrary, the finest hours of the presidency seem to have occurred during America's most perilous times. In this century, Franklin Roosevelt's legacy rests upon the unparalleled accomplishment of leading the United States through both a depression and a world war. Although everyone was traumatized by Kennedy's assassination, would the nation's deep sense of loss be as intense as it remains today had John F. Kennedy not brought it through the most daunting episode of the cold war—the Cuban missile crisis?

Americans are fond of looking to the United Kingdom for ideas about how executive leadership might operate more effectively here. As with U.S. presidents, British prime ministers who have led their nation in times of crisis have won the strongest reputations in the popular mind. David Lloyd George and Winston Churchill brought order to chaotic war efforts. Yet British prime ministers who have distinguished themselves in handling crises also have left a deep imprint on how their country's executive branch does its business. That is, they have not stopped at addressing the crises of the day. They also have altered existing political and bureaucratic structures with a view to assuring that future governments might call upon better processes and machinery for treating episodes that threaten national viability.

During and immediately after World War I, Lloyd George pursued so many ambitious reforms of the British cabinet and bureaucracy that he continues to be regarded as a visionary even in the latter fifth of this century. His central organizational concepts, such as the need for a distinction between "inner" and "outer" circles of cabinet and the "garden suburb" of partisan policy advisers working exclusively for the prime minister, continue to guide the agenda for innovations within the British executive.[3] Indeed, Lloyd George's views have informed innovations on this side of the Atlantic. Winston Churchill's organization of the cabinet during World War II so impressed George Marshall and James Forrestal that they worked during and after the war for the adoption of a similar national security process in the United States.[4] While their reforms fell short of a panacea, the Joint Chiefs of Staff, the Department of Defense, and the National Security Council largely owe their existence to the efforts of Marshall and Forrestal.

A very important point emerges from the Lloyd George and Churchill cases. Under cabinet systems of government, leaders— no matter how inspiring during times of crisis—must be able to summon innate organizational genius. This has not been the case with U.S. presidents in this century. The U.S. involvement in World War I was too short to adequately test the organizational mettle of Woodrow Wilson.[5] His health gave out before he could begin to pursue adequately his ambitious plans for the postwar era. Notwithstanding the fact that many institutional reforms took place during his administration, Franklin Roosevelt gave little personal attention to organizational matters.[6] His intellectual adroitness and political skill made it possible for him to obtain most of what he wanted from the executive branch through sheer force of personality.

Kennedy inherited from Eisenhower the most heavily structured cabinet system the United States had ever known. Kennedy's advisers argued that Eisenhower's elaborate organizational machinery had preordained the lackluster quality of his administration by overcooking issues.[7] The new president decided, thus, to ignore or dismantle cabinet structures. He pursued this tack relentlessly. In fact, students of foreign affairs, in assessing Kennedy's handling of the Cuban missile crisis, suggest that it constitutes one of the most dramatic triumphs of personal judgment over organizational reflex ever documented.[8]

Why is it that presidents, even in times of impending calamity, rely much less on cabinet and bureaucratic organization than do prime ministers? Why indeed have U.S. administrations, even especially memorable ones, left much less of a lasting structural imprint upon the executive branch than have their contemporaries in the U.K.? The answer, however obvious, merits restatement. Presidents rely much less upon collegial cabinet dynamics and the resources of the permanent bureaucracy than do prime ministers.

U.S. chief executives' personal styles and agendas shape their administrations' policies much more readily than prime ministers' approaches determine the course of British government.[9] Presidents are not disembodied spirits. However, they more readily delude themselves into thinking they are than do prime ministers. Moreover, the U.S. public loves presidents to act decisively. That is, they expect them to exercise the broad prerogatives imparted by the Constitution.

A Liberal senator in Canada who created, minded, and restored the images of two Canadian prime ministers during the last twenty years coined a term to distinguish between the style of Pierre Trudeau and his perhaps too Canadian and therefore low-key predecessor, Lester Pearson. Trudeau, the senator noted, had "royal jelly." That is, he had a presence that left nobody asking, "Who's in charge here?" In the United States, royal jelly comes with the office of president. Incumbents can neglect, even override, organizational considerations so easily because the Constitution grants their office immense latitude for highly personalized executive leadership. Woodrow Wilson perhaps stated it best when he wrote:

> The president is at liberty, both in law and conscience, to be as big a man as he can; . . . his is the only national voice in affairs. Let him once win the admiration and confidence of the country, and no other single force will withstand him, no combination of forces will easily overpower him. . . . His office is anything he has the sagacity and force to make it.[10]

A Flaw Made Worse by Crisis Inflation

For nearly forty years now, the United States has not experienced a calamity. One must acknowledge the Korean War and those exceptionally tense days in October 1962 when it appeared that a nuclear holocaust was imminent. Even granting some exceptions, the period since the end of World War II has proved to be exceptionally dull. The United States simply has not faced an enduring military, political, or economic crisis that day in day out has riveted the national consciousness on a struggle for survival. Vietnam veterans can speak eloquently to this point. They came from the war theater to find that the heroics of their life-and-death struggle did not impress a populace that had lost interest in the war. Indeed, the reasons behind the war effort had been roundly denounced as wrong.

The American system of government and way of life became threatened fundamentally more by the war's continuance than by any external danger.

As early as 1867, Walter Bagehot noted—with special reference to the presidency—that the absence of circumstances capable of destroying a political system makes the task of a chief executive more difficult, not less.[11] To begin, public attention becomes extremely fickle. Chief executives find themselves grasping for issues that might congeal or strengthen their electoral mandate. By the time they have cajoled other political leaders and nudged the apparatus of state toward a course of action, public attention often has scattered in myriad other directions.

Here a very serious temptation, afflicting presidents more than prime ministers, enters the calculus of leadership. Chief executives can rekindle public interest through astute use of crisis inflation.[12] To maintain public attention, they can make matters appear more urgent than they actually are. Even in good times, they can inflate the credit due them by exaggerating the severity of previous conditions. Thus, Ronald Reagan spoke in January 1984 of the Carter years as "the long night of our national calamity."[13]

The adverse consequences of crisis inflation as related to the quality of executive leadership provided by presidents constitutes a central concern of this book. Crisis inflation allows incumbents to govern with smoke and mirrors rather than with the state apparatus. By its nature, it abuses the public trust and weakens the fabric of democracy. The rest of this chapter will examine why it is a particular danger in the United States. First, however, I will offer two accounts, one from Canada, the other from the U.K., that demonstrate the general nature of the problem.

In 1980, Canada's Pierre Trudeau canceled his plans to leave government when his party called upon him to lead it back into power. After a resounding victory, he set as his top priority completion of the constitutional reform process, called patriation, within two years. This would have allowed him to leave politics as the prime minister who finished the work left incomplete by the founding fathers at the time of Confederation in 1867. Brushing aside the counsel of career bureaucrats who had been inching discussions with the provinces forward since the election of Quebec's separatist government in 1976, Trudeau turned to a young political appointee who contrived an acrimonious constitutional convention.[14] This would serve as justification for unilateral federal action on the grounds that the provinces were trying to destroy Confederation. Unfortunately for Trudeau, the adviser's detailed plan was leaked to the government of Quebec which, in turn, made it public. Undeterred, Trudeau embarked upon his unilateral strategy until a humiliating Supreme Court rebuke forced him to abandon it two years later.

The other account has to do with Margaret Thatcher and the Falklands crisis of 1982. Even as early as summer 1980, Whitehall officials had identified flaws in Thatcher's leadership style which made the fact that the Argentinians ever attempted and completed an invasion eminently understandable. She had little respect for cabinet procedures and even less for the career public servants who managed the flow of business.[15] She tended to throw herself into frays case by case, with little reflection on the larger picture. Whitehall had plenty of warning about a possible Falklands invasion.[16] It simply could not get the issue into the overseas and defense machinery. Mrs. Thatcher had allowed it to become clogged with a battle between Her Majesty's Treasury and the Ministry of Defense over the size of the British fleet. Under James Callaghan, Argentinian rumblings in 1977 had led to British placement of a secret Falklands "trip wire," a nuclear submarine and two frigates, which could nip an invasion in the bud. Under Thatcher, the case did not reach the docket in time. She was too busy making sure she won her battle over the size of the fleet. Had she adopted a wider executive compass, the Falklands situation would not have slipped through her administrative net.

In these two illustrations, Trudeau and Thatcher got themselves into such trouble because they had failed to operate effectively as chief executives. That is, they did not utilize fully the resources at their disposal through cabinet-level mechanisms and the career civil service. It is important for students of the presidency to keep this in mind. Collective decision making and engagement of the permanent bureaucracy do not always occur properly even in cabinet systems of government. The *Times* of London made this point in March 1984 while reporting the cabinet's dissatisfaction with Mrs. Thatcher's highly personalized style:

> Ministers increasingly voice concern . . . about the way key decisions are being taken by Mrs. Thatcher and small groups of ministers without reference to the full Cabinet—a practice which they say has contributed to failings in the presentation

of policies. One minister said privately last week that Mrs. Thatcher probably has used Cabinet less than any prime minister since the war. Some MPs are calling for a return to genuine *Cabinet Government.*[17]

In this regard, presidents must exercise even greater caution because of the weakness of U.S. cabinet dynamics and permanent bureaucratic cultures. As well, presidents shoulder heavier burdens than prime ministers by virtue of the intensity of the challenges faced by the United States today.

The Gravity of Being President

A cluster of especially intense difficulties relates to conditions that arose in the 1970s and profoundly altered the geopolitical context of the presidency. Successors to Franklin Roosevelt had already discovered that it is indeed more difficult to wage peace than war. However, the debacle of Vietnam brought home to most Americans the futility of foreign wars not vital to national security and lacking public support. Yet, trying to ignore the taunts of lesser powers can prove too agonizing for the world's mightiest nation to bear. Even more devastating, the facility with which Third World countries obtain from one or another supplier the means to defend themselves frequently makes quick action in the face of clear provocation impossible for the United States. The Iranian hostage incident proved that. Some might say that the Grenada invasion shed new light on the matter. To the contrary, the widespread delight in the United States over such a modest achievement points up the severe constraints to foreign intervention.

In the vast majority of foreign affairs matters, the president must resort to negotiations rather than force while working toward resolution of crises. The normalization of U.S. relations with China and the Camp David Accords did not occur with the flick of a wrist. They required the steady hand of presidents who, whatever their failures, effectively utilized the state apparatus in these two instances to achieve stabilization against formidable odds. Such counsel applies doubly to U.S. relations with the Soviet bloc. Even the strongest advocates of nuclear deterrence must surely recognize that the current distemper in U.S.-Soviet relations makes a mockery of arguments mustered in support of the arms race as insuring "national security."

On another front, every advanced liberal democracy has encountered much more severe economic conditions in the 1970s and 1980s than it had during the 1960s. Americans have felt these pressures acutely in that they have signaled the end of the nation's unrivaled domination of the Western economy. The combination of high labor costs, increasing dependence upon imported oil, and the aging of the country's industrial plant would have undermined U.S. paramountcy even under the best of world economic conditions. The 1973 and 1979 jolts administered by the Organization of Petroleum Exporting Countries drove the message home in stark terms. More fundamentally, the U.S. economy had never really recovered from the Vietnam War. The nation's simultaneous pursuit of guns and butter from 1964 to 1971 lost ground for the United States that probably will never be recovered. Thus, since Vietnam and the energy crisis, presidents have inherited a much less resilient and less powerful economy than that taken on by any predecessor at least since Franklin Roosevelt.

The continuing sense of economic drift has prompted presidents to adopt extreme economic strategies even though these hold out little practical hope of full implementation and/or produce side effects as dire as the original conditions under treatment. For instance, President Carter thought he could bring the economy out of stagflation by achieving a balanced budget. The 1979 energy crisis erased any hopes of even approaching this goal. President Reagan concocted a combination of tight monetary policy, a 23 percent cut in personal tax rates, and budget deficits on the order of 200 billion dollars. Eventually, consumer and military spending sprees perked up the economy. However, the hangover has many wondering if the strongest possible dose of every drug known to man is a remedy at all.

The immense fragmentation of the U.S. political system has contributed to the difficulty of being president. Of all the advanced liberal democracies, the United States operates with the clearest distinction between the executive and legislative branches. In addition, the relative openness of the political system to particularistic claims serves as the hallmark of American democracy. Yet, many scholars of the presidency wonder if the U.S. system has placed too much trust in the dynamics of separation of powers.[18] They resort to terms such as "subgovernments," "iron triangles," and "atomization" to describe the current situation. That is, detailed policy initiatives present the administration of the day with the daunting necessity of accommodating entirely new clusters of interest groups and bureaucratic and congressional forces.

Under such circumstances, presidents can quickly hobble themselves by loading their plates with more detailed legislative proposals than they could ever guide through the Washington labyrinth in twenty, let alone four, years. Jimmy Carter almost embodied this style of presidential leadership. On the other hand, a president attempting to avoid the pitfalls of detailed initiatives might be tempted to promote only blunt legislative proposals. Such measures, of course, fail to satisfy American democracy's central characteristic: relatively evenhanded responsiveness to particular concerns.[19]

Key members of Ronald Reagan's staff acknowledged this imperative when they pressed the "fairness issue" in the White House early in 1983. However, the central elements of Reagan's legislative agenda have remained so sparse and so often reiterated that school children must be able to recite by rote the words, "Cut taxes and social programs and raise defense spending." The dysfunctions caused by working in such broad strokes have raised compelling issues. The tax cuts failed to adequately stimulate capital investment largely because they did not target sectors of the economy; cuts in social spending left so much "anecdotal" poverty—as it was styled by some adminstration officials—that Mr. Stockman's safety nets appeared patently ineffective; and increases in defense spending beyond the wildest expectations even of the Pentagon simply encouraged the services in their wastefulness and promotion of marginal programs.

A New Approach to the Institutionalization Issue

A growing number of knowledgeable observers of the presidency have shown interest in organizational issues. Many of these have argued for the enhancement of cabinet consultation.[20] They also have advocated greater use in the White House's policy shops of appointees with significant experience in Washington and seasoned civil servants. Such measures would allow presidents to engage themselves more fully in the positive art of statesmanship. As for presidents, both Jimmy Carter and Ronald Reagan styled themselves as "new brooms" who would approach their office untainted by experience in Washington. Reagan perhaps can thank the fact that California operates a more complex state government than that of Georgia. He at least made more astute use of cabinet-level committees and old Washington hands than did Carter. Nonetheless, executive leadership as a presidential art remains largely on hold. On many major issues, Reagan's sweeping and highly idiosyncratic agenda leaves little room for detailed input from cabinet secretaries and their departments.

An unresolved conundrum forms the backdrop for any examination of the institutional development of the presidency. In fact, raising the issue really unravels an intricate puzzle. By its nature, the problem throws back at us the question, "institutionalization for whom or for what?" Organizational developments within a specific administration might run counter to the long-term power of the presidency while serving an incumbent. We can envision, likewise, circumstances in which the opposite might obtain. As well, institutional changes might serve both the president and the presidency. Or they might advance neither. Indeed, struggles between incumbents and the legacy of their office frequently do not come out as events that fit neatly into win-or-lose categories at all.

It helps here to contemplate two intersecting axes (see figure 1).

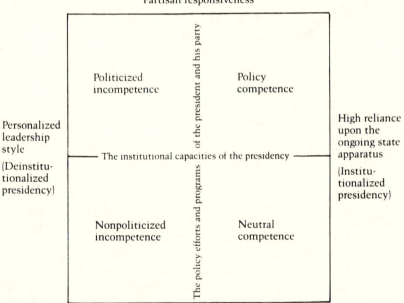

Figure 1. The President, the Presidency, and Policymaking

One depicts a *president* gaining or losing; the other, the *presidency* gaining or losing. With this scheme in mind, we can pinpoint myriad locations where winning or losing would be matters of degree. In all instances, the size of a president's victory or defeat would be related to the magnitude of the presidency's fate and vice versa. Studying how individual incumbents get along with the presidency is not like opening the sports page to find whether a favorite basketball team has triumphed again. Instead, it involves tracking an individual's performance within the context of an unfolding—often cyclical—historical process. Very few soundings will tell us definitively who/what won/lost. And we must interpret each occurrence within the wider frame of an unending process. This book thus departs from scholarly approaches eager to cast the institutionalization of the presidency in clear-cut, win-lose terms.

One such win-lose treatment, by Terry Moe, deserves automatic inclusion in future anthologies. Moe's work forms part of the Brookings Institution's assessment of partisan realignment in the wake of the Reagan presidency. It distinguishes itself by styling Reagan a winner in his bout with his office. However, it also sets itself apart by locating this outcome within a simple linear process. To Moe, a succession of dominant incumbents has eroded the institutionalized presidency's viability in the labyrinth of power. Moe becomes especially deterministic when recalling Nixon's efforts to politicize the Office of Management and Budget: "All of these fit into a larger pattern of institutional development; and they extended that pattern in ways that, while sometimes excessive and politically unwise, were consistent with both its historical trajectory and the institutional forces behind it."[21]

Such approaches as Moe's contain a faulty assertion at the heart. They correctly warn against the naive view that the presidency operates best when the norms of *neutral competence* prevail. Neutral competence criteria start from the premise that presidents best pursue and safeguard the interests of the United States when— while seeking information, expertise and coordinative capacity— they give due regard to the capabilities and integrity of established resources. These include the Office of Management and Budget, the cabinet, and the permanent bureaucracy. However, many critics of neutral competence press their case too far. They do this by setting up a false dichotomy.

Critics of the established resources of the presidency assert that incumbents are only vaguely interested in their potential capacity for neutral competence. In fact, they maintain that incumbents really seek *responsive competence.*[22] As employed by Moe, this term refers to the benefits accruing to presidents from centralization of the institutional resources in the White House and the politicization of the federal bureaucracy. Such measures offer to presidents the attractive combination of "responsiveness, flexibility, and strong incentives to circumvent established organizations and vested interests."[23]

We can err seriously if we assume that responsiveness of the state apparatus to *a* president assures its full and competent engagement in the pursuit of *his* goals. Too many presidents, not to mention their appointees, have failed at sorting out ends and means for us to retain the unquestioning trust that centralization will actually benefit an administration. As well, even badly bashed permanent bureaucrats under deeply politicized regimes take solace in the fact that "this too will pass." In other words, they devise strategies for limiting the damage.

Thomas Cronin has coined the term "presidentialists" for those who place exceptional stock in the capacities of the centralized and politicized administrations.[24] Such scholars, he maintains, betray strong reservations about the responsiveness of permanent bureaucracy and the administrative utility of the cabinet. They believe, in other words, that the president must almost singlehandedly orchestrate the affairs of state. Cronin views this perspective as wrongheaded. By its nature, permanent officialdom serves up "complexity, diversity, jurisdictional disputes, and bureaucratic recalcitrance."[25] Any president who only tries to override these institutional factors, rather than to master and redirect them, simply has not taken charge in the fullest sense of the word.

Along similar lines, Bert Rockman maintains that measuring presidential success involves at least four clusters of skills.[26] These include public presence, intraelite relations, organizational and management ability, and policy knowledge and analysis. Rockman argues, in addition, that the especially intense demands of the U.S. presidency place a premium on the adroitness with which incumbents activate their various skills as fully as possible: "The U.S. president, like leaders elsewhere, is engaged in multiple games, but is apt to be engaged in more of them, in more contradictory ways, and to be facing more formidable obstacles to achievement than leaders in most other industrialized democracies."[27]

Rockman registers his most serious concern when making the point that a president's political competence should not overshadow his policy competence. The latter complements and taps the immense capacity of the presidency to maintain its long-term legitimacy through policies oriented toward the national interest. Presidents tend to hold politics nearest and dearest to their hearts. Yet, policy competence permits them to attain some significant level of historical perspective. It also allows them to draw from any native "managerial propensity" whereby they might actually "move decisions along, effectively coordinate them, and have a sufficient informational base to make them."[28]

Figure 1 above represents schematically the conflicting objectives surrounding such terms as *neutral competence* (or *responsive competence*) and *policy competence*. It portrays two intersecting axes. The horizontal line represents developments that enhance the institutional capacity of the presidency. The vertical line represents particular presidents' efforts to make the state apparatus more responsive to their programs. Broadly, we can envision four conditions emerging from the interaction of incumbents' orientations toward the institutional presidency and responsiveness. *Politicized incompetence* results when exceptionally partisan, ideological, and/or egocentric presidents choose to ignore the state apparatus and do whatever they can get away with politically. *Nonpoliticized incompetence* characterizes the drift that occurs when incumbents succeed at neither redirecting nor fully engaging the institutional presidency. On the other hand, *neutral competence* emerges when presidents—while capably managing the day-to-day affairs of state—fail to leave their stamp through initiation and implementation of innovative policies.

Policy competence arises among incumbents who—along with ones ending up with politicized incompetence—harbor a compelling desire to leave their mark on history. However, those attaining policy competence successfully work from the premise that their goals can be accomplished best through use and reform of the institutional presidency. Thus they believe that they must tap a workable mix of three classes of resources. These include the White House staff and political appointments in departments and agencies, centers of neutral competence such as OMB and selected segments of the permanent bureaucracy, and the routinized dynamics associated with executive-branch control and coordination.

The Task of This Book

This work starts with the assumption that few presidents consciously eschew the requisite elements of policy competence. However, many find themselves incapable of achieving it. That is why the cases of Jimmy Carter and Ronald Reagan are so compelling. The former desired perhaps more than any president to creatively engage the state apparatus but failed miserably politically. The latter plays down—even disdains—the institutional presidency and continues to triumph politically. Yet even Reagan's avid supporters are hard pressed, when asked, to detail precisely how he has governed. In fact, slogans such as "Let Reagan be Reagan" suggest that even conservative ideologues question the degree to which Reagan remains master even of his White House staff.

Reagan's continued public support makes it vital for this book to get to the heart of the dangers of presidential aloofness from the state apparatus. Surely every attentive member of the public shudders when Reagan exposes his profound ignorance of the details of his own policies. To cite one horrifying instance, the president said in *three* separate segments of an interview with Soviet journalists before the November 1985 summit with Mikhail Gorbachev that the United States would not deploy the Strategic Defense Initiative (SDI) weapons (nicknamed "Star Wars") until after both superpowers eliminated their offensive missiles. Characteristically, this howler resulted in a White House correction. As well, the administration spokesman took the opportunity to coin a new term—"presidential imprecision"—when berating the press for writing stories on the apparent radical change of policy on "Star Wars."

The American public seems just as willing to interpret such errors as simply slips of the tongue. Yet any president who could make the same incredible misstatement three times reveals that he had not attained even an elementary grasp of the central plank of his nuclear policy. Such occurrences make it clear that enunciating sweeping policy objectives does not equal governance. The president might well believe fervently in SDI. However, he lacks the knowledge and motivation to provide leadership in this matter beyond incanting his pious aspirations. He also runs interference for administration ideologues. Even when the unreality of their schemes comes to light, they still can count on the firm believer.

Thus, Reagan's case presents as much as Carter's the need for students of the presidency to probe more deeply into the mix sought by individual presidents of responsiveness and reliance upon the state apparatus. They also must inquire more thoroughly into whether incumbents' desired mixes actually match their personalities and stylistic track record. Finally, upholding the standard of policy competence, scholars must examine much more critically apparent breakdowns in presidential performance and seeming instances of Camelot restored.

Chapter 2 will provide an overview of these themes as found in administrations since Franklin Roosevelt. This period covers, in fact, the modern era of the presidency. The chapter will set the stage by specifically outlining how the nature of U.S. executive authority—concentrated as it is in the hands of one person—differs from that of cabinet systems of government. It will then assess the approaches of each president from the standpoint of whether they believed their authority should be centralized or decentralized. From this issue emerge two clusters of corollary concerns. The first of these takes in presidents' views of the role of the cabinet. Here they can stress teamwork among their cabinet secretaries or let laissez-faire prevail; they can opt for regularized cabinet dynamics or for sporadic meetings; and they can strike several standing committees or permit ad hoc groups to develop issue by issue.

The second corollary centers on presidents' preferences regarding their advisory system. That is, they can organize their White House hierarchically or collegially; they can encourage or discourage competition between units potentially interested in an issue; and they can use policy-oriented staffs in the Executive Office of the President either to impose discipline centrally or to facilitate the collective resolution of issues among cabinet secretaries.

Chapter 3 examines in detail the models of the presidency, the cabinet, and the advisory system that have characterized the Carter and Reagan administrations. Regarding Carter, it will plumb the consequences of his insatiable appetite for detail and the inexperience of his staff, as well as the profound internal contradiction of his administration. On the one hand, he wanted to decentralize the actual exertion of executive authority. However, his failure to foster teamwork among his cabinet secretaries meant that issues perforce percolated right back into the Oval Office.

With respect to Reagan, we will examine how his image of nonchalance is of a piece with his noninterventionist view of the presidency. Under this rubric, tight controls over appointments, using the budget to drive policy priorities, and the inculcation of a "team" spirit among cabinet secretaries all create an aura of executive harmony. The fact remains, however, that people who tear a building down argue a lot less than those who construct it. The dependence of the Reagan brand of executive harmony on a limited policy agenda and the ideological fervor of many of his appointees raise serious questions about how his approach might be adapted for more proactive administrations.

Chapter 4 focuses on how Carter and Reagan set out their central advisory system in the White House Office and the Executive Office of the President. Of course, every administration attempts early on to enshrine its principal policy objectives and to organize itself so that, through monitoring and self-correction, it might optimize its realization of these goals. Yet conflicting cues and expectations pervade such processes. Chapter 4 looks at the interplay of four disparate and often conflicting activities on behalf of the president: (1) promoting his personal goals and political interests; (2) maintaining his partisan effectiveness and attractiveness; (3) nurturing and harvesting his congressional, media, and public support; and (4) safeguarding his prerogatives and interests as head of the executive branch. We will find that Jimmy Carter's nonhierarchical spokes-in-a-wheel format for organizing the White House greatly exacerbated the inherent disjunction between his style of operation and the exhaustiveness of his agenda. On the other hand, the quasi-hierarchical Baker/Meese/Deaver triumvirate of Reagan's first term achieved a rare detente between pragmatism and ideology within the White House.

Chapter 5 works from the assumption that the development and integration of economic and fiscal policies is a concern of any administration that overarches much of the rest of the policy process. As well, the sheer number of players claiming title to the various segments of this field makes the coordination of policies extremely complex and difficult. To begin, the Department of the Treasury operates in such a fragmented way that it rarely speaks with one voice. In addition, the Office of Management and Budget, the Council of Economic Advisers, the Office of the U.S. Trade Representative, the National Security Council staff, and White House units concerned with domestic policy all carve out areas where they press vigorously their interpretation of the president's interests. The parts actually successfully assumed by these various units differ greatly, according to their formal mandates for involvement in a field, the congruence between these and the policy preferences of the administration, and the standing their political leadership enjoys with the president and his closest advisers. During the Carter administration, clout weighed especially heavily. Thus economic policymaking tended to become ad hoc and personalistic. Under Reagan, the overriding commitments to ideological premises and the routinization of much of decision making in cabinet councils has contained many potentially contentious issues.

Chapter 6 moves the spotlight to OMB. This agency remains the nerve center for safeguarding the president's efforts to contain the size and cost of government, distributing resources according to policy priorities, and assuring that programs run efficiently and effectively. As an agency with a strong neutral-competence tradition, OMB has long viewed itself as the custodian of the long-term interests of the presidency. Jimmy Carter encouraged this role through his strong interest in budgetary and management issues. In fact, his desire to discern the "right" policy on the basis of the facts became so intense that he left too many immediate political exigencies begging for attention. If Ronald Reagan has ever encountered the concept of neutral competence, he probably has taken a dim view of it. At any rate, his budget director during the first term, David Stockman, regarded budget examiners as factotums with little to contribute to the administration's determination of the interests of the presidency.

Chapter 7 will look behind the scenes at the people within central agencies most intimately involved with trying to make the president's plan for executive leadership work. At the outset, the chapter will acknowledge that the analysis cuts across several cultures within officialdom. In reference to the respective universes of central agents during the two administrations, the chapter will probe the fact that the atmospheres contrasted sharply. For example, even career officials found themselves approaching bureaucratic life under Reagan in substantially different ways than they did under Carter. Regarding political appointees, chapter 7 accommodates the fact that both presidents used sets of criteria for selection of top advisers that worked considerable effects on their ultimate renditions of cabinet consultation. In addition, the chapter examines in detail two components to any appointive cohort—namely, "politicos" who primarily gained entry into the administration by virtue of their roles in the presidential campaign and "amphibians" who combine substantive policy expertise with the right political coloration.

Throughout, this book will rely most heavily upon material collected by me during two stays at the Brookings Institution—1979 and 1982–83. In all, 192 respondents from the most senior levels of U.S. central agencies were included. Of this number, 63 and 60 worked as political appointees under Carter and Reagan, respectively. Of the 69 who held career positions during the Carter administration, 37 still held their posts in 1982–83, under Reagan, and submitted to another in-depth interview. On average, the interviews took an hour and a half to complete. In all but four instances, respondents permitted the taping of their sessions. Much of the analysis, thus, will rely on verbatim transcripts of the interview materials. In addition, detailed coding of the transcripts permit statistical assessment of the hypotheses derived from the interview materials.

2. Presidents and Their Cabinets

Judging from the rhetoric adopted by presidential candidates at least since World War II, the man from Mars would certainly conclude that cabinet government had earned a cherished place within constitutional conventions connected to the operation of the U.S. executive branch. In practice, presidents have tended to set aside their notions of cabinet consultation once they contract the most virulent form of Potomac fever—incumbency. Strangely, one finds little scholarly attention given to cabinet consultation which, notwithstanding its spotty practical force, continues to appeal to the popular imagination. In fact, Richard F. Fenno's 1959 book, *The President's Cabinet: An Analysis in the Period From Wilson to Eisenhower,* serves as the most recent comprehensive treatment of the topic.

Jimmy Carter and Ronald Reagan have contributed to the utility of this fresh look at cabinet consultation. Both departed from many of their predecessors by clinging to their preincumbency rhetoric about greater use of the cabinet well into their administrations. Even more compellingly, the two presidents' blueprints and their success in implementing them have differed substantially. Carter chose a decentralized system whereby cabinet secretaries would resolve in their own departments all but the most "presidential" matters; Reagan opted for a highly collegial format in which department heads would prepare issues for presidential decision in an elaborate network of "councils."

In practice, Carter's penchant for programmatic detail and his inexperience with Washington combined to turn cabinet consultation into a ritual even though it continued as the administration's central theme until summer 1979. On the other hand, Reagan's approach has worked convincingly enough even to win over skeptics regarding the applicability of collective consultation in the U.S. executive. In short, the two administrations have presented themselves as laboratories for the "art of the possible" for cabinet government in the contemporary presidency.

While Reagan's overtures toward structured cabinet committees, especially as contrasted with Carter's laissez-faire approach, serve as its immediate rationale, this chapter looks more fundamentally at whether and to what degree the U.S. system allows for regularization of forums for collective cabinet-level consultation. To set the stage, I first examine the historical underpinnings of the British cabinet system. Certain developmental patterns can be identified that might help us to assess where the United States stands in relation to cabinet consultation as pursued in a stricter sense. The chapter then considers U.S. cabinets, including the degrees to which presidents have viewed secretaries as barons to be dealt with individually or as team members, have tried to institutionalize cabinet-level interactions, and have resorted to specialized committees to manage cabinet business within policy sectors. The administrations of the past fifty years, from Roosevelt to Reagan, will receive special attention in this brief historical treatment. Along the way, I will ask whether we can discern an evolutionary process toward structured cabinet consultation in the United States.

Finally, this chapter will study at length an issue that commands special attention in the United States. To be effective, cabinet-level committees must be able to tap the support of professional officials capable of managing decision processes in specialized policy sectors. Yet even presidents who have acknowledged this by setting up cabinet secretariats have found it difficult to keep such shops at arm's length. For this reason, this chapter devotes considerable space to issues surrounding how presidents have organized the White House staff, whether they have encouraged countervailing views from their advisors, and how well they have demarcated resources designed to assist cabinet consultation.

A Clarification of the British Model

Conventional wisdom in the United States views the U.K. executive as the archetypal collective cabinet government. As the theory goes, all British executive authority resides in the cabinet. This body, over which the prime minister presides as first among equals, determines collectively all major policy positions of the government. In turn, unwavering loyalty among the members of the government party in the House of Commons assures that cabinets can attain parliamentary approval of their legislative programs relatively easily.

Even if the system was ever this cut and dried, which is unlikely, developments during the past two decades have necessitated considerable modification of the theory of U.K. cabinet government. Most important, British voters might deny parties emerging victorious from elections an absolute majority in the House of Commons. The cross-pressures bearing on minority governments limit severely both what a cabinet can hope to achieve during its mandate and the internal coherence that it likely will maintain. Even apart from minority governments, factionalism within both the major parties often occasions cabinet retreats from legislative proposals and executive orders when it appears that these measures will face embarrassing desertions, even defeats, at the hands of backbench MPs.[1]

Under these conditions, executive harmony does not come as readily to British governments as Americans expect. More and more, prime ministers find themselves absorbed with the task of coordinating the executive. In consequence, the increasingly visible role of prime ministers, coupled with a gradual accretion of staff resources at their disposal, has aroused fears that cabinet government has yielded to a "presidential" model. A paradox arises from British use of such metaphors. While Americans clearly overstate the collectivization of executive authority in the U.K., Britons exaggerate the concentration of power in the presidency.[2]

While their systems operate out of two distinct constitutional legacies, greater accuracy would emerge if Americans and Britons reflected more on the fact that executives in both countries tackle comparable tasks. On the one hand, presidents and prime ministers want to give the political authorities responsible for the policies and operations of the major bureaucratic divisions a voice in matters that do not fit neatly into a single "portfolio." On the other hand, these principal executive authorities want to maintain the latitude necessary to allow them to intervene personally when chronic impasses and severe emergencies justify it. Historically, the British have tended to err on the side of wide consultation and the Americans in favor of chief-executive prerogative.

Cabinets first emerged in England as informal instruments of monarchical rule. That is, they developed under a system in which executive authority was concentrated in the person of the sovereign. This point of departure contrasts sharply with the current constitution in which the monarch serves merely as a figurehead. That is, discretionary control over U.K. executive authority is currently lodged in the ministers of government. These in turn must comprise a cabinet that enjoys the confidence of the House of Commons.[3]

The term *cabinet* did not appear until the early 1600s.[4] Indeed, constitutional tracts did not fully acknowledge the cabinet's legitimacy and its functions until the 1860s. The first cabinets operated essentially as executive committees of the Privy Council. The latter term itself had only emerged in the fifteenth century as a formal designation for the coterie of the monarch's most trusted officials. By the seventeenth century, the Privy Council had become too large, especially for coping with the turmoil of the times. The formation of cabinets allowed monarchs to consult in secret about the most sensitive matters they faced. Since cabinet members obtained their positions entirely at the pleasure of the monarch, they shared his authority only when he chose to share it.

As John P. Mackintosh has noted, British monarchs' use of their cabinets has not followed even lines.[5] James II (1685–88) convened his cabinet every Sunday and even assigned a clerk to arrange its business. George I (1714–27) ushered in a period in the eighteenth century in which the regularity both of cabinet meetings and the king's attendance fell off. Mackintosh has commented that George I was "both ignorant of English affairs and stupid and could never be at ease presiding over a wide-ranging discussion."[6] Thus even as a coordinative tool cabinets worked only for British monarchs desirous and capable of giving coherent direction to the myriad affairs of state.

During the nineteenth century, the monarchy declined considerably. Concomitantly, Parliament's power rose to the detriment of the executive. Initially, these developments resulted in the enhancement of the most prestigious ministerial domains to the point where some departments became virtual baronies. For instance, the cabinet normally considered only the broadest outlines of foreign policy. The foreign secretary, the chancellor of the exchequer, and the ministers of the two armed services worked out details either within their departments or between themselves. During the last half of the nineteenth century, various military crises and disasters sparked efforts to institutionalize consultation regarding overseas and defense policy. The principals largely frustrated such efforts by refusing to coordinate their activities beyond technical matters.

This baronial pattern persisted right through to 1916 when David Lloyd George became prime minister. He broke the impasse over the coordination of Britain's war effort by setting aside completely the cabinet's deliberative involvement and establishing a "war cabinet." A small group of ministers, largely detached from the operational responsibilities, helped him run the war from central, coordinative perches. The urgent circumstances caused by a brutal and seemingly intractable war, of course, greatly aided Lloyd George's imposition of coherence. Since the late 1800s the degree to which the electorate identified parties with their leaders had undermined cabinet baronies anyway. Lloyd George's institution of his war cabinet built upon an evolutionary process that was giving the prime minister greater discretion as to which cabinet ministers he consulted and authority in knocking ministers' heads together. Even after World War I, the enhanced position of prime ministers quickened by Lloyd George carried over to changes in how the cabinet conducted its business. Prime ministers stopped counting "pros" and "cons" after cabinet discussions. They preferred simply to state a summary of the "sense" of the meeting. They resorted increasingly to ad hoc committees to prepare the especially sensitive elements of policy initiatives agreed to in principle by cabinet.

As a partial response to the pressure for institutionalizing committees, near the end of the war Lloyd George created standing cabinet-level bodies for economic defense and development, home affairs, and postwar priorities. However, interest in such regularized committees sooned flagged. In fact, standing committees within the major policy sectors were not firmly established until after World War II. The current committee structure remains a state secret. However, known committees take in planning for legislative sessions and management of parliamentary affairs, economic strategy, overseas and defense policy, relations with the European Economic Community, home and social affairs, and security and intelligence. Networks of standing subcommittees operate within each of the broad policy sectors. Yet prime ministers still count heavily on "miscellaneous/general" committees to prepare particularly thorny issues ranging from replacement of the Polaris missile system to negotiation of fiscal grants to local governments.

With regard to staff support, the British practice has contrasted with that of the United States. The tendency in Washington has been for staff closely associated with the president to be organized around his requirements for advice on policy and political affairs. U.K. resources formally attached to the prime minister have gravitated toward facilitating cabinet decision making. Lloyd George's innovations during the latter stages of World War I planted the seeds for a more clearly prime-ministerial staff. A "garden suburb" of political advisers—so called because they were housed in temporary buildings behind No. 10 Downing Street—emerged along with a career-service cabinet secretariat.[7] However, the "garden suburb" concept fell out of favor soon after its wartime justification ceased. Not until Harold Wilson's second term (1974) have units in No. 10 successfully pursued Lloyd George's view that prime ministers should have at their immediate disposal five or six trusted policy advisers with partisan backgrounds. Such aides, it is thought, can best remind the government of their party's "manifesto" commitments during the previous election campaign.

Lloyd George's cabinet secretariat has developed into the highly differentiated Cabinet Office. This career public service organization includes over 350 officials in secretariats that support cabinet committees, plus many more public servants working in the Central Statistical Office, and, as of fall 1981, the Management and Personnel Office.[8] Brigaded under the secretary of the cabinet, the configuration, in relation to the prime minister, provides cabinet-related staffing rather than partisan-political advice.

Concentration of Executive Authority in the President

From the above section, we might conclude that the locus of executive authority in the United Kingdom has shifted around considerably. When the term *cabinet* first appeared in the sixteenth century, executive authority was concentrated in the monarch. By the mid-nineteenth century it had dispersed pretty widely among cabinet members to the point where individual ministers ruled over departments almost as barons. Since this era, three factors have intervened to greatly enhance the role of the prime minister in relation to the cabinet: the expansion of suffrage through the late nineteenth and early twentieth centuries, two massive shocks of global conflict and the residual fears about national security, and the growth of government in the mid-twentieth century. Yet constitutional conventions spun in the nineteenth century still bind the prime ministers to an institutionalized cabinet committee system. These constraints prescribe, within reasonable limits, that each minister concerned with a major government initiative should have his "day" in cabinet.

We will find in the pages that follow that U.S. presidents approach the cabinet from an entirely different perspective than do prime ministers. The bulk of constitutional theory in this century has sided with the view that all U.S. executive authority resides in the president. The Constitutional Convention clearly favored James Madison's position that the principal officers of the executive should be appointees under the control of the president.[9] It even rejected Roger Sherman's hope that presidents should emulate British monarchs by at least consulting regularly with their most trusted officers. The Constitution suggested only limply that presidents might request written advice from their department heads. As recently as 1980, a prominent panel assessing executive branch management for the National Academy of Public Administration held that the president's authority permeates the federal government. That is, the Constitution "instructs him to take care that the laws be faithfully executed."[10]

This rich constitutional endowment, contemporary scholarship hastens to acknowledge, carries the danger of presidential overload. For instance, Fred I. Greenstein asserts that the president assumes the dual role of constitutional monarch, a symbol of national unity, and of prime minister, expected to handle deftly a wide array of potentially divisive issues.[11] Nelson W. Polsby points with some alarm to the dangers inherent in extreme expectations for a president's fulfillment of either roles.[12] Americans who see the president as the embodiment of national sentiment run the risk of subject-like assent to imperial behavior based on the manipulation of public opinion. Those who consider him simply a prime minister cut him adrift in Washington's sea of checks and balances without party discipline and cabinet responsibilty.

In the face of the duality of the president's role, a wide band of scholarly opinion urges realism regarding what can be expected of incumbents. Lester M. Salamon reminds us that two presidents who appeared to mark an apogee of power over the executive, Lyndon B. Johnson and Richard M. Nixon, left a legacy of distrust that made it difficult for their successors to lead effectively.[13] Salamon believes that presidents have an obligation to maintain the credibility of their office. Thus, they must appear to be broadly cooperative with the rest of the executive branch, Congress, and other key elements of political power. Richard Rose and Stephen Hess add firmer counsel. Rose holds that the U.S. executive is a collective rather than a unitary noun.[14] Therefore, no single person wisely assumes that he can take complete charge of its various institutions. Hess underlines the fact that the Constitution and a great deal of U.S. statutory apparatus assigns the authority to run programs directly to department heads.[15]

These caveats intensify the difficulty of deciding whether presidents should involve themselves in only the most crucial executive branch affairs or engage themselves in administrative detail as well. The immense growth of government in this century and its expansion into programmatic areas in which evaluation defies any search for a "botton line" slipped the presidency to the "details" side of such a continuum.[16] The trend started after World War I when Congress was wringing its hands over the size of deficits accrued during the first two decades of the century. It decided to lodge responsibility for executive branch estimates more directly under the president.[17] The resulting Bureau of the Budget became in fact, though not in name, the president's department.

From the outset, BOB's power of "legislative clearance" over the expenditure implications of departmental proposals to Congress gave it added leverage.[18] Roosevelt, however, formalized the bureau's presidential mission by bringing it into the newly created Executive Office of the President in 1939. He assigned it the additional function of reviewing on his behalf the compatibility of departmental policies and programs with the substantive goals of the administration.

Harry Truman inherited from Roosevelt an immeasurably different presidency from that handed over by Herbert Hoover. Hess asserts that Truman's term corresponded with the period of greatest public acceptance of the presidency as the focal point of executive authority.[19] Salamon observes that Truman used BOB's clearance role to particularly good effect in pulling together his annual legislative program.[20] Some might view Dwight D. Eisenhower's administration as a retreat from the president's involvement in detail. Greenstein's recent assessment presents an entirely different picture.[21] Notwithstanding the widespread impression that Eisenhower was underemployed, Greenstein notes that he often engaged himself deeply in departmental matters. This was especially the case when the defects of top officials made his preferred tack, delegation, ill-advised.

John F. Kennedy, while trying to transcend Eisenhower's highly routinized legislative clearance and cabinet consultation, actually accelerated the centralization of executive authority in the presidency. In an effort to let in diverse and fresh views, he chose to work with cabinet secretaries one-on-one and to set up ad hoc task forces so unstructured that they often included individuals from outside government.[22] Johnson, as he did with so much of what Kennedy started, pursued this strategy with a vengeance. In the process, he tipped the scales toward presidential management of executive branch policy development and implementation, right down to the minutiae, from the White House.[23] Nixon, of course, took this "administrative" view of the presidency to its logical conclusion.[24]

Gerald Ford and Ronald Reagan both have contributed to reversing the trend toward a detail-oriented presidency. Ford chose his tack because the nation was still reeling from the shock of Nixon. Reagan has maintained relative aloofness because of his age, his lack of detailed knowledge of the Washington scene, and his uncanny ability to judge when to involve himself in the issues to achieve optimal effect. Jimmy Carter brought to the presidency just the "busy" view of his job that would ultimately result in Americans feeling too keenly a sense of déjà vu from the Nixon days.

Cabinet Secretaries: Barons or Colleagues

We have dwelt so far on the pervasiveness of the president's authority within the executive branch and incumbents' efforts to exercise this authority more collectively. However, countervailing pressures upon secretaries force us to question the feasibility of this quest. Cabinet officers head departments that are heavily reliant upon congressional mandates for their creation, organization, and operation.[25] Incessant congressional demands for information and testimony along with the heavy burden of brokerage in behalf of client groups, involve cabinet secretaries in subgovernment networks operating within numerous specialized issue areas. Sectoral brushfires often impose more intense demands for responsiveness than do policy signals transmitted from the White House.[26] Indeed, subgovernment politics permeate every department. This means that each cabinet secretary must learn to cope with highly entrepreneurial public-service cultures.[27] The relatively long tenure of career civil servants within specialized areas of departmental activities makes it doubly difficult for secretaries to follow cues from the White House.[28] In 1944, Pendleton Herring characterized the cabinet member as more part of a "feudal pattern of fiefs, baronies, and dukedoms than . . . an orderly and symmetrical pyramid of authority."[29] Nearly forty years of further embellishment of the presidency and its immediate resources have not altered this situation greatly.

This state of affairs often presents the image of two solitudes. On the one hand, we find the overweening constitutional view that the president enjoys ultimate responsibility over the entire executive branch. On the other, we recognize the harsh reality that no individual could possibly exercise this vast authority to its fullest effect. Faced with this paradox, most students of the presidency make one significant concession in favor of an enhanced role for the cabinet. As a collective body, it does not partake of ultimate executive authority. However, as Richard Fenno, Jr., observed in 1959, it can supply the chief executive with dynamics that will satisfy "the universal need . . . to consult with others and draw upon the advice of others in exercising this political power."[30]

The earliest presidents appear to have accepted such an instrumental role for cabinet much more than modern ones have. George Washington viewed Congress' institution of three administrative secretaries (state, treasury and war) and the attorney general as a recognition of the fact that one man could not perform all the business of state.[31] He convened these top advisers regularly for consultations on the weightier matters faced by the executive. Like Washington, Alexander Hamilton and Thomas Jefferson relied heavily upon cabinet. Neither viewed such consultation as a legal necessity. However, as the following passages indicate, both presidents spoke eloquently of cabinet consultation's advisability.[32] First, Hamilton:

> A president is not bound to conform to the advice of his ministers. He is even under no positive injunction to ask or require it. But the constitution presumes that he will consult them; and the genius of our government and the public good recommend the practice.

In Jefferson's words:

> For our government, although in theory subject to be directed by the unadvised will of the president, is, and from its origin

has been a very different thing in practice. . . . All matters of importance or difficulty are submitted to all the heads of departments composing the cabinet, . . . in all important cases the executive is in fact a directory.

Such views of the cabinet fared reasonably well through the remainder of the nineteenth century. Yet the institution has not stood up well during our current century in which presidents have increasingly emphasized personal leadership based on the mass appeal of their programs over their administrations' capacity for teamwork.[33]

Teddy Roosevelt's administration marked the first clear instance of leadership that left little room for cabinet consultation. To a similar extent, Woodrow Wilson viewed his role more as shaping and responding to the popular will than guiding his programs through the executive-legislative labyrinth. Franklin Roosevelt pretty much denied the collective significance of the cabinet, except when it served his convenience.[34] He involved individual secretaries in key decisions only when moved to do so.[35] When departments and agencies reached deadlocks over policy initiatives, he often imposed work schedules and conditions that forced the competing parties to reach agreements upon demand.[36] Harry Truman took a much more collegial view of cabinet than did Roosevelt. He was a good delegator—giving full backing along with implicit trust.[37] Although he initially hoped to use the cabinet as a board of directors for his administration, this degree of collegiality proved unworkable.[38] Cabinet discussions under Truman, thus, focused mostly on legislative tactics and political strategy.

Scholarly opinion supports the view that Eisenhower imparted to his cabinet a rare status variously described as a "team" with "coordinative power," a "major deliberative mechanism," and a forum for "spontaneous mutual coordination."[39] Eisenhower set the tone for his venture into cabinet consultation at a preinauguration meeting with his designated secretaries. His depth of commitment is revealed in the minutes:

My hope will be to make this a policy body, to bring before you and for you to bring up subjects that are worthy of this body as a whole. . . . I hope that before we have gone very long each one of you will consider the rest of you here your best friends in the world so that you can call up and do your own coordinating.[40]

For the most part, Eisenhower followed through on his pledge. Supported by the Bureau of the Budget, he vetted his 1954 legislative program in several cabinet sessions.[41] The practice of meeting regularly over various substantive policy issues seemed, as well, to have worked its desired effect of steeling secretaries' commitment to the administration. Both Hess and Greenstein have noted the development under Eisenhower of a sense of collective responsibility. That is, cabinet secretaries, beyond the norm in the United States, willingly drew flak away from the president by accepting blame for the administration's unpopular actions and mistakes.[42]

Cabinet consultation along structured lines did not survive the transition to the Kennedy administration. We owe this fact partially to the new president's personality. As Hess has observed, JFK probably was too impatient and mentally agile to tolerate a structured process of collective decision making.[43] More fundamentally, critics of Eisenhower had largely attributed his lack of imagination in responding to the more compelling issues of the day, especially in domestic affairs, to his highly institutionalized cabinet system.[44] Structure, it was widely thought, had led to a stifling lack of creativity. Kennedy thus went beyond merely eschewing tedious deliberations. He rarely convened cabinet meetings and ignored even statutory structures such as the National Security Council.

Under Johnson, cabinet continued to atrophy as a collective institution. The White House became increasingly obsessed with imposing programmatic discipline through Great Society task forces coordinated by Joseph Califano.[45] This spawned the Heineman Task Force which recommended a consolidation of departmental responsibilities that would make the president's authority over the executive branch more pyramidal.[46] The Heineman prescriptions left a clear imprint on Richard Nixon's view of how to bring harmony to an administration. In January 1971, Nixon proposed that four "superdepartments"—human resources, community development, natural resources, and economic development—be created to form, with State, Defense, Treasury, and Justice, an "inner cabinet." In theory, such an arrangement would force those concerned with the various elements of a policy sector to work out their conflicts in a single organizational framework.[47] The events surrounding Watergate, of course, dispelled even the illusion of this degree of administrative coherence.[48]

The three presidents following Nixon have all taken greater cognizance of cabinet secretaries. Ford placed considerable trust in his secretaries' ability to resolve their disputes amicably without necessarily involving him directly. For instance, his Economic Policy Board was considerably effective in coordinating the administration's economic policies.[49] Carter had less success. Initially, he viewed cabinet government as individual secretaries having greater discretion over their departments' affairs, combined with relatively free access to the president when warranted by circumstances.[50] Carter's immense appetite for detail soon made his plan unworkable.[51] His subsequent efforts to bring greater structure to interdepartmental coordination proved largely unsuccessful. Finally, Ronald Reagan reversed course back to the Eisenhower era of highly structured cabinet-level consultation. Indeed, he introduced a network of specialized cabinet and interdepartmental committees to both the domestic and national security fields, which embellished considerably the Eisenhower approach.

The Institutionalization of Cabinet Structures

The level of institutionalization of cabinet structures adopted by a president is a fairly accurate indication of how often he will consult cabinet secretaries while seeking greater coherence in his administration. Most presidents before Kennedy adhered faithfully to the convention whereby cabinet met at least weekly. The interval from Kennedy to Nixon thus constituted a departure from the normal practice.

George Washington, believing that his secretaries should review all executive proclamations, often called cabinet meetings on several successive days.[52] In 1959, Richard F. Fenno characterized customary procedure as sittings twice a week—usually on Tuesdays and Fridays.[53] In fact, he recounts that Abraham Lincoln failed in his efforts to limit cabinet sessions to times when the circumstances clearly called for a meeting. In our century, both Woodrow Wilson and Franklin Roosevelt succeeded in holding cabinet sittings only once per week during wartime.

Truman set aside the twice-weekly convention.[54] However, he took cabinet sessions seriously, initially even calling for votes. The Truman administration marked the emergence of the first standing cabinet-level committee, the National Security Council created by Congress in 1947. Initially, the Bureau of the Budget, concerned that the NSC might eclipse its role, convinced Truman that he should let the secretary of state chair most meetings on the president's behalf. However, the Korean War short-circuited this effort to limit NSC's significance. The president's ensuing direct involvement with this deliberative body soon diminished the significance of full-cabinet sessions. Eisenhower's cabinet met every Friday.[55] Unlike Truman, however, Eisenhower managed to make heavy use of cabinet and NSC meetings simultaneously. The NSC also met weekly, on Thursdays.

As we have already seen, Kennedy largely operated unencumbered by institutionalized cabinet-level meetings. Rarely holding full cabinet meetings, he preferred to grant private sessions to individual secretaries in rough proportion to his interest in their departments.[56] Even the statutory NSC system yielded almost entirely to issue-specific gatherings. These included only those aides whose advice was deemed most relevant to the matter at hand. Johnson did bring cabinet together on a regular basis. However, such sessions bore little resemblance to Eisenhower's. That is, they tended to amount more to briefings by secretaries on important developments in their departments.[57]

Johnson followed Kennedy's practice in the national security field. However, he initiated fewer issues himself and normally worked directly with smaller groups of officials. Nixon viewed meetings of the entire cabinet much as Kennedy did. He did give greater recognition to the NSC system by reintroducing a network of interagency study groups along with committees to coordinate them.[58] The NSC Review Group, chaired by Henry Kissinger, theoretically governed the process. However, the structures did not hold up well under the Nixon-Kissinger preference for holding national security issues close to their vests.

Ford revived weekly cabinet meetings.[59] He also adopted Eisenhower's format for support of the cabinet by assigning to a specific adviser responsibility for organizing its business. With Kissinger as secretary of state, Ford could do little toward reengaging the NSC process. Yet his Economic Policy Board marked the first highly successful use of cabinet-level committees to make economic policy. Jimmy Carter convened his cabinet infrequently. Like Johnson, he also let sessions run on as mutual admiration societies about departmental events. To Carter's credit, the NSC system experienced a notable revitalization during his four years. However, structure was not the order of the day on domestic issues. Carter's successor to the Economic Policy Board, the Economic Policy Group, took months before it "shook down" to include only principals representing the essential bureaucratic elements for management of the economy. The rest of the domestic sector operated with ad-hoc task forces set up to handle specific policy proposals.

Ronald Reagan initially wanted an inner cabinet comprised of supersecretaries along the lines of what he had used as governor of California and similar to Nixon's 1971 proposal. The more pragmatic among his advisers, principally James A. Baker III, talked Reagan into a compromise based on cabinet committees for each major policy sector. During Reagan's first term, seven of these bodies operated in domestic affairs and four senior interagency groups worked under the National Security Council umbrella. These NSC committees—dubbed SIGs—normally ran with subcabinent departmental representation. The cabinet rarely met as such. However, Reagan chaired cabinet councils and the NSC when they had reached the point on key items where they had largely settled their differences. The system produced at least one such session per week. Here a bias appeared toward national security and economic affairs issues. Presidential sessions operated on the domestic side as close-to-full cabinets. All secretaries had the right to request access to cabinet councils even if they did not belong. They tended to exercise this privilege when the president chaired the meeting.

At the beginning of his second term, Reagan collapsed the domestic side of the cabinet committee system into two bodies, the Economic Policy Council and the Domestic Policy Council. Both of these have met in presidential session much less than had their predecessors during the first term. With respect to the NSC system, three of the four SIGs have fallen into disuse. Currently, full NSC meetings chaired by the president occur almost twice a week. Reagan also chairs a more select body—the NSC Planning Group—which handles especially sensitive issues.

Specialized Cabinet-Level Units

We have already seen that cabinet committees did not firmly establish themselves in the United Kingdom until after 1945. We thus can excuse the relatively slow and sporadic development of these bodies in the United States. Considering the fact that the United States operates without the pressures for coordination inherent in British-style collective executive responsibility, we can marvel that these forums have emerged at all in Washington.

Even in the British system, the development of cabinet committees has had difficulty in achieving coherence between departmental policies. All relevant ministers should under normal circumstances make their contribution. Yet a prime minister must be able
to intervene effectively during deadlocks. Lloyd George's creation
of a war cabinet in 1916 successfully dislodged the government's
war effort from narrow technical concerns. However, the war cabinet's members, apart from Bonar Law, the chancellor of the exchequer, lacked departments. Thus the war cabinet served more as an
executive committee than a forum for mutual adjustment of departmental positions.[60]

During World War II, Churchill departed from Lloyd George's
approach by instituting a relatively large war cabinet—eight to
eleven members—consisting largely of ministers with departmental responsibilities. He also continued to convene the entire cabinet in order to solicit broader views on a host of policy issues.
Nonetheless, Churchill kept firm control over the war effort by
serving as his own minister of defense and chairing a committee
that coordinated the service departments. Thus, even with his
clearer acknowledgment of collective responsibility, Churchill
established a structural environment in which he could maintain
his firm guidance.

The circumstances under which Lloyd George and Churchill developed the first British committees to coordinate substantive elements of national security policies bear one distinct connection to
an early development in the United States. As we have noted, the
National Security Council came into being by an act of Congress in
1947. Its strongest advocates had been George C. Marshall and
James Forrestal. They believed that Churchill's coordinative machinery had provided much more effective management of Britian's war
effort than Roosevelt's ad hoc administrative style had to that of
the United States.[61]

In supporting the NSC, Truman used representation for the secretaries of the three services as an inducement for achieving their
support of unification under the Department of Defense. Although
the service secretaries would no longer belong to cabinet, they
would advise the president directly in the NSC. The secretaries of
state and defense would belong to the NSC. While the National
Security Act styled the president as chairman of the NSC, initially
the secretary of state often filled in on a pro-tem basis. In 1949,
Congress removed the service secretaries from the NSC and added

the vice-president. This set the stage for the body's operating more clearly as an instrument for coordination between State and Defense within a very broad array of national security matters. With the advent of the Korean War, Truman usually took the chair, and meetings increasingly became "principals only" affairs.

The development of the NSC under Truman provided the ideal framework for his successor's decision-making style. Eisenhower preferred to get information by listening and to form opinions after weighing others' views in discussions.[62] He used the NSC much more than Truman did, consulting it fifty-one times in his first year alone. He established elaborate procedures designed to enhance the consideration of various options by formal NSC sessions. After each meeting, a "record of action" was prepared and circulated to principals for comment. On many issues that required immediate operational coordination, Eisenhower would flesh out the details in the Oval Office with the officials essential to the implementation of a NSC decision. He did not content himself with indulging a preference for foreign affairs by introducing more structure to that field. That is, he established numerous other cabinet-level bodies in specialized policy sectors. These included committees or councils covering economic growth and stability, foreign economic policy, small business, trade policy, rural development, prices and costs, price stability, financial policies for postattack operations, and federal urban area assistance.

We have already seen that Kennedy disbanded or ignored the collective decision-making forums he inherited from Eisenhower. He preferred ad hoc bodies. His system evolved into a series of task forces, some of which included outsiders as well as administration officials. The same pattern was sustained by Johnson. However, one Johnson cabinet-level committee that has survived into the 1980s emerged in this period. This body, "the troika," consisted of the chairman of the Council of Economic Advisers, the secretary of the treasury, and the director of the Bureau of the Budget. It attempted to work out consensus memoranda on forecasts in order to bring more coherence to the various lines taken within the administration on the projected performance of the economy.[63]

Nixon initially tried to revitalize the NSC. He also created three cabinet councils responsible for urban affairs, rural affairs, and economic policy, respectively. These bodies and their various successors during the administration did not operate effectively as collegial organizations.[64] Nixon's habit of assigning responsibility for entire policy sectors to "czars" tended to negate efforts to involve cabinet secretaries in collective forums. The three most powerful czars under Nixon, Henry Kissinger (national security), John Ehrlichman (domestic affairs), and John Connally (secretary of the treasury 1970–72), drew upon clear presidential delegations to get what they wanted from departments and agencies even if these meant bypassing those formally in charge of a policy field.

Henry Kissinger continued to dominate national security matters when Ford became president. Thus, the NSC system still languished as a collective decision-making process. However, Ford's Economic Policy Board, in addition to being effective, reached the highest level of institutionalization achieved to that point by any cabinet-level body on the domestic side.[65] The committee, which included the secretaries of state, commerce, and labor, operated with an executive consisting of the secretary of the treasury, the chairman of CEA and the director of OMB. The smaller group met daily. The president attended about one in four meetings of the entire group. In Ford's absence, William Simon, the secretary of the treasury, chaired EPB. Simon also served as the administration's spokesman on economic affairs. Behind the scenes, L. William Seidman, a friend of Ford's from Michigan, worked in the White House as assistant to the president for economic affairs. With the help of a small unit (five professionals plus five secretaries), Seidman managed the EPB's business and briefed the president on its activities. The EPB process included six permanent subcabinet committees and numerous task forces. For the first time, a regularized cabinet committee with a secretariat stressing process management rather than advocacy emerged on the domestic side as an instrument of interdepartmental coordination.

Under Carter, notwithstanding the tensions between the secretary of state through most of his administration, Cyrus Vance, and the assistant to the president for national security affairs, Zbigniew Brzezinski, the cabinet-level machinery coordinating foreign, security, and defense policies experienced a revival. As we will see in subsequent chapters, reengagement of the NSC centered largely on Brzezinski's efforts to involve cabinet-level subcommittees in the preparation of key policy and coordination matters before they reached the president. Carter never effectively employed structured cabinet-level forums on the domestic side. For instance, his Economic Policy "Group" started with so many principals, assistants in tow, that someone had to fetch an additional chair when the vice-president appeared at its first meeting. It gradually shed participants, first by paring itself down to an executive committee and later to a steering committee. Ultimately it became a weekly informal breakfast meeting that resolved little between conflicting viewpoints.

Reagan adopted the most highly structured system of cabinet-level consultation ever employed in the United States. On the national security side, four senior interagency groups (SIGs) prepared issues for NSC meetings which the president chaired on a regular basis. SIGs took in foreign policy, where State had the lead; defense policy was governed by Defense; intelligence, by the CIA; and international economic policy, by Treasury. These bodies met with subcabinet deputies until reaching the penultimate decision points before going to the president. Several interagency groups (IGs) prepared issues in detail for SIGs. The seven cabinet councils created by Reagan during the first term on the domestic side took in economic affairs, commerce and trade, federal relations and health and human resources, natural resources and environment, food and agriculture, legal policy, and management and administration. The chairmen pro tem were, respectively, the secretaries of the treasury, of commerce, of health and human services, of the interior, and of agriculture; the attorney general; and the former counselor to the president, Edwin Meese III. Not all the councils met regularly. Economic Affairs convened about twice a week; Commerce and Trade came together every Wednesday; the others held sessions only as required for the resolution of specific issues. The president chaired approximately one out of four meetings.

During the current term, only the SIG on Intelligence remains active. The Crisis Preplanning Group chaired by the NSC staff's senior director for policy development coordinates the administration's management of major foreign policy emergencies. The Strategic Arms Control Group headed by the assistant to the president for national security affairs has supplanted the SIG on defense. And the Economics Policy Council has absorbed the entire case load of the SIG on International Economic Policy. On the domestic side, the elaborate cabinet committee system that prevailed during the first term has been collapsed into the Economic Policy Council and the Domestic Policy Council. James A. Baker III—the treasury secretary—and Edwin Meese III—the attorney general—have served offi-

cially as the respective chairmen of these committees. Under the
current arrangement, thus, Reagan rarely presides over cabinet-level
bodies considering economic or domestic issues.

Staffing the President and Cabinet-Level Bodies

This section advances a fairly straightforward proposition. To operate effectively, cabinet-level bodies must be able to call upon a staff
system designed to support a process of collective deliberation.
Only in rare exceptions in advanced liberal democracies are such
resources independent of those available to the chief executive.
However, the United States' concentration of executive authority
intensifies considerably the importance of central-agency personnel
and institutions to the president. Although many presidents have
started their administrations by making it clear that they wanted
sanctuaries of "neutral competence" for coordinating senior administration panels, the constitutional currents run against such
aspirations. Like all chief executives, the president bears the responsibility for assuring that the executive branch makes its decisions effectively and in accordance with the fundamental goals of
his partisan mandate. However, the president's personalized authority, in comparison to that of prime ministers with strong cabinets, can readily preempt collective claims on resources dedicated
in theory to cabinet operations.

Three issues arise in any consideration of the organization of resources designed to support the president and cabinet-level decision-
making processes. First, has the president opted for a hierarchical
organization of the White House, or does each senior adviser work
relatively independently of staff colleagues and enjoy direct access to
the president? The main concern of a White House staff is political
affairs. Thus, an overly hierarchical organization will produce a relatively partisan variant of neutral competence in a cabinet secretariat.
On the other hand, a laissez-faire mode will swamp a secretariat in
internal administration politics. That is, officials' energies will focus
on winning and keeping the president's attention. Relatedly, does the
president want to make decisions on the basis of limited options from
trusted sources, or does he encourage development of numerous
scenarios and intense scrutiny of views inside the White House?
Extreme tendencies toward either style could hamper the efforts of
staff members assigned to facilitate collective decision making.

Finally, has the president adequately partitioned secretariats in the White House? Here several related questions arise. Are the secretariats headed by officials at the highest rank? Do they divide into units with responsibility for specific issue areas and management of individual cabinet-level committees? Do they normally take the White House lead in horizontal communication with key policy development personnel in departments? Do they work in a significant degree under department heads who serve a committee chairmen? Do their staff complements blend workably political operatives with policy concerns, noted authorities and specialists from outside government and seasoned public servants? Or, do they overwhelmingly consist of political operatives and, therefore, become most responsive to highly partisan agendas?

Organization of the White House

U.S. presidents since FDR have increasingly grappled with the issue of how they should organize their White House. Each has taken seriously what seems to be an article of faith on such matters: presidents should organize their personal staffs in ways that will keep lines of communication open, both internally and outside the White House, and not stifle initiative and creativity. Unfortunately for presidents, the gradual accretion of staff and offices in the White House has not made it easy to realize the plans of those who hope to operate with relative openness.[66] Here enter attempts to bring more hierarchical structure to the White House. Such efforts, though increasing the economies of coordination between diverse personalities and functional responsibilities, reduce the directness of the president's relations with staffers and the variety of options presented to him on key issues.

Although the term had not been coined in his day, FDR followed a "spokes-in-a-wheel" style of organization that corresponded to a bias toward loose structure in the White House.[67] Under this format, a "chief of staff" would be antithetical. Roosevelt did not want his advice mediated. Working usually to resolve specific problems within clear time constraints, he preferred to select his advisers personally. He gave relatively little weight to jurisdictional lines, let alone to whose "turf" one or another issue belonged. Truman did pay more attention to the organization of his White House.[68] However, he served, like FDR, as his own chief of staff.

He also based his consultation of White House personnel much more on trust than upon their formal job descriptions.

In asking why Roosevelt and Truman eschewed formal organization of the White House, we should keep in mind the fact that the president's immediate advisers comprised a very small staff indeed when Roosevelt first took office. Until the Eisenhower administration, the White House Office's growth appeared mainly to respond to relentless ad hoc pressure on the presidency throughout the Depression, World War II, and the Korean War. Eisenhower was the first president with the luxury to ponder where the post-Hoover development of the White House was headed. He chose to structure it in a hierarchical fashion. Except that he only bore the title "assistant to the president," Eisenhower's most trusted aide, Sherman Adams, operated essentially as a chief of staff.[69]

Eisenhower's organizational preferences did not carry over into the Kennedy administration. In fact, both Kennedy and Johnson placed the same emphasis as did Roosevelt on organizational flexibility.[70] Nixon, if anything, followed a hierarchical mode more strictly than Eisenhower. The difference derived more from Nixon's personality than a substantially greater need for organization owing to the still expanding size of the White House. Nixon made of H. R. Haldeman, his chief of staff, much more of a gatekeeper than Eisenhower did of Sherman Adams. Haldeman kept to a minimum direct interactions between the president and his staff and cabinet secretaries, so that Nixon might pursue with few interruptions his solitary contemplation of the great affairs of state.[71]

The ignominious legacy of Nixon's White House only partially explains Ford's patterning his staff according to the spokes-in-a-wheel format. The style fit well his open personality. A chief of staff did preside over the White House. However, meetings of the top twenty staff each morning assured the circulation of fresh and countervailing ideas.[72] In addition, Ford used quite effectively oval office meetings with groups of aides working on key issues. These gave him face-to-face exposure to conflicting views. Carter wanted to follow this example.[73] For a number of reasons, he failed almost totally. He did not appoint even a Ford-style chief of staff; he tolerated a severe truncation of his advisory system—based on the ready access of a few trusted Georgians—which made some "spokes" much more vital than others; and he maintained extremely fixed ideas of his policy options that did not lend themselves to give-and-take sessions—even among Georgians.[74]

For his first term, Ronald Reagan employed a hybrid of the spokes-in-a-wheel and chief-of-staff designs. In fact, between early 1982 and late 1983 four key aides reported directly to the president. The chief of staff presided over a hub of his own, as fully six officials with the rank of assistant to the president reported to him. The counselor and assistant to the president for national security affairs ruled over secretaries responsible, respectively, for domestic and national security policies. The deputy chief of staff received many direct assignments from the president and governed most matters relating to his personal affairs, including scheduling. All four men enjoyed direct individual access to the president and frequently met in joint sessions with him. Thus not every person with the title "assistant to the president" enjoyed direct access to the Oval Office. However, each major sector of White House activity was headed by a superassistant who interacted freely with the president. Early in 1985, Reagan's first-term chief of staff, James A. Baker III, his counselor Edwin Meese III, and his deputy chief of staff, Michael K. Deaver, all left the White House. In their stead, the president installed his first-term treasury secretary, Donald T. Regan, as a strong chief of staff.

Room for Countervailing Views

As the case of the Carter administration suggests, selection of the spokes-in-a-wheel format does not inevitably lead to equal access to the president for all senior players in the White House. The presence or absence of a creative tension between divergent views appears to rest as much upon personality factors as structural ones. Thus, a president's temperament can severely limit competition in a spokes-in-a-wheel structure. Conversely, it can foster order in a hierarchical system without reliance upon an autocratic chief of staff.

Roosevelt charmed his staff much as he did the American public. He would work almost collegially with aides while addressing the problem of the day. He based such relations on the direct utility of a specific participant. This approach relegated some relevant parties to the status of mere spectators or, worse, left them completely in the dark. Truman defined White House responsibilities more clearly.[75] He even assigned specific aides to handle labor and minority relations. As well, he allowed presidential assistants to build up staffs assigned exclusively to their work. Eisenhower, of course, introduced a degree of hierarchical structure never before seen in the White House. Although the record now suggests that Eisenhower frequently dipped wherever he wanted for advice from his staff, his first chief of staff, Sherman Adams, produced an aura of efficiency that made him appear to be the president's surrogate.[76] In fact, Adams's departure in 1958 led to his replacement by Wilton Persons, a long-standing Eisenhower aide. Persons brought a balance between structure and openness more congruent with the president's preferred style.

While Kennedy repudiated the hierarchical model, he let his White House grow larger than Eisenhower's.[77] Through sheer intellectual agility and personal dynamism, he also tended to draw issues into the White House. Thus, Kennedy had personal aides working on virtually every key matter. Directed by a young man with a refreshingly creative grasp of the presidency, the system seemed to work well—at least up to the time of the assassination. The dysfunctions caused by the relative absence of structure showed up during Johnson's administration. At the outset, his White House was more subject to conflict than Kennedy's. Johnson's desire to maintain continuity between the two administrations had him holding over many Kennedy staff while adding others whom he trusted implicity. As one insider noted at the time, Johnson created a Noah's Ark with two of everything.[78] By necessity, Johnson opted more than Kennedy for ad hoc task forces, along Roosevelt's line, involving only the most essential participants. The very growth of the White House Office since Roosevelt made such particularism hazardous at best. In addition, Johnson's genius for executive leadership of this sort fell considerably short of Roosevelt's.

For those favoring the spokes-in-a-wheel arrangement, the Nixon administration began auspiciously enough. He had taken on three eminent policy advisers: Henry Kissinger, assistant for national security affairs; Arthur Burns, counselor; and Daniel Patrick Moynihan, assistant for urban affairs. All of these were to enjoy equal access to the president. The role of Moynihan, a Democrat, was particularly strange here. Although the two men shared no great political affinity, Nixon found Moynihan's briefing material so stimulating that he would search through piles of memoranda for his urban affairs adviser's submissions.[79] This relatively open structure failed to survive the departure of both Burns and Moynihan by November 1969. H. R. Haldeman filled the breach by playing to

Nixon's autocratic side. Soon little got to the president unless, in addition to being on paper, it was transmitted by someone he trusted completely.

More than in any other way, Ford was unlike his predecessor in providing a viable mix of countervailing scrutiny and structure. Carter struggled to strike a similar balance. However, his awkwardness with non-Georgians and his penchant for detail made for a serious disjunction between the administration's organizational plan and its actual workings. Like Ford, during the first term, Reagan found a much better fit between his personality and the organization of the White House than Carter. His famous one-page memos cut down drastically—some would say too much—on the amount of paper he read. Reagan preferred personal briefings from his most senior advisers. These officials would normally bring along the aide(s) most directly involved in the matter to be decided. Group sessions including all principal advisers and some key staff were frequent. It appears now, however, that Donald Regan has sharply curtailed the president's face-to-face encounters with other White House aides.

Secretariats

Earlier in this section I set forth the proposition that, to be effective, cabinet-level councils must be able to call upon central resources designated as facilitators of collective decision making in an administration. To say the least, acceptance of this view has come only slowly in the United States. The creation of the Bureau of the Budget (BOB) in 1921 marked the initial American effort to provide neutral-competence staff support to help achieve greater coherence in the executive branch.

BOB was not styled as a cabinet secretariat. Its staff focused narrowly on expenditure budgeting and saw themselves as servants of the president and creatures of Congress. The agency's first director, Charles G. Dawes, held his budget review sessions with cabinet secretaries in the Cabinet Room of the White House. He clearly viewed himself as the president's agent.[80] BOB remained in the Dawes mold until World War II. The budget office had become part of the Executive Office of the President in 1939. Its director at that time, Harold Smith, saw one of his principal tasks to be recruiting examiners with training in the social sciences and planning.[81] The clearer connection of BOB to the president, along with its strengthened analytic esprit, set it up as the perfect resource when Roosevelt sought a professional staff for managing the war effort.

As we have seen, the Truman administration created the National Security Council system in 1947. This was the first effort in the United States to formalize cabinet consultation within a broad policy sector. The new process allowed for a small secretariat of career officials on secondment from other departments or the military who worked out of the Executive Office of the President.[82] An executive secretary directed the staff and briefed the president on NSC business. The State Department Policy Planning Staff prepared NSC working drafts that would be circulated to "consultants" in member departments before submission to principals and, finally, to the president. Once the administration became preoccupied with the Korean War, the "consultant" system formalized into the NSC "staff." This consisted of departmental assistant secretaries for policy meeting twice a week. Cabinet-level committees along the lines of the NSC had yet to develop on the domestic side. However, Truman assigned a number of staff to White House–based policy development. His special counsel, Clark Clifford, played the most significant role among these advisers.[83] With the onset of the Korean War, the lines between the White House and BOB again tended to blur. That is, Truman aides did not hesitate to have their initiatives "staffed out" by BOB.

The 1952 election brought a firm believer in secretaries to the White House. When he stepped down as army chief of staff in 1948, Eisenhower had argued that the Pentagon needed a neutral secretariat for framing agendas of meetings between the secretary of the defense and the joint chiefs of staff.[84] On a modest but effective scale, President Eisenhower created a cabinet secretariat headed by a senior political appointee whose job was identifying and preparing issues for cabinet meetings.[85]

On the national security side, Eisenhower acted much more decisively.[86] He added greatly to the NSC staff housed in the Executive Office of the President and restyled the NSC's executive secretary as "the special assistant to the president for national security affairs." This official chaired the direct descendant of the NSC "staff," namely, the Policy Planning Board (PPB). The new body met for three hours twice a week to prepare for NSC meetings. PPB members, roughly the level of members of the "staff" under Truman, drew upon a new presidential order giving them access to any departmental information deemed necessary for their work. Although the NSC system was much maligned in the 1950s for overmanaging issues, recent research suggests that it served Eisenhower well.[87] It got competing interests talking at an early stage. Thus contentious points and potential agreements could be identified and worked on from the beginning of the interdepartmental process. The system served up many "split" decisions that could be resolved only by the president. Yet it stripped away enough departmental posturing to give the president meaningful options.

As we have seen, Kennedy and Johnson allowed the NSC process to wither on the vine. Both presidents kept national security secretariats exceeding ten professionals.[88] However, they did not construe these aides as neutral brokers. On the domestic side, the two presidents developed issues by assigning them to aides who worked through task forces.[89] BOB would come into play insofar as aides required analytic material beyond that provided by departments. While the system worked reasonably well under Kennedy, it began to burst at the seams under Johnson. So many Great Society initiatives competed for presidential attention or succumbed to departmental inertia by 1965 that Johnson assigned Joseph Califano the job of coordinating task forces and preparing the annual legislative program from a central White House operation with about seven staff.

Johnson took a top-to-bottom administrative approach. Stephen Hess quotes a former undersecretary in the Department of Housing and Urban Development who gives a worm's-eye view of the process:

> Confusion is created when men try to do too much at the top. In order to know what decisions are being made elsewhere in government, the White House tends either to spend time reviewing programs or to take more and more decisions on itself. The separate responsibilities of the White House, the Executive Office and the agencies are fudged, and the demarcations of who does what become uncertain. The result is a blurring of the distinction between staff and line, between programs and policy.[90]

One pronounced systemic difficulty became apparent under the process run by Califano. This was the lack of coordination between the administration's legislative program and its expenditure budget.[91] Much of the blame had landed upon BOB. Connoisseurs of executive office organization deemed BOB too hidebound by long-tenured career officials to examine policy initiatives creatively and help coordinate departments. That is, conventional institutional analysts diagnosed its problems along top-to-bottom lines similar to those exhibited by Califano.

As Nixon was frustrated in his efforts to bring about policy reforms, he began a concerted effort to impose rigorous adherence to presidential directions throughout the government.[92] His major innovations reflected a bias toward concentration of executive authority. BOB became the Office of Management and Budget (OMB) and took on a new layer of political appointees. The Domestic Council staff emerged as John Ehrlichman's fiefdom. It operated as a White House nerve center for the imposition of programmatic discipline on departments. The successful implementation of Nixon's plan for cabinet supersecretaries would have further tightened pyramidal control over departments and agencies from the White House.

We have already seen that the Ford administration was the first to have a secretariat assigned exclusively to a cabinet committee operating in a specific sector of domestic policy. As well as serving as an antidote to the Nixon years, the unit, under the direction of William Seidman, operated quite effectively.[93] Seidman and his staff embodied neutral competence by focusing their efforts on developing and maintaining more formalized cabinet consultative machinery on economic policy. In particular, Seidman has received praise for his evenhandedness in briefing the president on matters before the Economic Policy Board.

Rather than attempting to extend Ford's successful experiment into other domestic policy sectors, Carter dismantled much of the apparatus connected with what became the Economic Policy Group. While he renamed the members of the Domestic Council the "Domestic Policy Staff," he did not adopt a formal policy review system until September 1977.[94] This delay, along with the tendency of DPS appointees to be youngish policy advocates with relatively little experience in government, led to a bewildering patchwork of ad hoc groups on myriad policy issues.[95] Ironically, the Carter administration's resuscitation of collective consultation in the NSC system found the staff—now numbering seventy with over ten senior professionals—operating much more as a secretariat than it had since Eisenhower. That the NSC staff was on the whole older, and carried better professional credentials and had greater experience in government than DPS, contributed greatly to its relative success as a neutral-competence secretariat.

Initially in the first term Ronald Reagan failed to adequately complement his elaborate enhancement of the cabinet-level committee system with appointees to policy secretariats who could gain credibility as honest brokers. Starting with Richard V. Allen, Reagan's initial assistant for national security affairs who left the administration early in 1982, the first wave of NSC staffers came across as overly hawkish and/or lacking stature in their policy fields. A similar situation existed in the Office of Policy Development (OPD), DPS's successor, where Martin Anderson, the initial assistant for policy development, stayed only slightly longer than Allen. The administration made some satisfactory midcourse corrections with both the NSC staff and OPD. Reagan's seven cabinet councils drew upon "secretariats" for staff support. These bodies, chaired by executive secretaries from OPD, consisted of assistant secretaries for policy development from member departments. Small OPD staffs supported individual executive secretaries. Since the ascendancy of the hierarchical White House under Donald Regan, OPD has seen a substantial erosion of its role. On the national security side, lead departments chaired the functional equivalents to secretariats supporting senior interagency groups concerned with foreign policy, defense, intelligence, and international economics. However, the NSC staff retained its responsibility for briefing the president on all national security matters whether or not they went through the NSC process.

An Evolutionary Process

Table 1 summarizes various assertions, derived from the available literature, that have been made about presidents since FDR. These have related to presidents' views (1) of their authority, (2) of their cabinets, including the roles of secretaries, the need for structure, and the use of specialized committees, and (3) of their staffs, taking in organization of the White House, toleration of competition, and development of policy secretariats. I will now draw some broader conclusions by looking at each element of style to assess the trends since FDR's administration.

With respect to presidents' views of the scope of their authority within the executive branch, each administration up to Nixon tended to bring more issues into the White House. Thus, presidents' involvement in policy matters that conceivably could be resolved in departments or between relevant secretaries increased considerably through the decades. Truman's and Eisenhower's less pronounced instincts toward centralization did not amount to total remission of the trend. On the other hand, Nixon's imperial reflexes and actions brought home to Americans the dangers inherent in the overly concentrated exercise of executive authority. Ford, Carter, and Reagan have all struggled to rehabilitate public trust in the presidency after Nixon's excesses. Here Carter proved

Table 1
Presidents' Views of the Distribution of Executive Authority and Its Relation to Their Style

	Roosevelt	Truman	Eisenhower	Kennedy
Presidential authority	Centralized	Mixed	Mixed	Centralized
Cabinet secretaries' interrelationships	Baronial	Mixed	Collegial	Baronial
Cabinet structures	Ad hoc	Mixed	Institutionalized	Ad hoc
Areas of Cabinet specialization	None	National security	National security	None
White House organizational pattern	Spokes-in-a-wheel	Mixed	Hierarchical	Spokes-in-a-wheel
Relationship between units	Competitive	Mixed	Mixed	Competitive
Development of policy secretariats	None	National security[b]	National security[b]	National security[a]

a. President-centered.
b. Partially working under functioning cabinet-level councils.

the least successful. Although he initially pursued a decentralized form of "cabinet government," his penchant for detail largely canceled out his best intentions.

Of the presidents up to and including Nixon, only Eisenhower strove consistently to develop collegial relations among cabinet secretaries—although Truman's style gave some support to such esprit. The others viewed secretaries as barons to be dealt with largely

Johnson	Nixon	Ford	Carter	Reagan (1st term)
Centralized	Centralized	Mixed	Decentralized	Mixed
Baronial	Baronial	Collegial	Baronial	Collegial
Ad hoc	Ad hoc	Institutionalized	Ad hoc	Institutionalized
None	None	Economic policy	National security	National security; economic policy; domestic policy
Spokes-in-a-wheel	Hierarchical	Spokes-in-a-wheel	Spokes-in-a-wheel	Mixed
Competitive	Noncompetitive	Mixed	Noncompetitive	Mixed
National security;[a] domestic policy[a]	National security;[a] domestic policy[a]	National security;[a] economic policy;[b] domestic policy[a]	National security;[b] domestic policy;[a]	National security;[b] economic policy;[b] domestic policy[b]

one-on-one, or even forced into passivity. Of course, Nixon's views represented the latter of the two extremes. In a manner more consistent with previous constitutional practice, both Ford and Reagan—especially the latter—valued at least the instrumental utility in having secretaries relate to one another through collective forums. At the outset, Carter gave so much rein to cabinet secretaries that he resorted to a major purge during summer 1979 in a crash effort to bring a semblance of order to his administration.

Presidents who have viewed the cabinet collegially have institutionalized its meetings and procedures, while others have preferred ad hoc arrangements. There seems to be a gradual development toward presidents' greater use of specialized cabinet committees. The process started with Truman's and Eisenhower's use of the NSC; abated considerably under Kennedy, Johnson, and Nixon; and now has reappeared in the national security field under both Carter and Reagan. It was extended to economic policy under Ford and Reagan and to several additional fields of domestic policy under Reagan. Thus, greater institutionalization of cabinet dynamics characterizes post-Watergate Republican administrations. It remains to be seen whether the next Democratic president will continue this trend. However, as specialized bodies entrench themselves, it becomes increasingly difficult for incumbents to roll back institutionalization.

The accretion of units nominally or actually designated as secretariats for cabinet-level bodies can either complement presidents' commitments to collective decision making or increase their capacity for centralizing their administrations. Under some circumstances, secretariats can become exclusively focused on presidents' requirements for developing highly personalized policy agendas and monitoring the adoption and implementation of these goals in separate departments. In extreme cases, secretariats totally cease performing as facilitators of collective processes. Notwithstanding Greenstein's fine revisionist analysis, the perception of Eisenhower's contemporaries that his White House operated too hierarchically undermined the credibility of the NSC system as supported by its secretariat. Because of the widespread notion that Eisenhower administration structures "overcooked" policies, the NSC system, as a collective decision-making process, reached its nadir under Kennedy, Johnson, and Nixon.

Under Kennedy and Johnson, the neglect of the NSC as a cabinet secretariat, along with the emergence of a personalized domestic policy staff under Johnson, did not pose profound constitutional difficulties. The two presidents' spokes-in-a-wheel White House organizations and tolerance of countervailing advice kept their administrations from being extremely centralized. However, the absence of institutionalized and specialized cabinet-level consultation did cause serious dysfunctions in interdepartmental coordination during the Johnson administration. On the other hand, the hierarchical and noncompetitive nature of Nixon's White House intensified the personalization of policy secretariats to the point where his administration became obsessed with centralized control.

Ford began to extricate the White House from such compulsiveness. He particularly achieved success in mounting for the first time a viable economic policy committee with a functioning secretariat. The flexible organization of his White House advanced this effort greatly. Carter brought the NSC system back to life as a collective decision-making process. In domestic affairs, his unstructured, president-oriented staff resources collided head-on with the fact that he really trusted only Georgians and this hindered executive office policy development. Reagan, on the other hand, seems to have modulated various elements of his views of the presidency, cabinet, and staff to maximize the benefits of cabinet consultation. Notwithstanding the radical underpinnings of Reagan's brand of conservativism, his system seems to have worked effectively toward achieving his most cherished goals. A question arises as to whether the inevitable backlash to Reagan's policies will include another Kennedy-like repudiation of such structures.

3. Two Views of Cabinet Consultation
Carter and Reagan

Under Jimmy Carter, the cabinet drew upon little collective identity. In domestic affairs, cabinet-level committees were poorly delineated and did little by way of policy coordination. Thus, "cabinet government" meant each secretary for himself. An acronymic jumble of ad hoc task forces reflected more the burning issues of the day than sustained efforts to keep departments whose interests within policy sectors overlapped talking to one another. Ronald Reagan's administration, especially during the first term, has illustrated the fact that a diametrically different approach to Carter's can enhance the coherence of the executive branch. The belief that secretaries' relations with one another must be highly structured to adequately coordinate their departments' activities is the centerpiece of Reagan's perspective. That is, to operate as a team, the cabinet must have group dynamics. Early in the first term, this concept led to the embellishment of the National Security Council system with senior interagency groups and the creation of seven entirely new "cabinet councils" coordinating decisions in various domestic policy sectors. This chapter's detailed assessment of cabinet consultation under Carter and Reagan will begin by focusing on their views of presidential authority and whether the two leaders tried to centralize or decentralize its exercise, or to pursue a blend of the two strategies. How the presidents structured and used cabinet-level machinery will then be examined.

Jimmy Carter

Before treating Carter's approach to cabinet consultation, we should look briefly at the circumstances that Carter faced and the personal qualities he brought to office. Assuming the presidency in the aftermath of the Watergate scandal, defeat in Vietnam, and in an atmosphere of widespread concern about the growth of the welfare state, Carter served the nation during a period of intense stress. At the same time, atomization within the Washington political arena appeared to have reached an apogee. In the broader context of national affairs, continued economic stagflation following upon the 1973–74 energy crisis made for exceptionally gloomy economic prospects. To add to the constraints that the harsh economic times placed on fiscal policy, the specter of a taxpayer revolt, brought on by the approval of Proposition 13 in California, appeared to preclude any Democratic continuation of Johnson's Great Society in the expansion of social programs.

The fact that Carter was a moderate Democrat suggested that he would not be too adventuresome in the social policy field anyway. At first blush, his stress on a balanced budget and zero-base expenditure review fit the conservative times. In addition, these emphases did not come across as attacks on bureaucratic fiefdoms. Indeed, the search for savings along with efforts to reorganize agencies, departments, and the cabinet never evoked fear or hostility among career civil servants. However, deep bureaucratic dissatisfaction with the administration developed as it became clear that Carter and his most trusted aides were hobbled by inexperience. This defect—lack of familiarity with the Washington scene—presented the administration with very painful learning experiences in virtually all its significant initiatives. In fact, as one top White House aide recounted, the administration even found it difficult to discern those rare instances when minutiae really count because of the importance of those affected. In his words:

A couple of guys [in the Ford administration] told me that congressional liaison used to spend hours with Ford deciding which congressional trip went where and who got which airplane and the makeup of the delegation. Now Carter didn't know until he sent Bob Strauss to Egypt as special envoy that we didn't have all the airplanes we need or that there was any

question about who went in what airplane. . . . He didn't know
that some had windows and some didn't, which is very important to those people up there.[1]

Carter's own personality did not help here. He brought to his
work a ponderous style that tended to ritualize consultation and
caused him to devour factual information. Very early in the administration, senior career civil servants in the Office of Management
and Budget were astounded to find that they were to brief the
president personally on the defense budget. They worked feverishly
to develop a series of charts for their presentation. As an after-
thought, they brought to their meeting several back-up diagrams
for each of their main slides just in the case the president had a
detailed question or two. Their meeting, which started at 3:00 P.M.
lasted until 11:00 that night. By the close, the president had viewed
every single chart. In fact, Carter tipped off astute observers to his
style even before he came to the Oval Office. In his words:

> [My] exact procedure is derived to some degree from my scien-
> tific or engineering background—I like to study first all the
> efforts that have been made historically toward the same goal,
> to bring together advice or ideas from as wide or divergent
> points of view as possible, to assimilate them personally or
> with a small staff, to assess the quality of the points of view
> and identify the source of these proposals. . . . I like to be per-
> sonally involved so that I can know the thought processes that
> go into the final decisions and also so that I can be a spokes-
> man, without prompting, when I take my case to the people,
> the legislature.[2]

The Illusion of Decentralized Cabinet Consultation

At the time of my first interviews, 1979, top Carter aides still
invoked the principle of decentralized cabinet consultation as the
keystone of the administration. For instance, a member of the Domestic Policy Staff took pains to demonstrate that he dealt only
with issues that genuinely deserved presidential attention.[3] Over in
the White House, a very senior staff member told of the immense
restraint Carter used during a major review of the administration
in spring 1978. At that time, some cabinet secretaries and top
White House aides had complained bitterly of the lack of coherence in the administration.[4] Carter took a minimalist approach to

the issue. He mandated a weekly meeting of the senior subcabinet representatives of secretaries with White House senior staff in the Roosevelt Room. He also took review of senior appointments from Hamilton Jordan, who was woefully overloaded and notoriously neglectful of detail, and assigned it to Tim Kraft. Before this move, cabinet secretaries had exercised almost total discretion in choice of top management personnel in departments. In any event, interest in the Roosevelt Room meetings soon waned. However, a more intense "agency review process" won Carter's approval in fall 1978. Going beyond vacancies issuing from resignations, the review process attempted to identify political appointees who had done so well that they should receive more responsible positions or so poorly that they should be encouraged to think of resigning.

Even White House assessments of appointees attempted to avoid the appearance of centralization of presidential authority. Carter insisted that they remain secret. Thus, aides went to every length to comply—even talking reporters hot on their trail into not releasing leaked information. As well, cabinet secretaries were kept apprised of the review process as it went through their departments. Above all, Carter did not want a reenactment of Richard Nixon's 1970 purge, under the direction of Frederik V. Malek, of appointees deemed disloyal to the administration. In one observers words: "The president didn't want to unleash a junior team of Maleks, Haldemans, and Ehrlichmans who would run rampant through the departments and say, 'You've screwed it up and you're gone.' He doesn't operate that way and he wouldn't allow us to operate that way."[5] Unfortunately, the administration had so burst at the seams by summer 1979 that Carter set aside his pious thoughts entirely and allowed wholesale dismissals or forced resignations of appointees. He even sacked four cabinet secretaries. Only then was the rhetoric of decentralized cabinet government set aside. As one aide noted, "From now, the Cabinet will have to clear everything with the White House."[6]

This turn of events simply served to strip away an illusion. Every fiber of Carter's personal makeup had actually been conspiring all along to run a highly centralized administration. Here the president's tendency to engross himself in details served as the fifth column. Looking back in 1982, career officials drew a sharp contrast between Carter and Ronald Reagan with such comments as these: "[Carter] was almost too—not almost—he *was* compulsively oriented in the detail direction."[7] "He was down in the weeds . . .

he did not have this more global overview of what he really wanted."[8]

Especially during the first two years of the administration, Carter found in the budget process a major outlet for his love of detail. Career officials throughout the Office of Management and Budget marveled both that they were brought along to meetings with the president and that his desire for in-depth analysis appeared so insatiable. One strategically positioned political appointee justified Carter's involvement with the budget in terms appropriate to a centralized administration. Carter's interest hinged on the vital link between expenditure resources and the development and operation of federal programs. "A president like Carter is extremely active in the business of federal programs and what agencies are doing. He clearly sees the budget as his major way of making the system do what he wants it to do and making it not do what he doesn't want it to do."[9]

Another official who, like Carter, was trained in Admiral Hyman Rickover's nuclear submarine program confirmed that Carter had made a conscious choice to found his administrative style on an attention to detail. In addition, although Carter's closest aides had already taken him to task for floundering, our respondent remained, like many of his colleagues, a firm believer in the president's immense capacity for work:

> I've discussed this with him and his feelings, which I share because we came from a common background—both having been trained initially by Rickover—is that he doesn't know how to do a job well without looking at the details because it's the details that make up the whole. He complained that his closest advisers urged him to just concentrate on the big policy issues and leave the details to them. He pointed out to me that that wasn't his conception. I told him I shared his view based on my background. It's a warped view of how to operate. But, obviously, he manages to find the time to do this. . . . The only just criticism that I would find would be that in taking this approach, he doesn't have the time to handle all the important issues. But, he obviously does. He spends long hours.[10]

Interestingly, another graduate of Rickover's program serving as an appointee in the Reagan administration spoke of his severe disappointment when his expectations for someone with Carter's training proved illusory. That is, Carter appeared to have lacked the qualities, beyond intellectual curiosity and capacity for work, necessary for executive leadership:

> My reservations about Carter were not so much about over-work and attention to detail as they seemed to be about . . . political will and what appeared to be vacillation . . . venality and . . . his carriage; . . . the Carter administration . . . caved in all the time when there were hard decisions. . . . Jimmy Carter seemed always to be going through these great soul search-ings. . . . That to me is sort of an inadequacy that I would not have expected in a guy who was from the Naval Academy, who went through the submarine program. That is supposed to teach, *does* teach, a lot of self-reliance.[11]

A Cabinet of Barons

Richard F. Fenno noted over twenty years ago that presidents exer-cising tight control over many subunits of the executive branch will tend less than others to utilize collective cabinet dynamics.[12] Of course, the illusion sphere surrounding Carter's administration until summer 1979 did not admit to his slipping into a highly president-centered executive style. Up until that summer, the dep-uty head of a key agency in the Executive Office of the President still espoused the conventional line. The administration was de-centralized by virtue of "cabinet government": "The cabinet is by our standards a relatively strong cabinet administration. The presi-dent holds regular cabinet meetings. He relies very strongly on his cabinet. He does not have the strong central control that Nixon or Johnson had."[13]

In fact, those closest to cabinet operations gave little weight to their significance as collective dynamics beyond providing forums for sec-retaries' exchange of information and pep talks by the president.[14] At their height, cabinet meetings occurred once every two weeks. Over most two-week periods, the small White House cabinet secretariat only devoted about one day of work to preparing cabinet agendas and minutes. The rest of its time was largely devoted to screening cabinet secretaries' individual requests for time with the president. As one respondent put it, "Policy gets made on a one-on-one relationship between each cabinet secretary and the president."[15]

As we will see, the Carter administration was not devoid of machinery enabling groups of secretaries, not the entire cabinet, to meet on important issues. Some of these gatherings, such as those connected with the National Security Council process and the Economic Policy Group, took on a relatively formalized character. Others, operating around management of specific policy issues, were essentially task forces. Nonetheless, Carter's view of cabinet consultation failed to give even this modest array of bodies a sense of collegial enterprise. If cabinet officers ultimately settled matters one-on-one with the president, all the incentives favored baronial behavior whereby secretaries who enjoyed the president's favor could readily ignore their colleagues. As one Carter appointee who had also served briefly in the Ford administration noted:

> The Ford people had a fair-play system. A process was set up so that the president wasn't "blind sided." Any issue that involved other interests in the administration was quickly sent out for staffing and representative views. A maxium number of players got to play in a game before a decision was made. And their views were fairly represented in the decision papers that went up to the president. The Carter group has had a very difficult time, from day one, trying to set up an orderly process. It's been "ad hocary" at its best. Therefore, you find different players in different groups—a constant movable feast.[16]

Some Success and Notable Failures with Cabinet-Level Committees

Carter only half-heartedly pursued the use of cabinet-level committees in his administration. On the domestic side, this meant a massive retreat from the heightened formalization of such bodies under Ford. Chapter 2 has noted the poor performance of Carter's Economic Policy "Group" as compared to Ford's "Board." A recent study by Laurence Lynn, Jr., and David Whitman provides a detailed look at the disarray that prevailed in other domestic policy sectors.[17] In their treatment of Carter's welfare reform initiative, the authors assess how the administration's efforts fell between two jurisdictional stools: Health, Education and Welfare, and Labor. Among the many procedural faults described, the following seem particularly striking: because the principals rarely met face to face, disagreements between their officials were thereby deepened and prolonged; cabinet-level discussions included a consultant with Georgia connections and a Washington lobbyist whose ideas appealed to the president, which contributed to the truncation of interdepartmental processes by White House aides; and cabinet-level sessions with the president followed a formal briefing format, which forced HEW and Labor into lengthy preparatory negotiations about which graphs to display and how. Charles Schultze, a regular participant in meetings with the president, noted with dismay, "The thing got so goddamned complicated that nobody in the world but the three or four people who put it together fully understood it, and I doubt if they could fully."[18]

On the foreign policy side, however, Carter approved a major effort to revitalize the machinery for collective consultation between secretaries. These advances came about largely through the efforts of Carter's assistant for national security affairs, Zbigniew Brzezinski. As we have seen, Henry Kissinger permitted cabinet-level National Security Council deliberations to atrophy under Nixon and Ford. As Nixon's national security adviser, Kissinger had eased the burden of full NSC sessions by setting up and chairing personally a number of subcommittees on which departments were represented only at the subcabinet level.

Under Carter, Brzezinski first sought to consolidate the various committees operating in 1977 into seven, all of which would require principal-level representation.[19] The cabinet secretary whose responsibilities most clearly encompassed a policy area would chair the relevant NSC committee. Eventually, Carter balked even at this reduced level of complexity. Instead he approved two NSC standing committees. The Policy Review Committee—chaired, on an issue-by-issue basis, by the cabinet secretaries whose departments took the lead—treated broad initiatives and concerns in fields such as relations between Arab nations and Israel, international development, and matters centered on a specific country. Meanwhile, the Special Coordination Committee focused on more contingent matters in three functional areas—management of crises, specific intelligence activities, and development of U.S. policies concerning arms control. Brzezinski chaired the Special Coordination Committee on the grounds that contingent matters usually raise greater grounds for jurisdictional disputes and place more of a premium on timely action.

During the first half of the Carter administration, the new system appeared to work reasonably well. In fact, one career official intimately connected with its operation employed it as a model for proposed reforms of coordinative mechanisms in the economic policy field that he had submitted at the administration's request:

How do you emulate the National Security Council process? . . . Nobody is in charge. . . . You don't have people saying: "Mr. President, inflation is a real problem. We don't know how much of it is a problem of structural imbalances in the economy. We would like to know. . . . Let's do a study. Here are eight issues that ought to be addressed at a minimum. . . . It ought to be conducted jointly with the following departments." A report with options will be back by a prearranged date. The decision memo will go to the president: "Here are the things you can do about it, if anything."[20]

As one might expect, the NSC committee system did not really operate quite as smoothly as our career official suggested. Brzezinski himself observed that even very early on in the administration the president's penchant for detail made it difficult to maintain the system's integrity:

At times, Carter's impatience produced circumstances in which he would make decisions ahead of the NSC coordinating process, prompting me to complain to him. Moreover, whenever I tried to relieve him of excessive detail, Carter would show real uneasiness, and I even felt some suspicion, that I was usurping his authority.[21]

This situation became chronic as Cyrus Vance, secretary of state through most of the administration, appeared increasingly dovish in Carter's eyes. Simultaneously, a succession of thorny foreign affairs crises seemed to confirm Brzezinski's more skeptical world view and skew the distribution of work between the Policy Review Committee and the national security adviser's Special Coordination Committee in favor of the latter. The National Security Council, as such, rarely met; thus the ascendancy of the SCC in relation to the PRC intensified an "escalator" process whereby cabinet secretaries felt bound to attend the SCC even if a deputy would do just as well. As a former NSC staff member now working elsewhere in the Executive Office of the President observed, the SCC increasingly pandered to the president's preoccupations rather than providing arm's-length preparation of stances and initiatives:

"When you had a continuing crisis, as you did with the hostages, you were more or less locked into endless high level meetings by the SCC. The president made a tremendous issue out of the hostages. The system they had set up almost demanded that it be dealt with at the SCC level. It took up a tremendous amount of top-level time which is the most precious commodity there is around the White House.[22]

Ronald Reagan

Ronald Reagan, in sharp contrast to Jimmy Carter, conveys a nonchalance about the details of government that has prompted many commentators to question the degree to which he has applied himself to his job. Yet his first year in office proved to be one of the most successful on record—using, of course, the narrow yardstick of a president's ability to enact essential elements of his legislative program. In fact, his achievement of huge tax cuts, massive curtailment of spending on social programs and lavish embellishment of defense funds by summer 1981 brought on howls of protest that Congress had slipped into impotence. Although we increasingly find evidence of the erosion of the Reagan hegemony, no one can deny his exceptional exploitation of a strong election mandate and a Republican majority in the Senate. No matter what nightmares all this has evoked in the social consciousness of his critics, those who deplore Reagan's policies no longer can dismiss him on the grounds of ineptitude. In addition to being one of the most winning souls to occupy the White House, he has used his cabinet and White House resources exceedingly well.

A parable is in order here. During the 1980 Canadian federal election, a political scientist then teaching in Toronto was asked to be policy adviser to a young Liberal candidate. The request was couched in urgent terms. The candidate had never graduated from high school. He needed special help with issues. At last the political scientist had something to do with his nervous energy during the doldrums of the winter term. He started feeding the candidate reams of newspaper clippings and briefing notes on every conceivable topic that might, and did, come up in all-candidates forums—including why the Liberals had got rid of Canada's only aircraft carrier back in the 1960s. He soon found to his dismay that the candidate was not using these materials—except to cure his insomnia in the wee hours after a day of, among other things, shaking hands outside subway stations in subzero weather. The political scientist quickly took another tack which proved more effective. He briefed the candidate in "smokers" in which campaign workers would present contrasting viewpoints. As well, he provided a series of "bullet sheets" that enabled the candidate, while taking a question during a town hall–style meeting, to find on one short page a few very basic points which he wove into a passable answer.

In the end, the candidate lost—the Liberals had never won that seat. However, he so impressed the party leadership that he obtained a senior political appointment in Ottawa. While the reluctant student went on to fame, his tutor returned to obscurity on his campus. Virtually all of us from academe could recount several similar experiences. Why then do we find it so hard to understand Reagan's success? Do we too often expect the level of comprehension that comes from studiousness to inform our political leaders? In real life, many of them operate much more like indifferent underclassmen who simply want to grasp enough to pass the exam.

This trait in Reagan comes through clearly in Lou Cannon's biography.[23] At first blush, Cannon seems to present conflicting evidence about Reagan's intellectual ability. As a child, Reagan came off as a prodigy—apparently learning to read before he went to school and demonstrating a precocious memory. However, one of his college professors complained that he never opened a book. His brother asserted that Reagan's "photographic memory" enabled him to spend "a quick hour" with a text the night before an exam and pass. The case to the contrary, which Cannon does not address fully, suggests that Reagan has never in his adult life displayed a strong intellectual command of public issues. In fact, Cannon uses on occasion terms such as "monumental ignorance" to portray the policy-issue acumen of this most successful leader whose advisers, since his days in California, have spoon-fed with one-page mini-memos, boiling even the most complex matters to the bare essentials.

One of Cannon's anecdotes so aroused my curiosity that I consulted several specialists in learning skills for their impressions of Ronald Reagan's intelligence as reflected in his delivery of speeches. As Cannon presents it, Reagan, who allegedly read at age five, encountered serious difficulty reading radio scripts when he got a job as an announcer after college.[24] Only after memorizing a passage and repeating it out loud could he deliver it with reasonable spontaneity. This suggested some sort of a disability. Indeed, my experts speculated that, while Reagan might well have been a precocious performer for his mother and early teachers, he might not have, by his young adulthood, gone beyond visual perception—decoding what appears on a page—to comprehension—grasping difficult concepts. A deficiency in comprehension would sharply reduce spontaneity in delivery of a script prepared by someone else. The experts identified traits in Reagan's current delivery that suggest the condition has not been overcome. He comes across as bright but shallow.

Pointing up that "we read with our acumen," one expert suggested that Reagan probably would tire even in an attempt to cope with a fraction of the formidable memoranda that Carter devoured. In other words, his shallow comprehension urges would fail to respark his interest when it waned. Another indentified a five-step cumulative process leading to full comprehension of written material. While a person with a studious disposition like Carter's would by nature go through even the most laborious steps to grasping material, the upper levels can be delegated. Thus, we find Reagan managing reasonably well on a diet of mini-memos supplemented by oral briefings.

Delegation with a Reagan Touch

We should not be deceived by Reagan's inattentiveness to detail and nuances buried in briefing books. It does not necessarily mean that he is only a semiengaged president. In fact, Lou Cannon notes that while Reagan was governor, a lack of mastery of detail did not prevent him from employing "the authority of his compelling personality" to take charge in those situations which he believed demanded his attention.[25]

From the outset of his first term, Reagan imposed exceptional discipline on his administration. The White House perhaps never before exercised such control over subcabinet appointments.[26] The ideological compatibility of nominees with administration views was an exceptionally strong factor in determining whether they eventually obtained posts. However, the budget and David Stockman's command of its intricacies provided Reagan with his most potent instrument for altering the course of the vast administrative apparatus he inherited in the U.S. government. Stockman operated through two mechanisms. First, with clear guidance from the White House, he worked out dramatic changes of the budget while secretary-designates were still assembling their teams and had yet to encounter career officials in their departments-to-be.[27]

To top off these bilateral sessions, Reagan used a series of full cabinets, in which his budget prodigy shone, to assure that the central programmatic implications of the budget revisions came across clearly as a "team" effort:

The cabinet was assembled often during the first few weeks to confirm these policy program directions. It was a highly disciplined operation in which OMB was clearly acting on behalf of the president. It was in the driver's seat—at least as far as the civilian agencies were concerned.... So, the early cabinet meetings were Stockman, on behalf of the president, and the other presidential advisers just laying out, "Here's what we're going to do, fellows, and I expect you to support it." ... The cabinet met often ... but just to receive their marching orders and to hype each other up: "We've all got to get on and ... if we start to make special pleas for our programs, we're going to be in difficulty."[28]

The success of the initial use of the budget to impose a stringent regimen both on secretaries and their departments should not suggest to us that Reagan, or even Stockman, was going to mire himself in programmatic detail. The entire venture came off in global terms, with detailed programmatic implications taking a back seat to macrostrategies. In domestic policy areas, which were to experience ruthless curtailment of expenditure and the termination of many programs, the macro approach left virtually no room for modulating cuts according to efficiency and effectiveness. In national security, where defense was "off on a growth path,"[29] Stockman, by his own admission, failed to apply even a modicum of analysis to the development of budget projections.[30] Here Stockman's tack led, in the words of one OMB career official, to the enshrinement of figures "beyond the wildest expectations of the defense establishment."[31] As another respondent put it, the president had adopted figures following directly from his unvarnished view of defense expenditure as the administration's top priority:

Defense issues, especially the big ones—like the size of the budget or whether you cancel this or that major program, or whether Defense is made to put money in for a major program that they don't want—all those issues are settled with the president; ... he's got to be in on it. Now the biggest hawk in the administration happens to be the president himself. So, when the issue goes that far, the outcome is predictable.[32]

The inherent problem with Reagan's administrative style appears to be too much thrust, largely owing to the president's and his advisers' black-and-white views of issues, behind dubious policies. The questionable nature of the policies stems largely from their strongly ideological skewedness. Within the margins, however, the president could conceivably have worked to moderate the more eccentric elements of his administration. As we will see when we examine more closely how his White House operated during the first term, the "implementation" side of the West Wing under James Baker played with tangible success to Reagan's desire to succeed, as well as his interest in matters of deep ideological significance.

Almost all the political appointees among the respondents gave Reagan credit, notwithstanding his neglect of detail, for energetically engaging himself in some issues. One appointee stated,

> One thing that Reagan does is, when push comes to shove, he'll stay up all night. I mean he will get involved at the important moment. . . . Reagan is usually above the fray except where he thinks the president's getting involved will make a difference. He's probably been through 20 hours of budget meetings in the last week . . . so if something's important, he'll put everything else aside. But, he has a ruthless sense of priorities. He really knows that he can accomplish a few things. He's going to pick some good people and let them handle the rest.[33]

All this depends on Reagan's being able to discern which issues merit his attention. In turn, these judgments require a grasp of policy fields which, in fact, he lacks in key areas. This point was brought home by a member of the National Security Council staff:

> At least in the national security area, the president himself does not have the background and the middle-level grasp of the machinery that he does in the domestic area. So, we really operate a bottom-up system. The president has a good overall idea of where he wants to go. When specific decisions are brought to him, I think he makes them with enormous good sense and skill. But, there's not really much push coming from him in the form of initiatives or unifying policies at an early stage. It's more waiting for the issues to come up when they get critical.[34]

The Team

Through attention to screening appointees, the early imposition of discipline, and the use of cabinet councils in key policy sectors, the Reagan administration projected during the first term an image of harmony rare to the U.S. executive branch. Indeed, career officials consistently stress these ingredients in explaining the coherence of the administration. As one said,

> This administration has, through the people that it appointed, through their early indoctrination and through the various cabinet committees, done a better job of keeping their agency heads aligned with and responding to their priorities than any other administration I've seen. This is much more of an ideological administration. I think there's a consistency in what the various agencies are doing.[35]

Central to the above assessment is the assertion that close vetting and careful orienting of appointees do not explain entirely the apparent harmony of the Reagan administration. In addition, cabinet councils supposedly take us beyond the usual rhetoric offered by administrations about cabinet consultation. They allegedly engage secretaries in a collegial deliberative process that helps maintain the value placed on teamwork inculcated at the beginning of the administration.

The introduction of cabinet councils itself involved finding a middle ground. Initially, Edwin Meese and other Californians who had served Reagan while governor sought to tranplant Sacramento's supercabinet system to Washington. Here cabinet members, free of operational responsibility for line departments, would serve as coordinative officers for large umbrella policy sectors. A premium would be placed on departments, under subcabinet heads, to resolve disputes between themselves. Only the residual issues that proved intractable at a lower level would rise to cabinet deliberations. There, in frequent sessions with the president, secretaries would feel free to offer comments outside their specific areas on the grounds that seeking solutions in this order of issue required collective consciousness and effort. As one Californian reflecting on the Sacramento experience put it:

> The kinds of items that would come up for business were either differences that couldn't be resolved at a lower level because of some sort of impasse between departments, or were of a magnitude that they should receive the attention of the governor before policy decisions were made. . . . While each of the cabinet members had a general functional area, . . . when they sat in the various meetings they were encouraged by the governor to speak out on any subject.[36]

Members of the Reagan transition team with Washington experience were skeptical about the national-level viability of what had worked in Sacramento. A compromise presented itself when some of the non-Californians began thinking of an extension of Ford's success with the Economic Policy Board to other policy areas. In the words of one observer,

> I don't think you can have the secretary of defense considering matters that might normally fall within the province of the secretary of the interior. . . . We ultimately decided not to go with a supercabinet. But, based on my experience in the Ford administration and the EPB, I thought that you could have smaller groups of cabinet officers who have a particular interest in a certain issue. They could get together and work on that issue as a group and do so productively. And that's how we came to form our cabinet council system, patterned after the EPB.[37]

Although respondents pointed to cracks in the process, most indicated that the cabinet council system contributed greatly to the orderly handling of business in the administration. Several, both political appointees and career officials, believed that the tendency (in White House vernacular) to "roundtable" issues made it difficult for cabinet secretaries to work bilaterally with the president. First, the White House guards the president from situations where he might be privately lobbied by a secretary and, second, he likely will defuse such an overture by reminding the secretary of the cabinet council process:

> As long as they know that the president doesn't want to hear from them or their colleagues independently or in private sessions, they know they've got to play this game and do what they might otherwise resist. That is, expose themselves to arguments against their point of view from their colleagues. . . . We just don't make time on his schedule for people to come in and privately review matters with him or lobby him on some issues. . . . If they happen to do it, during a photo opportunity or some other thing . . . he's not at all reluctant to turn to me and say, "We've got to get this on the agenda." At that point the integrity of the process is protected, the cabinet officer is satisfied that he's raised the issue, and we have a forum for dealing with it.[38]

Interestingly, many respondents who stressed the force of the round-table norm noted that it succeeded in large part because of the homogeneity of the cabinet. In addition to sharing compatible world views, most secretaries bring from their experience in the corporate world a relatively detached view of winning and losing. One official, viewing the current administration from the vantage point of long experience in the Executive Office of the President, stressed that Alexander Haig did not fit well into the ethos of cabinet government:

> Since Secretary Haig left, I think that you have a fairly homo-geneous group sitting around the cabinet table. I mean, they are men who are used to winning *and* losing in their corporate existence. They don't make a life-or-death issue over every problem that comes before them. That's where I felt Secretary Haig was different from the others. He was very, very uptight. He made much more of winning or losing on each issue than anyone else in the cabinet.[39]

Despite their praise of the system, most officials warned of clear limitations to cabinet councils. Many, working in staffs serving these bodies, cited instances where cabinet secretaries had by-passed the process entirely on some key issues. Respondents in the two central agencies with programmatic responsibilities in addi-tion to advisory roles—namely, Treasury and the Office of the U.S. Trade Representative—gave a glimpse of how line departments de-velop ways to protect traditional turf from collective scrutiny. First, in areas where the department's lead responsibility is firmly established by statute or convention, the strategy is to run with the ball until someone blows a whistle. Second, try to get extremely sensitive issues—because of national security and/or political rami-fications—privately to the White House, and eventually to the president, arguing all the way that the administration cannot afford the danger of leaks presented by roundtabling.

More fundamentally, a significant number of respondents won-dered if the cabinet council system had not overly channeled con-flict in the administration. In time, some believed, such delibera-tions become pro forma since participants, operating under a norm of cordiality, find they can only lose by criticizing too intensely. When the president attends a cabinet council session, deference to his office further constrains conflict. In fact, some departments had learned how to exploit the greater reserve of secretaries in sessions with the president by arranging to have their issues considered first in his presence without the normal preparatory work in meetings led by pro tem chairmen. One observer noted,

> The effect of having the president there is to suppress most meaningful controversy. This is too bad. The participants seem to be much less willing to express their views forcefully if the president is there than if he isn't. It's doubly unfortunate in that several agencies have arranged to have their first cabinet council review of an issue in front of the president. This gives the proposing agency extraordinary leverage. You're faced, in many cases, with all-or-nothing types of choices rather than meaningful alternatives.[40]

This account of cracks, and ploys to exploit them, in the cabinet council system should not lead us to the conclusion that it was never meant for the U.S. presidency. Any account of cabinet in the United Kingdom would note similar defects. One respondent in the West Wing, not entirely a devotee of cabinet councils, gave them credit for managing a host of issues of a large enough order that they cannot be handled by a department acting on its own, yet less compelling among the constellation of issues calling out for presidential attention. In his words,

> It works extremely well on the issues that are, on a scale of zero to ten in terms of the president's political interest, ranging to about six or seven level. When you get things that are really close to the guts of the administration, it becomes essential for the president's staff to mount an effort to get around the council process. That's when we really need to get deeply involved; . . . beat the drum and figure out how to get it through the Hill.[41]

Institutionalization and Specialization

The Reagan administration, through its elaborate system of cabinet-level committees, attained simultaneously in the first term the greatest regularity and differentiation of such bodies in the history of the presidency. The very density of activity meant that cabinet secretaries frequently found that they had attended committee meetings in the White House three or more times a week. Any twelve-month period might have seen in the neighborhood of two hundred cabinet-level meetings, of which a third would have been attended by the president. As a rule of thumb, secretaries made every effort to represent their departments personally when the president took the chair. Other meetings, which were held in the Roosevelt Room instead of the Cabinet Room, might only draw deputies from departments not vitally concerned with an issue.

As we saw in chapter 2, a three-tiered committee system operated on the national security side. This included the NSC proper, four senior interagency groups (SIGs) that prepared issues for NSC meetings, and interagency groups—normally working at the assistant secretary level—which did the spade work for the SIGs. This system attempted to reduce the susceptibility of the NSC to policy obsessions such as those that occurred during the Carter administration when the Special Coordination Committee, usually a principals-only affair, was often taken up with day-to-day management of crises such as Iran and Afghanistan. As one respondent with experience under both the Carter and Reagan administrations put it:

> If you had a continuing crisis such as one of those today, you could start it off at the NSC. They would come out with a National Security Directive which would task a SIG and an IG to deal with it. So you would have three levels at which such a crisis could be dealt with. You could push it down as it became possible to handle it at a lower level.[42]

Nonetheless, the Reagan NSC system operated poorly through the first year and a half of the first term. Here the forcefulness of Alexander Haig and the weakness of Richard V. Allen, then the national security adviser, impaired the process. Things improved notably under George Shultz and William Clark. This fact, along with the NSC system's near demise during the Kissinger era, suggests that such machinery works well only when the principals' assertiveness is reasonably well balanced. In addition, Clark, no expert on foreign affairs, enjoyed strong personal relationships with two other principals—Shultz and Caspar Weinberger—both of whom he knew well from California.

The seven cabinet councils operating on the domestic side included Economic Affairs (chaired pro tem by Treasury), Commerce and Trade (Commerce), Federalism and Health and Human Resources (Health and Human Services), Natural Resources and Environment (Interior), Food and Argiculture (Agriculture), Legal Policy

(Justice), and Management and Administration (chaired by the counselor to the president—formerly Edwin Meese). A midterm planning process in fall 1982 provides an illustration of how the cabinet council system handled administration issues. Before the November congressional elections, Meese and Edwin Harper, then assistant to the president for domestic policy, called cabinet councils designed to produce policy proposals that would serve as key agenda items for the rest of the presidential term. Disappointing congressional election results reduced the utility of this exercise for assuring that the administration identify goals helping it to "stay" its conservative course. Yet several of the policy ideas that became public immediately after the election evolved from the planning process. These included the "user tax" for highway improvement, payment of farm subsidies in surplus food rather than cash, taxation of unemployment benefits, taxation of health insurance premiums paid by employers beyond a certain level, and an accelerated phase-in of the tax reduction scheduled for July 1983. These proposals had appeared on shopping lists submitted to cabinet councils by the Transportation, Agriculture, Labor, Health and Human Services, and Treasury Departments, respectively. While two—Labor's and Treasury's—were ultimately discarded, the president endorsed the others. In fact, the Transportation proposal won congressional approval during the lame duck session that ended in late December 1982.

At the beginning of the second term, of course, Reagan collapsed his numerous cabinet councils handling domestic affairs. Thus, two standing bodies currently function in this field. James A. Baker III chairs the Economic Policy Council and Edwin Meese III chairs the Domestic Policy Council. The first body has operated the more effectively. For instance, it conducted through 1985 major reviews of both trade and agricultural policies. This does not mean that its performance has been flawless. Both of the issue reviews ran up against matters that required closer management by the White House and, ultimately, the intervention of the president. Interestingly, Baker has frequently exercised the treasury secretary's prerogatives by not taking policies that clearly fall under his department's jurisdiction to the Economic Policy Council. This has been the case both with tax simplification and efforts to work with the economics secretaries of four other leading advanced industrial nations toward stabilization of the key trading currencies.

Meanwhile, Mr. Meese's Domestic Policy Council has become a

bit of an administration backwater. This may be caused by the ideo-logical character of his central policy concerns. For instance, the council spent much of its time during fall 1985 and early 1986 trying to reconcile deep divisions over whether affirmative action guide-lines for government contractors should be lifted. Mr. Meese led those who sought suspension, while the labor secretary, William E. Brock, headed those fighting to maintain the system.

Conclusion

Although every president since Truman has grappled with the is-sue, cabinet consultation has not commanded much serious atten-tion from those who have studied the presidency. For the most part, scholars have found it difficult to reconcile the notion of collective deliberation within administrations with the simple con-stitutional fact that, ultimately, U.S. executive authority resides in a single person—the president. Thus, assessing the limits within which cabinet secretaries might share in this authority, either as individual administration officers or collectively, becomes a much more formidable task than that confronting students of the cabinet in prime-ministerial systems.

A logical starting point presents itself to students of the U.S. presidency who wish to probe the role of cabinet consultation. While it might not mean giving it a collective authority, consulting the cabinet might ease the president's decision load. This role emerges in situations (1) where the president essentially delegates a large proportion of issues to be worked out by secretaries within their departments, (2) where he establishes cabinet-level bodies that attempt to settle interdepartmental differences before options reach the president for his decision, or (3) where he employs a mix of both approaches.

Several caveats come to the fore as we examine a president's im-plementation of his model for cabinet consultation. First, he must know himself well and assess the degree to which personality traits might undermine his approach. Here the Carter case suggests that a president's penchant for detail can override a preference for a decen-tralized form of cabinet consultation that might otherwise allow secretaries greater latitude in deciding departmental issues on their own. Second, a president cannot set aside entirely the legacy of institutional development. If a relatively formalized cabinet-level committee has operated with reasonable effectiveness in previous administrations, a president must recognize that an instrumental imperative might make such a mechanism essential to preparation of issues within its policy field. Here Carter reversed the neglect of the National Security Council as a deliberative body dating back to Kennedy's repudiation of Eisenhower's "government by committee." However, he did not follow through rigorously enough on the lessons derived from Ford's success with a cabinet-level body developing major issues in economic affairs.

Third, while cabinet-level bodies have pretty well proven their utility in national security and economic policy, expansion into other areas should occur gradually. Not every sector presents compelling issues on a weekly, even monthly, basis. Also, in some fields, such as legal policy, one lead department (Justice) pretty well overshadows the legitimate interests and expertise of other potential parties. Although the dysfunctions had become less apparent by midterm, Reagan's enthusiasm about cabinet government brought about a network of cabinet councils with a degree of specialization greater than the business within some policy sectors could justify. In addition, overlapping jurisdictions brought considerable confusion to some issue areas. Here trade policy, where the statutory Trade Policy Committee, the Cabinet Council on Commerce and Trade and the NSC Senior Interagency Group on International Economic Policy all vied for issues, serves as the worst case. In part, Reagan's second-term streamlining of the cabinet council system simply responded to the diminishing returns of an overly elaborate network of standing committees.

4. Mapping, Adhering to, and Changing Administrations' Strategies

In another work, I proposed that administrations might take one of four approaches to strategy.[1] A *priorities-and-planning* method starts by delineating several key objectives for the administration and requiring departments to adjust their policy commitments and programmatic schedules accordingly. Since the tack places a strong premium on detailed follow-through, it works best in cabinet systems of government in which department heads share a common respect for the "mandate" and long-standing experience in collegial decision making. The former condition existed under Reagan to an exceptional degree for an American administration. The latter simply does not present itself in the United States owing both to the the weakness of cabinet mechanisms and to the high proportion of secretaries lacking previous experience as agency heads. As well, the fragmentation of the U.S. political system—especially the difficulty of presidents obtaining what they want from Congress even if their public support remains strong—argues against incumbents adopting a planning and priorities format. No matter how finely tuned and agreed to within the executive branch, the various elements of administration strategies still must run the congressional gauntlet.

A second approach, *broker politics,* fits the realities of the U.S. executive-legislative complex much better than does the priorities-and-planning style. Here administrations set out their objectives only in the most general terms. Secretaries receive fairly wide latitude in which to work out the detailed ramifications for their departments of the overarching strategic commitments. On some critical issues, it might well become necessary for the White House to prod a department along the desired course. Some intense jurisdictional disputes between secretaries will require that they either work together toward a solution "out of court" or take the matter to the president. In the latter case, secretaries run the risk of coming out with decisions that fall short of their departments' best interests. The White House rarely has the time and resources to take all of the relevant nuances of the issue into consideration. Also, it might conclude that, since secretaries have failed in one important instance to resolve differences, it should keep a watching brief on related issues.

Both the priorities-and-planning and broker-politics styles make some allowance for attempts within the administration to reconcile conflicting claims over priorities and disputes about their actual implementation. Broker politics fits the U.S. system better than priorities and planning because it permits greater realism about the level of integration that can be achieved between departmental policies and programs. It also recognizes that the weakness of collective decision-making machinery in the U.S. executive branch counsels lower expectations from cabinet-level consultative forums.

Two other styles frequently emerge in the U.S. presidency. *Administrative politics* develops when incumbents cannot keep secretaries' efforts focused collectively even on broad administration goals. In other words, cabinet officers pretty much determine their departments' priorities without reference to wider administration goals. A "law of the jungle" emerges for disputes between agencies. That is, the assertive secretaries with the prestigious departments and the most links into the White House and with the president will gain virtual hegemony within policy sectors. Rather than stemming from a presidential strategy, the administration's agenda will run pretty much on the basis of fighting brush fires on an ad hoc basis.

Administrative politics arises when presidents do not take special steps to integrate competing views within their administration. On the other hand, *survival politics* comes about when incumbents actively limit the presentation of contrasting positions. Nearly every administration experiences episodes in which it must "draw the wagons into a circle." Survival politics characterizes a presidency that attempts to establish total discipline within the executive branch. Under such circumstances, the president and the White House staff will review centrally many routine administrative issues. In addition, they will undertake extreme measures to assure that political appointees within agencies toe the White House line. Survival politics emerged at the beginning of Richard Nixon's second term, even before the devastating consequences of Watergate had taken hold, in reponse to the administration's belief that the bureaucracy had undermined its programs. Even though he terms the resulting syndrome simply "an administrative strategy," Richard P. Nathan's description of Nixon's approach in 1973 conveys well the us-against-them thinking that permeates survival politics:

> The legislative agenda was pared down. No longer was the cabinet to be composed of men with their own national standing disposed to go their own way. Unprecedented changes were made below the cabinet level. Trusted lieutenants who were tied personally to Richard Nixon and had no national reputations of their own were placed in direct charge of the major bureauracies of the domestic government.[2]

The preceding chapter focused on Jimmy Carter's and Ronald Reagan's use of cabinet consultation. The former adopted a decentralized view whereby cabinet secretaries would receive maximum discretion to decide matters falling within their jurisdiction. Theoretically, such delegation, would allow Carter to concentrate his efforts on the genuinely presidential decisions. The administration, thus, eschewed elaborate strategic scenarios for its four-year mandate. The president would work case-by-case on matters worthy of his attention. In short, Carter set up his administration as if he were following administrative politics. Here two paradoxes enter our assessment. Carter's inability to control his own penchant for detail resulted in his immersing the White House in analysis of issues to a degree more akin to priorities and planning than administration politics. When it became clear that this approach had hopelessly foundered, Carter resorted to survival politics. Significantly, Carter's approach spilled over from executive leadership to political operations. That is, the ill-fated 1980 reelection campaign virtually gutted the White House of its top officials.

Reagan, on the other hand, stands as one of the few presidents who started his administration on a survival politics footing. Arguing that the nation was in dire straits internationally and economically, he called for radical increases in defense expenditure, huge tax cuts, and severe reductions in domestic programs. Even with these radical commitments, however, Reagan chose to stress teamwork in implementing his policies. To be sure, the relatively broad strokes of his approach discouraged even modest tailoring of specifics to departmental considerations. For example, the White House and David Stockman imposed the strict regimen of domestic budget cuts upon cabinet secretaries, before they took charge of their assignments, as "give-at-the-office" propositions. However, once putting his wide-gauge policies in place, Reagan fostered a collective approach to key administration decisions. Here his relatively structured cabinet councils played an especially important role. After summer 1981, thus, the Reagan administration inched toward broker politics.

Carter's Spokes-in-a-Wheel Model

The organizational mode chosen by a president for the White House greatly influences the degree to which resources for coordination of interdepartmental treatment of issues divide on the basis of neutral process management. An overly hierarchical White House will tend to draw virtually every issue on the the desk of a chief of staff and eventually into the Oval Office simply through the stringency of clearance requirements. Thus, officials in secretariats such as the National Security Council staff or its domestic policy equivalent will become surrogates for the president rather than process moderators. On the other hand, a loosely structured White House might lead to an excess of overlapping authority. As aides in the West Wing compete more intensely for the president's respect and time, those across the way in the Executive Office of the President will find it necessary to become equally entrepreneurial in getting attention for their issues. Those most astute at the game of coalition building will become free-standing advocates.

Jimmy Carter followed sentiment more than design in setting up his White House. The continuing national hangover from Richard Nixon's hierarchical White House made it extremely tempting to adopt a spokes-in-a-wheel organizational model. Here all senior aides would have equal access to the president. Not even a "weak" chief of staff would be designated. We have seen that cabinet dynamics were to consist of secretaries attempting to decide matters on their own and resorting to one-on-one encounters with the president when all else failed. Likewise, a spokes-in-a-wheel White House would assure maximum possible discretion for individual aides who, nonetheless, could readily consult the president if the need arose.

Apart from senior staff meetings a couple of times a week when crises came to a boil, no collective councils regularly reviewed White House management. Deputies thus conferred with one another only in informal gatherings. One respondent supportive of the lack of structure reported that everyone related to the next person, including the president, on a need-to-do-business basis. In his words:

> There is no single person who exercises the gatekeeper function or is somehow a little more equal than the rest in the management of the staff. There are members . . . who have a special relationship with the president. But none of them exercise the White House staff management function that a chief of staff would. It has taken people some time to learn to live with that fact. What we do now is informally have frequent deputies' lunches and other groups where we meet and just kind of coordinate ourselves into a collegial body with nobody serving as chairman.[3]

More than anything else, the Carter approach underestimated the difficulty of switching roles from a campaign cadre, the upper echelons of which mostly had worked with the president in Georgia, to a White House advisory system. Students of the presidency such as Richard E. Neustadt and Stephen J. Wayne noted this fact very early.[4] In his study, Paul Light came upon a Carter White House respondent from Georgia who put the situation in an especially straightforward manner:

> We spent a great deal of time simply learning how to do things, and even then we made more than our share of mistakes. The president told us that we should do things pretty much the same as we did in Georgia. But Washington isn't Georgia, and the White House isn't the governor's mansion.[5]

The Functions of the Various Spokes

In examining the role of any White House in devising an administration's strategy, assuring that substantive decisions adhere to it and making adjustments along the way, we should keep in mind the multiplicity of units that play at least some part in the process. It helps, thus, to consider four broad sectors of White House activities that relate to the most critical ways in which the president must be supported by staff. Figure 2 portrays these sectors as present under Carter's spokes-in-a-wheel format for organization of the White House. They include advising the president on matters most strongly associated with his *personal* prerogatives, duties, and schedule; handling his relations with other key elements of *government*—namely, departments and agencies, Congress, and state and local officials; attending to his *partisan* affairs and standing; and

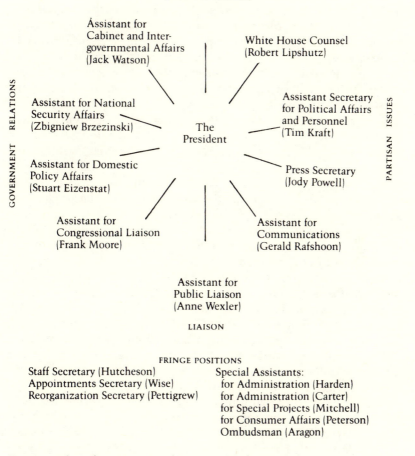

PERSONAL MATTERS

"Assistant"
(Hamilton Jordan)

Assistant for
Cabinet and Inter-
governmental Affairs
(Jack Watson)

White House Counsel
(Robert Lipshutz)

GOVERNMENT RELATIONS

Assistant for National
Security Affairs
(Zbigniew Brzezinski)

The
President

Assistant Secretary
for Political Affairs
and Personnel
(Tim Kraft)

PARTISAN ISSUES

Assistant for Domestic
Policy Affairs
(Stuart Eizenstat)

Press Secretary
(Jody Powell)

Assistant for
Congressional Liaison
(Frank Moore)

Assistant for
Communications
(Gerald Rafshoon)

Assistant for
Public Liaison
(Anne Wexler)

LIAISON

FRINGE POSITIONS
Staff Secretary (Hutcheson)
Appointments Secretary (Wise)
Reorganization Secretary (Pettigrew)

Special Assistants:
for Administration (Harden)
for Administration (Carter)
for Special Projects (Mitchell)
for Consumer Affairs (Peterson)
Ombudsman (Aragon)

Figure 2. The White House under Carter (Early 1979)

maintaining *liaison* and general bonhomie among various groups and the public at large.

Central to understanding the actual operation of this scheme is the role of Hamilton Jordan, who had also served as Carter's most trusted aide during his gubernatorial career in Georgia. Although the president did not bestow him the title "chief of staff," Jordan found he could put a gloss on the inputs of virtually any White House unit. This raised serious difficulties as Jordan was notoriously inattentive to process management and time constraints. To make matters worse, the administration followed the spokes-in-a-wheel motif so uncritically that ancillary support functions normally brigaded under a chief of staff operated as separate, although very thin, spokes. Most important here, the staff secretary attempted to manage the flow of paper through the White House for clearance purposes, while the appointments secretary struggled with the presidents schedule without clear coordinative mandates.

One office in the Carter White House operated in the gray area between the president's prerogatives, duties, and schedule, and his relations with various elements of government. Carter appointed an "assistant to the president for cabinet and intergovernmental affairs" to head a secretariat responsible for cabinet business, and state and local relations. In practice, the Carter cabinet ran on a relatively unstructured basis. This meant that the assistant to the president through most of the administration, Jack Watson—another Georgian—did not support an institutionalized process. The intergovernmental affairs side to Watson's responsibilities, on the other hand, marked the first effort on the part of an administration to centrally coordinate departments' policies and programs in relation to state and local issues. In this respect, the staff complemented offices already established in most departments and agencies for liaison with state and local governments. This formalization of White House involvement led to two significant attempts to provide more comprehensive policies, namely, reviews of urban and rural policies. For the most part, however, the intergovernmental affairs staff functioned essentially as a switchboard for handling governors' and mayors' relations with the president.

With respect to the administration's policy strategies, the assistants to the president for national security and domestic policy affairs played the strongest roles. A later section looks into these in greater detail. We have already seen, however, that National Security Council machinery as restructured under Zbigniew Brzezinski found no parallel in the interdepartmental consultative process on the domestic side. This state of affairs owed partially to Stuart Eizenstat's eschewing of structure within the Domestic Policy Staff and the lack of experience among DPS members. The relative absence of hierarchy and routinized decision processes in the White House exacerbated conditions.

By midterm, Carter became deeply disturbed about the difficulty of winning congressional approval for his legislative program. However, the transparent inadequacy of two offices, congressional and public liaison, drew some of the potential blame for the administration's failures from internal confusion in the White House and a chaotic interdepartmental decision process. Frank Moore, who had served as Carter's legislative assistant in Georgia, had proven seriously deficient as the assistant to the president for congressional liaison. By 1978, two of Moore's aides, Les Francis and James M. Copeland, received a broad mandate to spearhead a greater involvement of the congressional liaison office at the preparatory stages of the president's legislative program. Francis participated heavily in the annual process whereby the vice-president sifted through department's claims for high rank among the administration's priorities and then informed secretaries of how their plans fitted in with the overall legislative strategy. Copeland began monitoring much more closely than the office had during the first two years the activities of interdepartmental task forces preparing policy initiatives for congressional action. Insofar as it impressed upon task forces due regard for the art of the possible, the reoriented congressional liaison office began to take a significant part in establishing the contours of the administration's legislative plans.

Relatedly, the office of the assistant to the president for public liaison found its role in the uppermost deliberative forums of the administration enhanced the more Carter's legislative program foundered. While headed by Margaret ("Midge") Costanza, the office served only as a lightning rod for various organizations' grievances with the administration. Costanza's successor, Anne Wexler, changed the thrust of the office along the lines of mobilizing interest group support for key Carter initiatives. This emphasis simply acknowledged the need, given the fractiousness of Congress, to make sure that key administration stances would win the approval of a viable coalition of affected publics. Once struck, well-built coalitions would more effectively bring the necessary pressure to bear on Congress so that it would act more in accordance with the administration's plans. The concept granted interest groups considerable access at the earlier stages—even in the most private councils—of Carter's policy apparatus.

On the partisan affairs side of figure 2, the White House counsel attends to the president's legal affairs relating directly to his personal prerogatives and duties. This position concerns most clearly the partisan side of the White House. That is, it monitors the administration's adherence to legislation guiding the selection and activities of political appointees. It also reviews from the standpoint of probity White House efforts to maintain or expand the president's support among the electorate. In short, the counsel serves as the president's legal watchdog and, when things go awry, his personal attorney. For most of the Carter term, Robert Lipshutz, an Atlanta lawyer, occupied the counsel position. He failed to become a major official in the administration. Carter replaced Lipshutz with Lloyd N. Cutler, a prominent Washington lawyer, during his summer 1979 effort to add prestige to his flagging White House. Cutler readily extended the counsel role to cover other sectors of the White House. For instance, he insisted upon attending all but the most sensitive meetings of the National Security Council.[6]

Tim Kraft, who started out in the administration as Carter's appointments secretary, assumed the title Assistant to the President for Political Affairs and Personnel in spring 1978. Before, these responsibilities had lodged with Hamilton Jordan. By 1979, Kraft had immersed himself in two major partisan exercises. He directed Carter's gearing up for the 1980 election and he supervised the administration's summer 1979 purge of appointees deemed incompetent and/or disloyal. Carter had resisted the idea of a purge when it had been recommended in spring 1978. His 1979 U-turn reflected the White House's deepening frustration with the lack of discipline in the administration. In fact, it fit well the tendency for administrations without collegial leadership to slip into survival politics.

Beginning in spring 1978 as well, two offices managed Carter's media relations. The Office of the Press Secretary under Jody Powell maintained day-to-day briefing responsibilities; the Office of the Assistant to the President for Communications under Gerald M. Rafshoon directed the administration's attempts to garner greater media attention and support for its central themes. As Georgians with long-standing Carter associations, both Powell and Rafshoon wielded considerable influence over the substantive elements of policy issues. In fact, only Hamilton Jordan's impact on Carter exceeded that of Powell. This fact probably makes Powell the most influential press secretary in the history of the position.

Georgians Sticking Together

In assessing the operation of the spokes-in-a-wheel format, we have to ask whether it achieved its intended effect. Did it provide Carter with diverse views upon which to base his judgments? Did it actually allow sufficient access for various players to introduce adequate cross-pressuring of the president to improve his decisions while not inundating him with details?

Carter's advisory net extended much further than that of perhaps any other president in modern times. We have seen, for example, that career officials in OMB, especially early in the administration, enjoyed personal contact with the president through White House meetings. Even after these subsided, most OMB officials believed that their views, including ones at variance with the director's, at least received mention in memoranda to the president. Senior political appointees working in the Old Executive Office Building, and who were therefore one step closer to the West Wing, told of ways in which they could press their views personally and obtain direct guidance from the president. Yet, career officials and appointees alike frequently spoke of a pro forma dimension to Carter's accessibility. To many, he seemed to have observed the letter but not the spirit of the spokes-in-a-wheel principle. Carter's organization model was short-circuited by two failures. First, Carter, in his personal encounters with aides whom he did not know well, avoided overt conflict. Second, the advisers he trusted implicitly, mostly Georgians, demonstrated deep suspicions about both fellow political appointees not in their charmed circle and career officials.

The two faults tended to reinforce one another. For instance, several officials with direct exposure to Carter but lacking a Georgia background told of relatively stilted encounters with the president. A number made special note of Carter's aloof personality as dampening give-and-take in his presence. One respondent commented:

I would say you have to begin with the personality of the president. In Carter's case, I found him a somewhat shy, withdrawn person who is guarded in the trust and confidence he places in people and consequently there is a circle of people whom he really trusts a lot.[7]

Correspondingly, much of the president's communications were on paper. As one OMB political appointee noted, even sessions with staff could find participants pretty much glued to briefing books and graphs:

> As you know, the president does not hold as many working meetings as some of his predecessors have. He does more of it based on paper inputs. The man is amazing in his ability to absorb in true depth things presented to him that way. . . . In doing briefings . . . he likes to use these view graphs on the screen. . . . Here are the alternatives. If we know, we will reflect how the staff and the departments have voted on the issues. Then we will make our points about what we think is relevant.[8]

The second defect arose from the fact that Carter chose mainly Georgians for senior staff positions. A clannishness developed among this group. In turn, the insularity of Carter's staff reflected their profound insecurity in Washington. This came across vividly in the remarks of one Georgian:

> I came with a dedication to demonstrate that not everyone from the South is dumb and not everybody from the South could not come into a new situation, develop, do well and help Jimmy Carter run the country. Then I'll go home when I'm through and not become a hanger-on in Washington. When I get through I'm going home.[9]

Lamenting this approach, many Washington-wise appointees and career officials pointed up the tendency for Georgians to tighten their wagons into an ever contracting circle.[10] One non-Georgian responsible for several major administration initiatives, but not in the most intimate ring, stressed that the resulting truncation of formal networks relegated important elements in key administration initiatives to the sidelines. In his words:

> There may be a formal leadership that includes everybody with a stake in the outcome. But then there will be informal ad hoc groups which are not advertised that involve the real heavies. They will meet confidentially in rump sessions and make most of the decisions. . . . This administration, far more than any other that I've ever read about or experienced, tends to pigeonhole people. It does not invite opinions outside your chosen

sector. . . . The real difference is that this administration has got that little clutch of Georgians.[11]

Entrepreneurial Secretariats

I have asserted above that loose organization of the White House proper will foster entrepreneurial styles among aides in the executive office. The workings of the West Wing under Carter promoted such dynamics. Officials responsibe for coordination of cabinet consultation and briefing the president in various policy sectors were most effective if they obtained and held on to the West Wing high ground through political adroitness and the right contacts. Under such circumstances, the National Security Council staff and the Domestic Policy Staff both fell short of the criterion of neutral competence.

Here the NSC staff strayed the least from a brokerage role. The fact that it enjoys a statutory mandate and has operated under various levels of institutionalization since 1947 gave it a much stronger legacy than that available to the DPS. I. M. Destler has noted a weakness in the aides the Carter administration brought to the NSC staff.[12] They appeared to be "idea people" identified with specific schools of thought more than the professional policy management "types" thought to be the norm for the NSC. Yet one would be hard pressed to find Carter appointees from outside government who could not claim very high levels of expertise. In addition, Carter's NSC maintained a significant complement of officials on loan from within government and well acquainted with the bureaucratic politics of national security. Some respondents observed that the NSC staff under Brzezinski ran less hierarchically than usual. However, Brzezinski took this avowed stylistic preference of the administration much less literally than did Stuart E. Eizenstat, to whom the DPS reported. Finally, Carter's revitalization of the NSC's cabinet-level deliberative machinery after several years of neglect, if anything, renewed the NSC staff's original raison d'être.

Notwithstanding these factors that helped keep the NSC staff more or less on course, Carter's own style and, relatedly, the fixation of the national security community on crises during the last two years of the administration hampered the secretariat role. One career official involved in an assessment of the national security decision process dwelt on certain dimensions to the president's personality—his penchant for detail and selectivity in trust—that confounded the agreed-upon design. Here supposed custodians of neutral brokerage, like Brzezinski and OMB director James McIntyre, found it difficult to eschew advocacy. In the official's words:

> According to Carter's Reorganization Plan No. 1, the nature of the Executive Office of the President is supposed to be one of coordinating with and processing the views of departments . . . not duplicating their efforts, or substituting for them, or overriding them. . . . It really hasn't completely worked out that way. The reason why, to some extent, is the personality of the president. . . . He may have a very close relationship with McIntyre, for example, and McIntyre might end up taking a very substantial policy role, . . . not just a staff role, but he directs the cabinet . . . and says, "you will do this." . . . The same thing with the relationship with Brzezinski. . . . I'm not sure if there's an ideal way of doing it. So much relies on personalities. . . . He can use the NSC any way he likes. He can get advice from anybody he wants. He can talk to his mother, or his wife in bed at night. But . . . there ought to be a way of trying to clarify responsibilities so that everybody understands what their role is.[13]

In comparison to cabinet-level mechanisms for deliberations within the national security sector, similar systems on the domestic side left a great deal to be desired during Carter's administration. Likewise, the Domestic Policy Staff (DPS) never really attained credibility as a secretariat. This fact derives largely from the role of Carter's assistant for domestic affairs and policy. Especially in economic policy, Stuart Eizenstat attempted to dominate decision processes to such a degree that even W. Michael Blumenthal, Carter's treasury secretary until summer 1979, often found himself ostracized for having crossed a Georgian.[14] In Blumenthal's case, intermittent exclusion undermined severely the credence given U.S. economic policies by foreign finance ministers. Too often, carefully developed international agreements were embarrassingly scuttled at the hands of the White House.

Given Eizenstat's approach, DPS reached the highest level of freelance advocacy ever achieved by a domestic policy secretariat. The DPS's meager hierarchical structure, denoted by the distinction between "associate" and "assistant" directors, concealed the fact that all the professional staff pretty much drew up their own job descriptions and reported personally to the director, Bert Carp, who, in turn, reported to Eizenstat. Eizenstat had mainly recruited youngish policy advocates with relatively little experience in Washington's executive-bureaucratic arena. The administration's preference for ad hoc task forces over standing cabinet-level committees in all fields except macroeconomic policy freed most DPS officials from the routine business that normally absorbs the time of members of a policy secretariat. One staff member described, with obvious disaffection but considerable accuracy, this free-floating DPS as a brood of overachievers requiring a facilitator to channel the energies of the alleged coordinators:

> I think also one of the things I would do, I would provide a staff psychiatrist. This probably sounds really off the wall. But, I think, because it is a world of highfliers, that you will find that there is a lot of competition between people. For instance, I have never worked before this in an atmosphere where information is hoarded. Part of your strength and position comes from hoarding and being very careful about whom you say things to.[15]

Reagan's Modified Spokes-in-a-Wheel Pattern

As we have seen, Carter embraced the spokes-in-a-wheel model for organizing his White House largely in order to avoid an overly hierarchical format. In other words, he believed he would eschew the pitfalls of the Nixon administration whereby far too many issues ended up being resolved in the White House and process managers became surrogates for a greatly overloaded president. Carter's plan failed because the president could not restrain himself from detailed review of policies. As well, the clannishness of his trusted aides, overwhelmingly Georgians, meant that access to the president depended more on personal familiarity than hands-on responsibility for key elements in executive-bureaucratic coordination.

With Carter's experience as a backdrop, Ronald Reagan's administration faced potentially a much more difficult design problem as it began the first term. The new president's age, his preference for a relatively short work day, and his inattention to detail all suggested that a hierarchical White House in which all reporting lines ended up in the chief of staff's office would present a real danger. A strong chief of staff under Reagan might soon become, both in the eyes of other players and the public, the de facto chief executive of the adminstration. Yet the president's years, work habits, and detachment from particulars argued equally well against the spokes-in-a-wheel model. Notwithstanding his irrepressible personality, Reagan probably would not hold up well under a free-floating format, such as Kennedy's, which placed a premium on drive, intelligence, and an *acute*, rather than simply unfailing, sense of humor.

During the first term, Reagan functioned with a modified spokes-in-a-wheel format to help himself out of his conundrum. Initially, three senior advisers with direct and immediate access to the president formed a triumvirate encompassing three White House clusters. Edwin Meese III, the counselor to the president, belonged to the cabinet. At the beginning of the administration, he oversaw cabinet administration and issue development for national security as well as domestic policy. Under the formal title "chief of staff," James A. Baker III guided White House units responsible for the "implementation" of policies. These offices included intergovernmental affairs, legislative affairs, public liaison, communications, the press secretary's office, political affairs, personnel, and the counsel to the president. Michael K. Deaver, assistant to the president and deputy chief of staff, headed several offices concerned with travel preparations, scheduling, special support services (i.e., military aides-de-camp and the president's physcian) and the first lady's office. William P. Clark transformed the triumvirate into the "Big Four" when he succeeded Richard V. Allen as assistant to the president for national security affairs in January 1982. Unlike Allen, Clark—who left the White House in December 1983—enjoyed direct access to the president and, therefore, absorbed completely Meese's former role in the national security field.

The Reagan scheme appears effectively to have provided a middle ground between hierarchical White House and one attempting to offer equal access for all senior assistants. Essentially, the model added four hubs to the spokes-in-a-wheel format so that officials responsible for numerous "shops" in the White House reported to the president through the manager of a cluster of related functions. A meld of functional justification for access and personal ties attained greater success than did the Carter arrangement in avoiding truncation of the advisory system. That is, access did not run on "blood lines" alone. Baker joined the Reagan campaign through George Bush's and enjoyed strong lines of communication with moderate elements of the Republican party garnered through extensive experience in Washington. One respondent from California dwelt at length on the significance of Baker's appointment both for the operation of the White House and what it tells us of Reagan's ability to trust advisers on the basis of ability as well as friendship:

> Reagan pretty much demonstrated his openness to views from various directions within the Republican party when he took on Jim Baker as chief of staff. I think of him now as one of us— even as a conservative. But, I think it is a little unusual; . . . it shows that the president is an extremely secure individual. He just does not feel threatened because somebody didn't work for you for twenty years or has been in another camp.[16]

Three members of the quadrumvirate, Meese, Clark, and Deaver, called upon considerable personal familiarity with Reagan based originally on their fulfilling key staff functions while he was governor of California. Deaver's relatively meager list of responsibilities concealed the fact that he enjoyed the strongest personal relationship with the president and involved himself fully in meetings of the "Big Four," either with the president or alone, in such forums as the Legislative Strategy Group. Deaver's formal responsibilities gave him custody over the president's time. Thus, he ultimately judged the merits of his colleagues' requests for a hearing for one or other of their "constituents." In addition, his intimate knowledge of the president gave him considerable insight into the issues the administration should be focusing on and how these should be presented to the public.

A Look at the Spokes

Figure 3 presents schematically Reagan's modified spokes-in-a-wheel format as it functioned at its height. The imposition of four hubs worked considerable effects on the operation of various White House units. This section focuses on offices reporting to James Baker and Michael Deaver. Along with structural features, it examines personality factors that influenced the role of each spoke. Fred Fielding—one of the few members of the Nixon White House left untainted by Watergate—occupied the position "counsel to the president" throughout the first term. Ironically, the post-Watergate accretion of reporting and conflict-of-interest legislation governing political appointees has greatly increased the workload of the counsel. Fielding played a significant role in broad judicial matters of special interest to the president. For instance, he had chaired weekly meetings with Baker, Meese, and other top White House aides on judicial appointments. As well, he had participated as a designated member on the Cabinet Council on Legal Policy. Here he kept a weather eye for matters of interpretation or enforcement that related to the president's constitutional duty to uphold the law.

The Presidential Personnel Office functioned under three different directors during the first term. Most notably, E. Pendleton James, a professional "headhunter" from New York, guided the personnel selection process for the first two years of the administration. Although faulted by some for taking overly long to fill appointive vacancies in departments, James actually achieved the narrow aims of the administration. That is, his system identified and placed a corp of dedicated Reaganites within virtually every department. Each appointment was cleared with the candidate's

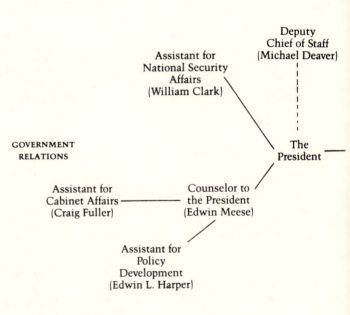

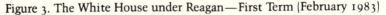

Figure 3. The White House under Reagan—First Term (February 1983)

prospective cabinet secretary, the counselor to the president, the White House counsel, the chief of staff and his deputy, either the national security adviser or the assistant for policy development, and, finally, the president.[17] Even after James's departure, his successors—Helene von Damm and John S. Herrington—continued to meet each Wednesday with top White House staff to vet personnel issues and appointments before reviewing these with the president on Thursdays. In cases where the administration had not arrived at an acceptable candidate, departmental units without political heads have frequently merged under those for which an acceptable appointee could be found. Much more than Carter's, Reagan's political appointees have drawn a curtain around their deliberations that usually excludes career officials from departments' inner circles. In short, the personnel process created by James laid an exceptionally strong foundation for ideolgical allegiance within the administration.

The Political Affairs Office under Reagan has played less of a role

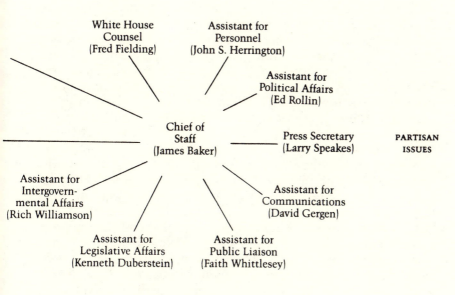

in shaping substantive White House policy than Tim Kraft's office did during the Carter administration. The fact that the assistant to the president responsible for this unit lacked control of appointments contributed the most to its relatively modest role. In fact, the first incumbent, Lyn Nofziger—a Reagan stalwart from his California days—left early in the administration largely because he could not find how to relate his concerns to other parts of the White House apparatus. His immediate successor, Edward Rollins—another Californian—seemed content to concentrate his efforts on coordinating the White House involvement in the 1982 congressional elections and preparing for the president's running for a second term. In fact, he left the White House late in 1983 to direct the Reagan-Bush '84 campaign. He returned for only a short period in 1985.

The administration's management of media relations did not get off to an auspicious start largely due to the tragic shooting of the press secretary, James S. Brady, during the assassination attempt against the president in March 1981. In addition, Reagan had not drawn very clear lines of authority between the principal aides working in this field. On paper, David Gergen, the assistant to the president for communications, ultimately reported to James Baker on all matters concerning the media. However, Michael Deaver, the deputy chief of staff, took from the outset a very strong interest in communication issues. That is, he viewed his job as making sure that the "true Ronald Reagan" got across to the public.[18] He thus spent as much time working with Gergen and Larry Speakes—the latter filled in for Brady after the shooting—than he did fulfilling the more mundane functions that fell under his formal jurisdiction.

Even with Brady, the administration did not want the press secretary to assume the high profile taken by Jody Powell. As a result, Speakes has suffered from a narrow mandate as well as the awkwardness of filling the press-secretary role without the formal title. Until his departure in 1983, Gergen shouldered responsibility for providing "off-the-record" briefings to reporters. As well, the first-term Reagan White House tolerated considerably more direct contact between senior officials and members of the media than was allowed under the Carter administration. From time to time, this relative openness led to leaks that proved embarrassing to the president by exposing internal White House conflict. Reagan reacted on occasion by trying to limit press access to his aides. For instance, he gave an order in January 1983 instructing senior officials to clear all press contacts with Gergen. Here individual resourcefulness came into play. Officials who did not want to be told whom to see and which phone calls to return inundated Gergen with requests for clearance. The always amiable Gergen soon turned clearance into an implicit permission.

This is not to say that Gergen did not leave his mark in the communications office before his departure from the White House. Although not a Reaganite, he enjoyed—at least until the months before his departure—the confidence of Baker. He gained access to the most senior administration panels, including most meetings of the Legislative Strategy Group and Monday "issue lunches" with the president. Gergen thus made his presence felt in discussions about the thrust of the administration and how adjustments might help the White House come across better to the public. His clearest contribution occurred during winter 1982–83 when he effectively impressed upon Reagan and his top aides the necessity of doing more to address the "fairness issue," namely, the widespread public concern about the consequences of the administration's policies for the poor.

By their very nature, genial and straightforward players such as Gergen are uncomfortable with White House politics. Gergen began to fall out of Baker's graces. He also became increasingly agitated about recurrent efforts to tighten the flow of information and investigations into national security leaks. With Gergen's departure, Michael Deaver took direct control of the administration's media relations. Election years, of course, tend to put communications issues at the center of White House concerns. Here Deaver took the initiative by calling a daily Communication Strategy Meeting beginning December 1983 and including Baker and several other senior aides. The early morning meeting tried to assure that various elements of the White House pursued the same "line of the day" on key issues as they arose. Deaver also intensified the activities of the Blair House Group which, from the beginning of the administration, had met occasionally to track the progress of long-term communication issues. Also a top-drawer gathering, this body convened weekly or more during 1984. Interestingly, Larry Speakes inherited Gergen's former access to Deaver's groups and other key White House panels such as the Legislative Strategy Group and issue lunches.

Reagan's Office of Public Liaison has never attained the prominence within the White House that it did under Anne Wexler during the Carter administration. Reagan's first assistant to the president for public liaison, Elizabeth H. Dole—the Senator Robert Dole's wife, now transportation secretary—never achieved a status whereby she could consistently insert her views into the tightest ring of the White House. In the absence of such access, the more astute interest group leaders found little utility in working closely with the public liaison office. Dole's immediate successor, Faith Ryan Whittlesey, made matters worse by catering excessively to conservative groups concerned about school prayer, tuition tax credits, and antiabortion legislation. That is, she had little time for the main-line business, religious, labor, ethnic, and women's groups simply interested in making an impact on more conventional policy concerns. As a result, Whittlesey found herself increasingly in a White House limbo. For instance, Michael Deaver excluded her from a special group he formed in 1983 to work on improving the administration's response to women's issues.

One could not find a sharper contrast between the Carter and Reagan White Houses than by comparing the two presidents' congressional relations staffs. To begin, Reagan's assistants to the president for legislative affairs all brought to their work extensive experience in the field. The first, Max L. Friedersdorf—who again assumed this position during the first year of the second term—had worked in White House congressional relations as far back as the Nixon administration. Friedersdorf was followed by Kenneth Duberstein, who had handled legislative liaison work for two separate agencies under the Nixon and Ford administrations. Duberstein's successor, M. B. Oglesby, had served Reagan for three years before taking the top legislative affairs post. He had brought to the White House considerable experience on congressional staffs. When Friedersdorf returned to the White House at the beginning of the second term, Oglesby stepped down. However, he remained on the congressional affairs staff. Thus he regained the title of assistant to the president upon Friedersdorf's second departure.

Perhaps more important than the high qualifications of the assistants to the president for legislative affairs is the responsibility they are entrusted with. Reagan has given exceptional priority to congressional relations from the beginning of the administration. He has not hesitated to undertake telephone campaigns and breakfasts to urge his views personally upon congressmen and senators.

During the first term, this level of presidential keenness about congressional victory prompted James Baker to style the most exclusive body of the "implementation side" of the White House the

"Legislative Strategy Group." The legislative affairs assistant served on this committee throughout the first term. He also attended daily meetings of the senior White House staff in Baker's office at 8:00 A.M. Baker thus interpreted executive leadership as the ability to pursue partisan principle within the constraints of the art of the possible. Here legislative affairs assistants played an instrumental role in laying the groundwork for maximizing congressional support. However, both the president and Baker made their task relatively easy by investing time in winning votes and following the counsel for compromise when the "numbers" held out little hope for doctrinaire stances.

The Reagan administration took Carter's decision to give the cabinet secretary responsibility for state and local relations a step further by establishing a separate office for intergovernmental affairs under the chief of staff. Rich Williamson, the first appointee to hold the new position, started off auspiciously enough by recognizing that he should organize the office according to jurisdictions rather than issue areas. That is, his assistants divided the burden of contact along state and local lines. Williamson appeared to have carried off a coup in January 1982 when he managed to place his comprehensive plans for reform of revenue sharing as a central element to the president's State of the Union address. However, the initiative foundered in the face of exceedingly stiff opposition from governors and mayors. As well, Williamson operated too independently by half for the taste of James Baker. He left the administration in 1983 to become ambassador to Austria. He was succeeded by Lee L. Verstandig who concentrated his efforts on day-to-day handling of governors' and mayors' representatives and improving interaction between department and agency officials responsible for intergovernmental affairs.

What Strife?

Even during its heyday, the Baker-Meese-Deaver triumvirate— which became a quadrumvirate when William Clark joined the White House in 1982—ran into difficulties that evoked press comment questioning whether it could maintain its delicate balance indefinitely. In fact, virtually every crisis in the administration stirred afresh speculation that White House harmony had come to an end. Many commentators concluded, thus, that Clark's and Meese's nominations to cabinet posts had fulfilled all the gloomy prophecies. To the contrary, the fourth-year shift into a precampaign mode of operation takes us further in understanding the Clark and Meese nominations. Both men found it difficult to conceal their designs on departmental posts. As experienced political operatives with strong ideological commitments, they recognized that the White House's preoccupation with the election during 1984 would drown out their incantations of pure Reaganism. Most important, they had achieved about as much of their ultraconservative agenda as any "conscience" of a president could reasonably expect to fulfill in a four-year interval.

Two members of the triumvirate and subsequent quadrumvirate attributed their success to the right mix of personalities, a lot of hard work, *and* an assassination attempt that concentrated minds. In their words:

> This has worked better than I thought it would. It is hard work for all of us to make it work. You have some strong egos. You have some people who feel very strongly about policy and how it needs to get done. But, as I say, we have made it work. One of the things that changed this whole chemistry in here was the shooting itself; . . . it forced us to work closely together and we learned how to. That isn't to say there haven't been problems—there have been a lot. But, it's like marriage—you have to work at it to make it work.[19]

> We had a situation here in the White House that we had to work at making work . . . in this fishbowl atmosphere . . . in the glare of publicity and the press constantly trying to drive wedges. . . . What ultimately happened quite frankly is that . . . everybody has so much to do there can't be any problems of turf.[20]

Both our respondents, in emphasizing "work," partially alluded to the fact that they spent a great deal of time with one another in meetings. In this respect, they served almost as the antithesis of Carter's most trusted advisers. For instance, during the quadrumvirate, the four members, along with their key assistants, met every Monday with the president for an "issue briefing lunch" designed to keep him up to date on the administration's main issues. Although Baker, Meese, and Deaver seemed to have dispensed with the daily breakfasts which were the ritual until late 1982, they convened each day at an 8:00 A.M. meeting of all senior staff in the White House. Around 9:00 they went to the Oval Office where Clark joined them for the national security briefing at 9:30.[21] During the week, Baker, Meese, and Deaver called Legislative Strategy Group meetings any time particularly thorny issues emerged requiring the implementation and policy sides of the White House to resolve differences in the face of adverse reactions to administration positions and initiatives. During the budget season, Baker and Meese worked with David Stockman through the Budget Review Board in handling appeals from departments. Even paper transactions underwent considerable coordination. Two key players emerged here: Richard Darman, Baker's deputy, and Craig Fuller, the assistant to the president for cabinet affairs. Their roles, which White House colleagues termed the Darman-Fuller process, involved the former collecting views from various units in the White House and the latter gathering them from cabinet secretaries. In addition, Darman served as the conduit for all position papers reaching the president.

As we might expect, officials operating short of the quadrumvirate level in the White House Office and the Executive Office of the President, gave mixed reviews of its effectiveness. One favorable commentary, acknowledging that direct access to the president was constricted by the "Big Four," still gave full credit to the benefits accruing from good circulation of paper right up to the president:

> The way I judge openness is the availability of information. You have to have the ability to make input from the bowels of the White House and get all the way to the top so that it's acted upon. That happens with amazing frequency as far as I'm concerned; . . . we get excellent feedback all the way from the top. . . . It's not as important that I see the president . . . in terms of operation you're better off limiting those who actually have direct access to the president.[22]

A more senior official working in the West Wing had his reservations. First, the quadrumvirate presented burdens of internal clearance in the White House that could become quite onerous. Thus the system operated well when one very large burning issue had focused everyone's attention. However, it did not respond well in overload situations. The official noted,

This is a cumbersome process. You generally have to build consensus for things to go forward. You have to check here and here and here. . . . We tend to be very, very good when we have one major problem out there that we all have to work on together. . . . We have much more difficulty coping with three or four simultaneous problems.[23]

Second, the concentration of four very high-profile aides in the Reagan White House and the intricacy of their intramural processes tended to sharpen the distinction between staff in the White House and those across the way in the Old Executive Office Building (OEOB). In other words, our respondent believed that less senior White House staff housed in the OEOB and members of the policy offices in the Executive Office of the President found it more difficult than in other administrations to gain access at critical decision points. He observed,

There's a geographic distance that's longer than the half a block between here and the OEOB. I thought the Nixon administration did a better job of distributing power between the two buildings. There were power centers of their own in OEOB and people at junior level had access into those power centers. It's very hard for a lot of people over there to feel that they're closely tied in when, after all, the Big Four are all in this building.[24]

Remarks by respondents in the Old Executive Office Building reflected similar concerns. One deputy head of an executive office agency lamented the fact that the ascendancy of Baker, through the White House's emphasis on implementation, eclipsed somewhat Meese's role in development of policy issues. As a result, ideologically committed members of the EOP found that they had to yield to the premium that the White House placed on consensus politics. As this aide expressed it,

The primary development that has taken place in the White House is the growing role of Jim Baker and his immediate people. Initially, the division of labor between Meese and Baker was that the former was supposed to handle policy matters and the lattter legislative strategy matters. But anybody who's been around town for thirty minutes knows that's not a very clear distinction. Baker has gained an increasing role on policy matters, although he was not part of the original Reagan team. . . . We generally find that we are losers if we are an outlier on an issue. . . . So, coalition building internal to the administration consumes a good bit of time.[25]

Another deputy head in the EOP styled himself a Reagan conservative, that is, "more revolutionary in a traditional sense, much more willing to change and get things done . . . a man of principle." He openly regretted the departure from the administration of several fellow members of the "California mafia." Though much more ideological in their approach, many had simply replicated the misfortunes of Carter's Georgians by lacking sufficient knowledge of Washington and placing too much trust in the capacity of personal contacts in carrying the day. As a survivor, our respondent believed he had learned how to attain the right mix of use of the system and personal ties to make a difference on select issues:

I didn't feel initially the structure problem that the White House presents. That was not healthy for me. . . . I came in a kind of a blithe spirit—good for the country and motherhood, the white knight and that kind of thing. It was only after a year and I had been beaten on two or three major issues and not even known it that I realized the structural problems; . . . you decide the power center you're going to be part of. . . . And that's what I've done. . . . I've cast my lot with Meese.[26]

Secretariats—A Struggle to Place Process Before Ideology

We saw earlier that the loose organization and operation of the White House under Carter fostered entrepreneurial styles among officials working in the National Security Council staff and the Domestic Policy Staff. Our assessment of Reagan's White House during the first term suggests that the preoccupation of key aides in the West Wing with process worked a considerable effect on the roles of less senior officials in the Old Executive Office Building. In this respect, the more structured White House augured well for more neutral, brokerage-oriented secretariats in the NSC staff and the Office of Policy Development. However, a major disturbance makes this inference much less straightforward than we might expect. As Ronald Reagan's ideological commitments run deeper and farther from the center than did Carter's, so administration personnel initially selected to work in the NSC staff and OPD generally professed much stronger stances than did their opposite numbers under Carter. Especially while the overarching White House process was establishing its legitimacy, ideologically oriented officials in the NSC staff and OPD used their status as true-blue Reaganites to short-circuit the process by winning over the president through a sympathetic contact in the West Wing of the White House. While this condition subsided somewhat in the OPD, it persisted to a more significant degree in the NSC staff.

Further into the first term, Reagan did make important personnel changes in appointing William P. Clark as Richard V. Allen's replacement and Edwin L. Harper as Martin Anderson's. Clark drew upon a close friendship with Reagan and cordiality with George P. Shultz to dampen the acrimony that prevailed in the national security sector when Haig was secretary of state. Harper claimed considerable exposure to both the White House and the Executive Office of the President dating back to 1968, experience in private sector management positions, good ties to Republican moderates and a previous high-level Reagan administration position as deputy director of OMB. The administration made similar improvements through lower level NSC staff and OPD replacements.

For instance, Roger Porter, who worked in the secretariat for Ford's Economic Policy Board, eventually served jointly as Reagan's executive secretary for the Cabinet Council on Economic Affairs and director of OPD with responsibility for coordinating its operations. He reported to the assistant to the president for policy development who, in turn, reported to Meese. All along, Meese had working directly to him Craig Fuller, another Californian, who oversaw clearance of issues through the entire cabinet council system and briefed the president when Reagan chaired meetings.

Although most observers saw improvement after the departure of Allen, the NSC staff continued to receive strong criticism for its poor performance under Reagan. In fact, many NSC staff members discussed their organization's problems with great candor. Generally, it encountered its early difficulties as a result of members' overly strong ideological commitments, relative inexperience working in key roles within Washington's national security community, and a lack of clarity in the assignment of responsibilities in the staff. To quote one official:

> I've also noticed a big difference in the two years I've been here in terms of people just settling into their jobs and getting to know them. . . . [Before Reagan] there was an identifiable

political-military set of officials who moved in and out pretty freely and pretty well knew each other—you had quite a bit of continuity. Most of those faces left with the old administration and new people came in, many of whom were sort of on the periphery—I mean they were coming from the conservative side. They had been unfashionable for a long time; . . . it took them a while, number one, to know the job, and to get to know each other.[27]

A career official, deeply concerned about what he considered the collapse of the NSC staff under Allen, tore into a Reagan appointee whose outspoken comments eventually precipitated his unceremonious dismissal from the administration. He also reflected less charitably than the NSC staff member quoted above on how the NSC staff had, under Allen, ceased operating effectively as a secretariat:

The previous guy . . . was impossible to work with. He would take whatever you gave him and send it to his old department for staffing; . . . he was kind of a violent guy. If he didn't agree with you, he would threaten to practically throw you out the window. . . . The Allen NSC was particularly weak because they did little more than staple the papers together. They did almost nothing about structuring the arguments and laying out the pros and cons. . . . At NSC meetings, "Cap" [Weinberger] would read his brief and Haig would read his and the president would decide. There were some disastrous decisions made because the president didn't know what he was signing up to. I think it's getting better somewhat; . . . there are still cats on the NSC staff who are ideologues. They have their own personal agenda. Their mission in life is not to lay out arguments but to get their will done.[28]

This tenuous situation did not appear to extend to the Office of Policy Development. For the most part, career officials in other central agencies gave the OPD higher marks for its performance in neutral brokerage than they accorded Carter's DPS. As one respondent put it:

This is a pretty unified administration within the Executive Office of the President when it comes to policy. You don't have quite the activist role of the OPD that you did with DPS. Now, there are some people who have been very active in certain things. But, these are not quite the crusaders that we had under the Eizenstat regime. . . . I guess we haven't felt it in any overwhelming sense, but there is a systematic kind of staffing process that goes on.[29]

During the Reagan first term, Roger Porter clearly received the highest praise for his management of the Cabinet Council on Economic Affairs. Virtually every respondent in a position to assess the operation of the CCEA made a point of stressing Porter's effectiveness. Respondents acknowledged that Porter's strong personal relationship with the CCEA's chairman pro tem, Donald T. Regan—the first-term treasury secretary—gave him a credibility that other cabinet council executive secretaries did not enjoy to the same degree. In addition, they recognized that Porter could become acquisitive in his zeal to have economics issues "roundtabled." Nonetheless, their descriptions of his strengths left one with the impression that he had become the broker par excellence: "His role is genuinely that of an honest broker. He will assure that papers are well written, that—when decision papers—they offer very clear choices that are presented in as unbiased a way as possible, and they'll often be written or at least reviewed by a work group."[30]

Not all of the executive secretaries received this order of praise. Some drew critical remarks based more on their becoming captive of their chairmen pro tem than being overly entrepreneurial. In other words, respondents believed that effective executive secretaries serve their committee process and not just their lead cabinet officer. Although (at the request of the respondent) it appears without names, the following comment gives the flavor of what officials judged to be less than a sterling performance:

[He] views himself as working for his chairman pro tem. The papers that go to his cabinet council are not necessarily unbiased. They may be written by the chairman pro tem's department. They may not present the other side of an issue. He doesn't view himself as an honest broker. He would like to be, but he feels constrained by his chairman.[31]

Let Regan Be Reagan

On January 8, 1985, Ronald Reagan made a change in personnel that radically altered the nature of his White House advisory system. James Baker and Donald T. Regan—the treasury secretary—

were to switch jobs. The impending departures of Edwin Meese III and Michael Deaver from the White House probably spelled the demise of the modified spokes-in-a-wheel format for organizing the West Wing anyway. However, the appointment of Donald Regan as the chief of staff pretty much sealed this outcome.

Very much enamored of his success as chief executive officer of Merrill Lynch and Company, Regan did not bring to his work an immense respect for the higher crafts of executive-bureaucratic politics as practiced so well by Baker. Soon after his appointment, one administration official prophetically contrasted Regan's likely style with that followed by Baker:

> Baker was a lawyer, a negotiator, a chief of staff who tried to make his case for his client through negotiation. Under Baker there wasn't a hierarchy—there were three or four senior partners with access to the president. Don [Regan] will eliminate parallel sources of access; . . . as a businessman by nature he operates in a hierarchical manner rather than a negotiating manner. He seems like an uncharacteristic person for the job.[32]

Indeed, nearly a year later, a journalist who gained access to one of Regan's 8:00 A.M. staff meetings caught a glimpse of just how imperious a hierarchical chief of staff could be. Brooding over a leak regarding planned spending cuts, Regan berated his senior personnel like so many school children:

> I'd say "good morning," but that's just a phrase. . . . Anyone who wants to leak confidential information can resign. . . . If any of you think you know better than the president about what ought to be communicated, you don't belong here.[33]

One simple fact permitted Regan to speak to the top West Wing personnel in this way. While certainly a "staff," they no longer constituted a senior assemblage. Donald Regan did not like the chief/Indian ratio when he took over the White House. He therefore demoted several advisory positions from "assistant to the president" to "deputy." In the process, some formerly freestanding offices merged with others under a single appointee at the assistant to the president level. The former communications and public liaison domains now came under the director of communications. The political affairs and intergovernmental affairs portfolios now fell under the assistant to the president for political and intergovernmental affairs.

At the outset, Patrick J. Buchanan assumed the communications job and Edward J. Rollins and Max L. Friedersdorf returned to the White House to take up, respectively, the political and governmental affairs and legislative affairs positions. As well, John A. Svahn—a former undersecretary in the Department of Health and Human Services who held top posts in Reagan's California administration—remained assistant to the president for policy development, while Robert C. McFarlane—a member of the "Big Four" during the first term—continued as assistant to the president for national security affairs.

Observers thus can be forgiven for concluding that Regan's hierarchical approach would allow for some diversity. By the end of the first year, however, the reality had departed sharply from such expectations. McFarlane, Rollins, and Friedersdorf had all left the White House. None of their replacements equaled them in stature. Further, Regan had marginalized both Buchanan and Svahn. Instead of relying upon a quasi-collegial system based upon consultation with functioning office heads, Regan turned increasingly to a cadre of advisers who came directly under him. All of these officials had worked for Regan in the Treasury Department and were beholden to him for their rapid career advancement. They function, thus, more as surrogates than as colleagues.

Why has a president who appeared to thrive under the modified spokes-in-a-wheel format tolerated such a decided shift toward a hierarchical White House? Three factors suggest themselves in addressing this question. To begin, the Baker-Regan trade enabled the administration to cope with James Baker's desire to leave the chief of staff job without submitting to feverish infighting over his replacement. For instance, some archconservatives had already rallied behind UN ambassador Jeane J. Kirkpatrick as a candidate for Baker's position. Second, observers perhaps underestimated Donald Regan's force of personality. Although virtually every commentator registered warnings about his hierarchical manner, few anticipated the degree to which he would follow this approach in the White House. Finally, a major miscalculation concerned the president. His engagement in the quotidian affairs of state—especially on the domestic side—simply has not equaled even his relatively modest involvement during the first term. This point comes through most significantly in the fact that—even with a dramatically simplified committee system—he now rarely chairs cabinet-level policy councils concerned with economic and domestic affairs. The president's age, his summer 1985 illness and creeping "lame duck" factors all exacerbated Regan's propensity to operate hierarchically.

Conclusion

Presidents must pay close attention to the effects of their White House organization and operation both on cabinet secretaries' roles and the functioning of policy shops in the Executive Office of the President. The experience of the last several years suggests that a mix of the hierarchical and spokes-in-a-wheel models as found in broker politics best serves the president in pursuing the often conflicting goals of executive branch harmony and access to the Oval Office. A pure spokes-in-a-wheel format would best fit presidents who have opted for a priorities-and-planning approach to their administration. However, the fragmented nature of the U.S. executive branch and its relations with other segments of the policy arena suggest that priorities-and-planning formats would collapse under their own weight.

On the other hand, the spokes-in-a-wheel pattern might win by default when a president has failed to induce even the moderate amount of central guidance present in broker politics. Here the Carter administration presents a paradox. Carter's embracing administrative politics fit well the generalized national repudiation of Nixon's imperial presidency. However, it would be hard to conceive of a president willingly embracing this design to the degree that Carter did. In the event, Carter's leadership style, especially his penchant for exhaustive policy agendas and his personal immersion in details, undermined his administrative politics format and severely overloaded his White House. Especially gifted presidents such as Franklin Roosevelt or John F. Kennedy might find that they can err in this direction. Carter could not.

During the first term, Ronald Reagan found a workable mix between a hierarchical and spokes-in-a-wheel format. In the first year, the White House imposed extreme discipline on secretaries and stood its radically conservative ground in relations with Congress. Yet it worked in very broad strokes—avoiding at all costs engrossment in details. Here the view prevailed that getting the macropolicies right would force the specifics into line. Along the way, the presence in the White House of considerably more senior appointees with extensive experience in Washington than was true of Carter's staff contributed greatly to the Reagan administration's relative success with maintaining the support of Congress, the media, and, in general, the electorate. By midterm, the division of the White House between Meese and Clark on the "president's conscience side" and Baker and Deaver on the "implementation side" allowed for a relatively smooth transition from the radical stances taken earlier in the mandate to the "do-able" goals isolated in the last two years. In sum, Reagan spared himself from becoming manifestly one of the least engaged presidents in this century by knowing how to organizing his White House to maximum effect.

With respect to policy secretariats, presidents wishing to use these as coordinative mechanisms must assure that the conditions exist whereby they can adequately fulfill cabinet secretaries' and committees' need for neutral brokerage of divisive issues. Normally such matters do not reach resolution without reference to the senior White House staff and the president. However, they must be sufficiently developed before they reach the West Wing. Here working within an identifiable and effective decision process in the White House proper can lend discipline to secretariat staff who might otherwise give excessive time to their pet issues. As well, presidents must assure that those in charge of secretariats not select aides with so little experience in Washington that they get in the way of, rather than facilitate, the development of issues. Both Carter and Reagan failed in this respect. In addition, the Reagan administration initially brought on board too many ideologues firm in the belief that true-blue conviction can move mountains.

5. Keeping Economic and Fisal Policies Dancing in Step

More than in any other policy sector, Jimmy Carter and Ronald Reagan faced a similar challenge in the state of the economy when they first took office. Both presidents confronted the problems caused by economic recession. The simultaneous conditions of high inflation and unemployment left very little room for maneuvering in applying the macroeconomic policies of times more amenable to "Keynesian" instruments. That is, finely tuned spending programs and tax measures held out little hope, while it appeared that only a jolt of major proportions would revive the economy. Only radical proposals would engage the popular imagination. The attractiveness of pleas for a balanced budget before both Carter's and Reagan's incumbency, and the allure of promises for massive tax cuts before Reagan's accession to office made bold action almost imperative.

Contrary to historic expectations, America's diminished place in the world commuity suggested strongly that the domestic economic policy process could no longer afford to be insular. In the wake of the Vietnam War, the nation found that not even the world's soundest economic base allowed it unrestricted military engagements. Of course, the West experienced during the period two especially alarming economic shocks in the form of the 1973 and 1979 energy crises. In addition to driving home the vulnerability of a gas-guzzling people greatly dependent on imported oil, the energy crises underlined the relative noncompetitiveness of many sectors of the U.S. economy. Carter and Reagan both faced compelling evidence of the fact that domestic and international economics had become so clearly linked that getting only the former right no longer ensured prosperity.

This chapter presents the case that the adverse economic times intensified and complicated by new international imperatives, brought the U.S. economic policy process to a crossroads in its development. Since World War II, the difficulty of coordinating policymaking within the national security field has argued strongly for institutionalization of cabinet-level consultation in that sector. As we have seen in Chapter 2, Truman created the National Security Council in response to the perception that Churchill, by virtue of regularized committee structures for interservice and interdepartmental consultation, had coordinated his war effort better than Roosevelt had his. This chapter asks whether a similar process toward institutionalization, quickened by the economic conditions of the past fifteen years, has taken hold within the economic policy sector. It examines, thus, Carter's and Reagan's approaches to machinery intended to coordinate the principal participants in development of economic policies.

After presenting the agency-related issues connected to economic policy, the treatment moves to Carter's and Reagan's approaches to cabinet-level integration within this sector. To what degree did the two presidents recognize the instrumental utility of regularized cabinet consultation on economic policies? Did the systems they set up fit their personalities and the styles of their administrations? As well, did they build adequately upon machinery already employed in previous administrations? What about the operation of White House and executive office policy units in the scheme of things? To what extent did they occupy a stance of neutral brokerage allowing for facilitation of interdepartmental coordination?

Whenever Two or More Gather in the Name of the Economy, There You Have Confusion

Looking at advanced liberal democracies, one would find it difficult to suggest any more routinized process of interdepartmental coordination than that provided by the U.K. cabinet committee system.[1] In relation to development and integration of economic policies, an irony emerges here. In the United Kingdom, Her Majesty's Treasury retains control over all principal elements of economic policy. The only other central agency in the play, the Cabinet Office, confines its efforts largely to running the machinery in which Treasury

presses its view of the economy to clusters of operational departments. These gather in specialized committees such as "economic
strategy," "nationalized industries policy," "European Economic
Community policy," and "home affairs and social policy." On the
other hand, the Department of the Treasury in the United States
must contend with stiff competition from several other organizations which enjoy central-agency status. In a very real sense, the
U.S. arrangement heightens the necessity of ongoing cabinet-level
coordination. However, presidents have been loath to install adequate machinery in this sector.

The Executive Office Complex

The fact that all of the central agencies that compete with the U.S.
Treasury for turf operate out of the Executive Office of the President did not come about by accident. In an executive branch
centering unambiguously on the head of government, it falls upon
the president to take direct responsibility for segments of central
coordination and control which seem not to operate well. This
process started in a modest way with the creation of the Bureau of
the Budget in 1921.[2] Established to enhance the president's ability
to control expenditure estimates going to Congress and—in the
long haul—improve the economy and efficiency of government,
BOB remained part of Treasury until 1939. During the war, Franklin Delano Roosevelt seized upon BOB's utility as a career staff
distinct from White House aides. Thus it helped him through the
crunch by serving as a management planner and sorting out fiscal
priorities.[3]

The onset of other rough patches, although less dire, has argued
for the same approach. For instance, the Council of Economic Advisers can mostly trace its lineage to the National Resources Management Board, which Roosevelt had created to spearhead elements
of the New Deal and which Congress had abolished in 1943. Eventually, Harry Truman provided for the CEA in a package of economic planning proposals that led to the 1946 Employment Act.
On the basis of an independent reading of the economy, this agency
was to advise the president on the means toward achieving full
employment. The Office of the U.S. Trade Representative (1980)
takes the place of the Office of the Special Representative for Trade
Negotiations, which was created in 1962. The latter agency owed
its existence to Congress's wish, as the "Kennedy round" of multi-

lateral trade negotiations began, that the administration be able to develop coherent policies from the conflicting goals of operational departments interested in trade issues. The Council on Wage and Price Stability (CWPS) received its mandate in 1974. Although in that year the Nixon administration lifted mandatory wage and price controls, CWPS set out to supply the president with an independent source of data on pay and prices in various sectors of the economy. The agency did not stand the test of time, principally because its responsibilities overlapped excessively with those of the CEA and elements of OMB. Ronald Reagan dismantled CWPS shortly after becoming president.

The Office of Management and Budget (OMB). As the agency that develops the president's expenditure budget, OMB controls a central element of the fiscal framework. This in turn embodies the administration's tax and spending targets intended, in aggregate terms, to stimulate or slow the growth of the economy. OMB's domination of expenditure review gives it an integral role, along with Treasury and CEA, in the development of the administration's economic forecasts. These normally involve technical consultations among staff economists that lead to negotiations between the heads of the three agencies on the final figures. In addition to OMB's involvement with forecasting exercises, the pivotal importance of spending plans to macroeconomic policy warrants OMB's contribution to decision making on major economic issues and crises that develop independently of the president's annual economic report and budget.

OMB's associate director for economic policy assists the agency's director in consultations over the forecast and in reviewing the fiscal framework and other key macroeconomic policies. This official, a political appointee, serves as a brain truster assuring that OMB's contribution to the administration's economic policies reflects its mandate as a budget office. Normally, the associate director comes from academia and brings to his work some practical experience in government posts. During Reagan's first term, Lawrence A. Kudlow was an exception. Kudlow brought from his career in the financial community virtually no formal training in economics. This deficiency notwithstanding, he doubled his office staff to ten professionals and, more effectively than any predecessor, swung OMB's weight in forecasting exercises. He accomplished this largely through the astute use of the OMB budget review division. That is, he made extensive use of this unit's career officials, who normally focused on straightforward stewardship of the aggregate budget figures, for generating alternate macroeconomic analyses to those being served up elsewhere in the administration.

The pragmatic bent of David Stockman, the agency's director during Reagan's first term, played a vital role in upgrading OMB's involvement in macroeconomic policy. Stockman viewed forecasting and budgeting as exercises in finding the package that would achieve the administration's programmatic objectives and obtain a viable level of congressional support. Such realpolitik struck a responsive chord with the "implementation" side of the White House, ruled over by James A. Baker III. Kudlow maximized his own role by adhering to Stockman's approach and confounding analysts used to a more open-ended process. One career official in Treasury put it well:

> They went and negotiated over this budget [fiscal year 1983], the president and his men with the chieftains on the Hill. We didn't know who did . . . the comparative analysis of the economic effects of various alternatives. . . . When some people from the Council of Economic Advisers wanted to do some data analysis on their own, the White House called them and said, "Just lay off." Even my political boss, who, after all, was hired to do these things, said he was in the dark. . . . So, I was trying to figure out who knows anything. Well, it turned out that the OMB and the White House itself [produced the figures for the budget], period; . . . there were no economic impact studies of specific measures.[4]

The Council of Economic Advisers (CEA). During the Carter administration, the CEA fulfilled reasonably well its formal mandate. Staffed for the most part by academic economists who normally stayed for only two years or so, the CEA took as its main responsibility pursuit of consensus forecasts from disparate government sources. Here it worked mainly as ringmaster for the "troika." This mechanism, consisting of representatives from Treasury, OMB, and CEA, operated at three levels. T[roika]3 brought together technicians preparing the fundamental elements of the annual forecast. These analysts employed models that often made substantially different economic assumptions. T[roika]2 consisted of the policital appointees in each agency responsible for forecasting. These included Treasury's assistant secretary for economic policy, OMB's assistant (now "associate") director for economic policy and the member of the CEA who took the lead in macroeconomic matters on behalf of the council's chairman. Finally, T[roika]1—meetings between the treasury secretary, the OMB director, and the CEA chairman—would iron out remaining differences. Largely through the forceful personality of the chairman, Charles L. Schultze, and the acumen of the council's member for forecasting, Lyle E. Gramely, CEA effectively chaired the various levels of the troika. Thus it assumed under Carter a leading role in enforcing analytic probity—insofar as this is politically possible.

Under Reagan, economic modeling has run forecasting less clearly. Thus, the CEA has found itself in an ambiguous position. CEA's chairman from 1981 to 1982, Murray L. Weidenbaum, found fruitless his attempts to reconcile the wildly contradictory projections of supply-siders and monetarists in Treasury and the stringency-minded in OMB. By the time he left his post, the strongly political nature of administration forecasts had become transparent to attentive publics and insiders alike. Weidenbaum's immediate successor, Martin Feldstein, benefited at the outset from the fact that the administration had lost by summer 1982 its most doctrinaire supply-siders. He also acted more aggressively to imbue the 1983 annual report with analytic probity. In fact, the administration made assumptions for the 1984 budget which soon appeared too pessimistic when the 1983 economic recovery proved stronger than CEA forecasts had allowed.

To be fair, the difficulties Reagan's CEA encountered during the first term in fulfilling its mandate stemmed significantly from the turmoil in the economics profession during the post-Keynesian era. One career official in the Treasury cited the diverse views among his political masters. He also noted the substantially different approaches in OMB and CEA. He concluded that the absence of common presuppositions permeated even analytic processes:

At the technical level, whereas we formerly sat down and worked out a forecast to be passed along to higher levels, it wasn't easily done in this case. I think in previous administrations the various appointees came in with pretty much the same economic outlook—a more or less Keynesian view of how the world operated. So, it was easier to narrow differences. Previous appointees might not accept a technical-level forecast or might say, "Go back and do this or do that." Yet, the differences weren't nearly so wide and it was much easier.[5]

When Feldstein entered the debate, Treasury and OMB had locked themselves in a battle over the size of the budget for fiscal year 1984. The former held that a strong recovery would increase revenues, thereby producing a smaller deficit, while the latter argued for tax increases. At this point the terms "structural" and "cyclical" deficit joined the American political lexicon. "Structural" refers to the part of the deficit produced by systemic defects in fiscal policy as related to long-term weaknesses in the U.S. economy; "cyclical" denotes the segment of the deficit that would disappear if economic recovery were to restore revenues to a more robust state. Under Feldstein's guidance, CEA began through the late summer and fall of 1982 to attempt to distinguish between the two elements of the deficit. In the end, most of the analysis never reached the public forum. However, it reflected an ingenious attempt to restore the internal dialogue to a higher level of analytic integrity. In the words of one respondent:

> We really did an awful lot of work—it almost went into our annual report—on the concept of the cyclically adjusted GNP. . . . you try to extract from the data the underlying trend free from cyclical fluctuations. . . . So, I was trying to construct something that would have wide appeal. That is, it would be viewed as impartial—not being subject to manipulation for the political needs of the day. . . . [Regarding the actual deficit figure chosen by the president,] people wonder to what extent it is really backed by some solid analytic work, and to what degree it is simply pooh-poohing the size of the deficit.[6]

CEA does not confine its role to participation in the development of administration economic forecasts. Allowing for differences in the specialities of council members, the agency involves itself in any economic policy issues in which the president has a clear stake. Relatedly, the chairman belongs by convention to the big three—including the treasury secretary and the OMB director—who emerge as the principal economic advisers in any administration. Of the three, the chairman least often attains the highest level of intimacy with the president. Yet, his very small agency—three "members" and fewer than twenty professional staff—finds myriad openings for advice by virtue of the chairman's access to the very highest decision councils of the administration.

Under Schultze, the CEA intervened especially effectively on a number of international issues. Schultze himself used his chairmanship of the economic policy committee of the Organization for Economic Cooperation and Development to become an unofficial White House coordinator on international monetary affairs.[7] For instance, he, more than Treasury Secretary W. Michael Blumenthal, masterminded the October 1978 package to rescue the dollar from foreign exchange pressures. In the same period, CEA played an active role in vetting U.S. agreements connected with the Multilateral Trade Negotiations, concluded in Geneva in 1979. Under Reagan, CEA has found less of a part in international monetary and trade issues—largely because such matters have preoccupied the administration less. However, it has continued a very active role in regulatory policies. Here, it relied heavily during the first term upon a council member with wide academic and practical experience in this area, namely, William A. Niskanen.

The Office of the U.S. [Special] Trade Representative (STR). As mandated by statute, the STR works primarily with formal coordinative bodies centering on the issues before the Trade Policy Committee (TPC). This committee, chaired by the U.S. trade representative—a cabinet-rank appointee—and specified by the Trade Expansion Act (1962), includes the political heads of some fifteen agencies with some interest in trade matters. Matters coming under the purview of the TPC must pass through two committees before reaching the cabinet-level body. The first of these, the Trade Policy Staff Committee, functions mainly with agencies' career public servants most vitally concerned with trade. The second, the Trade Policy Review Group, operates with political appointees below the cabinet level attempting to resolve outstanding issues before reference to TPC. During the Carter administration, the preparation of U.S. positions in the Multilateral Trade Negotiations saw the creation of around twenty-five ad hoc committees—all chaired by STR officials—that tried to iron out interdepartmental conflicts on items relating to various economic sectors.

The positions taken by the various trade committees do not command juridical force within an administration. That is, the U.S. trade representative can make recommendations to the president at variance with the TPC consensus. Here the standing of the trade representative with the president and Congress comes into play. Carter's trade representative, Robert Strauss, benefited greatly from his friendship with the president and his very high credit with key Democrats. He therefore proved to be highly successful despite the general chaos of interdepartmental coordination during the Carter administration and the overload created in STR by the Multilateral Trade Negotiations.

On the other hand, Bill Brock—Reagan's first-term U.S. trade representative—found himself at a relative disadvantage. First, he did not enjoy the access to Reagan that Strauss did to Carter. Second, the cabinet council system instituted under Reagan crowded somewhat TPC's statutory prerogatives in connection with preparation of trade issues for presidential decision. At the outset, Reagan's Cabinet Council on Commerce and Trade partially replicated the mandate of TPC and legitimated the commerce secretary's taking a more active role in coordinating departmental views on trade. Subsequently the National Security Council staff and the Department of Defense began pressing for restrictions on trade of advanced technology into Eastern bloc countries.

The latter coalition led in summer 1982 to an embargo against the sale of pipeline technology to the Soviets by U.S. firms and their foreign subsidiaries. The NSC recommendation advocating this hard line contributed to Alexander Haig's pique that led to his departure from the administration. His successor as secretary of state, George P. Shultz, calmed the waters by advocating the creation of a Senior Interagency Group under the National Security Council system that would, among other things, prepare trade issues with especially serious national security implications for the president's decision. The resulting SIG on international economic policy, chaired by the treasury secretary, provided yet another forum in which many STR positions ran the gauntlet before reaching the president. In the words of one career official who compared the Reagan arrangement with that under Carter, the involvement of two additional committees vitally concerned with trade made life considerably more complicated for STR:

> There's the Cabinet Council on Commerce and Trade, CCCT—sounds very Soviet or something—which is run out of the White House and which the president often chairs. Then we've just recently seen a new SIG formed for international economic policy. . . . The whole thing is a bit difficult to figure out how it works; . . . It's considerably more intricate and a lot less orderly than it was before.[8]

The Council on Wage and Price Stability (CWPS). As noted above, CWPS came into being in 1974. It obtained a sizable staff and set out on the relatively technical task of gathering data on how various industrial sectors were adhering to the spirit of voluntary wage and price controls. Initially in the Carter administration, Charles L. Schultze chaired CWPS as well as the CEA. Barry Bosworth, a Brookings Institution colleague of Schultze's, actually directed CWPS's operations and gained prestige in the administration through frequent and accurate augurings about where inflation was leading the economy. However, Bosworth receded into the background at the most critical point in the administration's efforts against inflation.

Early in fall 1978, Alfred E. Kahn, previously the chairman of the Civil Aeronautics Board and largely responsible for implementing the Carter administration's massive decontrol of the airline industry, became the president's senior adviser on inflation. This took CWPS from Schultze's to Kahn's domain. The latter used CWPS simply as a base for promoting deregulation in other sectors. By the end of the Carter administration, CWPS could offer few arguments against the judgment that it had performed all along as a fifth wheel among executive office economic policy shops. However, after its abolition, some CWPS units survived by being grafted on OMB under a new office entitled "Information and Regulatory Affairs."

The National Security Council Staff (NCS Staff) and the Office of Policy Development. In addition to executive office units with specific statutory responsibilities for aspects of economic policy formulation, the National Security Council staff and the Office of Policy Development gain considerable access to the president by virtue of their responsibilities for coordination of "presidential" matters. The NSC received its mandate within the foreign policy field through a 1947 statute. Increasingly, it has successfully argued that many international economic matters raise national security issues that require it to have a separate input. The Office of Policy Development, on the other hand, derives from the practice, beginning with Nixon in 1970, whereby the president collects advisers coordinating various sectors of the White House review of domestic policy in one office. This body took the title "Domestic Policy Council" under Nixon and Ford and "Domestic Policy Staff" under Carter. Especially under Carter and Reagan, it has enjoyed considerable leverage in the administration's treatment of economic issues.

The Department of the Treasury

A look at the organizational chart of the Department of the Treasury becomes daunting if we do not keep an important distinction in mind. That is, some units merit consideration in this treatment because they are actually involved with higher-level policy deliberations made by the central agency complex at the very top of the executive bureaucracy. Other units mainly administer programs adopted by the more cerebral parts of Treasury. The policy-oriented units all belong to the Office of the Secretary. During the Carter administration and Reagan's first term, they included the offices of the undersecretary for monetary affairs, the assistant secretaries for international affairs, domestic finance, economic policy, and tax policy, and the fiscal assistant secretary. This discussion will focus on the roles of these offices. It excludes other units in the Office of the Secretary, which support the policy arms—namely, legislative affairs, public affairs, public liaison and consumer affairs, and the general counsel—as well as units that monitor the various bureaus and services reporting to the treasury secretary—namely, enforcement and operations, and administration. The various agencies coming under the Treasury's umbrella include the Bureaus of Alcohol, Tobacco and Firearms, Engraving and Printing and the U.S. Customs and Internal Revenue services.

Notwithstanding the vastness of the treasury secretary's responsibilities, his department does little to coordinate issues before they reach his desk. This state of affairs stands in stark contrast to the British Treasury, in which several strata of coordinative panels within the department attempt to maintain continuous consultation between units responsible for various elements of the government's economic program. One Reagan appointee put the U.S. Treasury's approach succinctly. He noted that coordination very often depends upon who is called into the secretary's office for a major briefing:

> The real mechanism for coordination is simply the meetings held by the secretary. He tends to hold large meetings—surprisingly large, with eight to ten people. They frequently include the deputy assistant secretaries and above most involved with an issue. It's not really that formal even. It's not really so much designating a level. It's just who gets involved. It's in these meetings that we find our greatest impact on other offices. It's in those sessions that difference of opinion are aired and discussed.[9]

In comparing the Treasury under Carter and Reagan, officials did note some important differences in the department's operations under W. Michael Blumenthal and G. William Miller in the former administration, and Donald T. Regan in the latter. Specifically concerning personalities, the managerial style of Donald Regan received higher marks than that of either Blumenthal or Miller. That is, Carter's secretaries did not pay enough attention to bringing on board political appointees with management experience. As well, they adopted uncritically the Treasury way of doing things—that is, allowing everyone his day in court through private sessions. One official put these points in very strong terms. "Blumenthal has said publicly that he didn't hire managers because in government you only need to make policy and be brilliant on issues. So, he had a great many intellectuals who had brilliant ideas which, two offices down the corridor, couldn't be implemented."[10]

In making his second point, the respondent added a criticism of the deputy secretary throughout the Carter administration, Robert Carswell. The official believed that Carswell received too much delegated authority by the two secretaries and, as a lawyer, worked too much on a case-by-case basis:

> There was no management at all in the place. It was totally absent. You had a lawyer whose management style was to deal with everyone personally. . . . It was just associates. Everyone was an associate running in to see the partner . . . nobody cooperated with anybody. They had a lot of personal conflicts and everybody had to stay here until the dying day. So, they just seethed for the next three years after they'd had their fight in the first.[11]

Much of the Treasury's haphazard, even dysfunctional, organization owes to a fact of the American bureaucratic life not present in the United Kingdom. Short of ministers, the U.K. Treasury assigns the uppermost offices to career civil servants. These have developed a community of interests based on many years of working within the various sections of the same department. Any U.S. administration's appointees to the highest echelons of Treasury, on the other hand, will differ substantially among themselves both in backgrounds and approaches to the economic agenda of the day.

Although it is far from being spared the effects of the appointive system, Reagan's Treasury has demonstrated a greater capacity for harmony than did Carter's. Even the divergence between supply-siders and monetarists fell within a relatively narrow band of highly conservative, market-oriented economic thought. The administration, in part, replicated on the departmental level what it accomplished throughout the government. That is, it selected only political appointees who passed "Reaganite" ideological tests and gave them very clear missions. These steps reduced the likelihood that appointees would become the captives of office directors and other career officials never at loss to present personal agenda items when the new political masters arrive at their desks. In some cases, career officials had the good fortune to preside over pet projects that fit especially well with the new administration's goals. However, these would comprise a minority.

Most career officials expressed the view that the political appointees' adherence to the administration's conservative dogmas drove a wedge between them and their immediate political masters. As one such respondent said:

> I'm just trying to describe my personal frustrations. I don't think I'm able to communicate with them as well as I could. . . . I have no hesitation at this stage to mention that I've been a life-long Republican. So, if I were looking at it from that standpoint, I don't even have any political problems with the folks. For better or worse, I never voted for the opposition in my life, . . . but I'm frustrated in trying to establish some rapport with them. . . . In previous administrations . . . you got a sense of where they were going, what they were trying to do. . . . I think we could be more responsive that way. Now, a lot of things I get to respond to are second- and third-hand. There might have been hours of discussion of a problem. Then they would come down to me with a question.[12]

Relating to this theme, another respondent felt that much of Treasury's longer-range analysis has suffered greatly under the Reagan administration. Units have found that they work mainly to "what-if" exercises attempting to flesh out practical dimensions to schemes concocted entirely at the political level. The respondent thus gave the administration full marks for accomplishing what it had set out to do. However, he faulted it for ignoring many of the more complicated issues that still required attention: "In the Treasury the desire is for quick results . . . and that is good, because it does create an atmosphere of setting priorities and going after the 'do-able' things. . . . Some of us have reservations about other more basic things that simply can't be done in a short period of time but are necessary."[13]

Independent of administrations, organizational efforts designed to improve in-house Treasury coordination have not met with spectacular success. For instance, the assistant secretary for economic policy under Carter, Daniel Brill, assumed his appointment on the condition that all Treasury units responsible for various aspects of economic analysis would be housed in his office. In effect, this meant that analytic shops that formerly had reported to the assistant secretary for the international affairs moved under Brill's part of the organizational chart. Their clients remained policy units under international affairs. However, they observed the new protocol whereby projects undertaken for international affairs had to receive the approval of Brill's office. This requirement led many international affairs policy units to upgrade their own analytic staff so as to conduct research unencumbered by the additional bureaucratic loop. The Reagan administration returned the international analytic units to their original place under the assistant secretary for international affairs.

The Treasury reforms attempted under Reagan apppeared to be much more sweeping. Here the undersecretary for monetary affairs during the first term, Beryl W. Sprinkel, was to assume added responsibility for all international affairs issues and domestic finance, which would have made the assistant secretaries responsible for these offices much more subject to his direction. As well, the administration created a new position, undersecretary for tax and economic affairs, with the view that its incumbent, Norman B. Ture, would coordinate the activities of the assistant secretaries for tax and economic policy. The first of these efforts met with modest success, while the other ended in failure. In both instances, the fragmentation of the U.S. bureaucratic culture—even within departments—appears to have prevailed. In fact, Sprinkel's departure from Treasury to serve on Reagan's second-term Council of Economic Advisers spelled the abolition of his former post.

In the Sprinkel case, the administration's strong emphasis on monetarism focused much more on domestic than international policy. During Reagan's first term, the Treasury worried a great deal more about the supply of money at home than the value of the dollar abroad. Apart from the continuing threat of major loan defaults by developing countries, the United States had not had to rescue a foreign currency as it did with the British pound in 1976. Nor had it found it necessary to race to the assistance of the dollar. All this left little latitude for Sprinkel to gain a tighter hold on the Treasury's international affairs office. The fact that domestic finance is more concerned with regulation of the banking and securities communities and managing government debt than with domestic monetary affairs likewise gave Sprinkel only a limited entree.

With respect to Ture, his strident pursuit of supply-side economics—focused on the alleged centrality of radical tax cuts to economic recovery—made the already difficult attempt to coordinate two disparate units next to impossible. One political appointee with experience in a previous administration spoke incisively to the issue: "From the past here I didn't think it would work. And, it didn't work. In tax matters you get so quickly to the specifics. So you have to get involved in details. Otherwise, it's just very difficult to make a judgment on what's right or wrong. On the other hand, if it goes beyond detail you will have to go to the secretary anyway. Thus, there is no need for an intermediate coordinator."[14]

Of course, the domestic economic objectives of the administration amounted largely to running tax policy more by the grander macroeconomic strategies of the supply-siders than microeconomic concerns related to tax structures. In the words of a surviving political appointee caught in the struggle between Ture and the recalcitrant office of tax policy, the plan meant that the magnitude of the tax cuts would simply have to override much of Treasury's traditional concern for specifics:

> The whole cadre of people over there saw philosophically the tax code as fulfilling the principles of progressive taxation and redistribution. So, the undersecretary was created because this administration was pursuing tax reduction at the margin. The undersecretary was to make sure that there was nothing inconsistent about tax law and regulations, including the development of those, and the administration's economic philosophy.[15]

Notwithstanding the restrained tone of this assertion, such thinking offended the sensibilities of other political appointees. As one official noted, Ture's approach came across so abrasively that even the secretary stopped listening: "[Ture] was an ivory tower type in his bearing and his way of presenting things. After all, Regan is simply a bond salesman. . . . Ultimately, he stopped inviting him to meetings and so on."[16] The administration discontinued the position of undersecretary for tax and economic affairs when Ture left Treasury in 1982.

The Office of the Undersecretary for Monetary Affairs. Under Carter, the official in this position lacked career staffers reporting directly to him. However, the assistant secretary for international affairs and the fiscal assistant secretary both reported to the undersecretary for monetary affairs. In theory, and for the most part in practice, the undersecretary effectively called upon any support he needed as the principal Treasury officer responsible for advising the secretary on foreign and domestic monetary matters.

Beryl Sprinkel, as we have seen, added the Office of the Assistant Secretary for Domestic Finance to the other two gathered under his jurisdiction. However, his attention centered most intensely on domestic monetary affairs, while international matters loomed less large in the administration's mind. To match these circumstances, Sprinkel created an office of domestic monetary affairs—a career unit working under a political-appointee director and reporting to the undersecretary. In the words of one well-placed official, the undersecretary required more immediate access to such staff support:

> Domestic monetary policy is, after all, the primary responsibility of the Federal Reserve. So previous administrations and undersecretaries put relatively little importance on the domestic monetary policy issues. . . . Sprinkel was appointed to his job with the explicit agreement that he would take more of an interest in domestic monetary policy—that he is an expert in the field is the primary reason that he's there. . . . But there was no staff-level group whose primary responsibility was monetary policy. So he established one.[17]

The Federal Reserve System (the Fed) under its chairman, Paul A. Volcker, wields independent authority over the "discount rate" extended by the Federal Reserve banks to private banks and trust companies. This rate, in turn, sets the trend for interest on loans made to borrowers in the open market. By mid-1982, a major dispute broke out between the administration and the Fed. The former held that the economic recovery induced by its tax cuts had foundered on the Fed's erratic regulation of the money supply which, in turn, had kept interest rates excessively high. As noted by a top appointee, the administration's frustration brought on a major effort to review the relationship between the Fed and Treasury:

There are really two sides to the issue. On the one hand, you want to maintain a considerable degree of independence. I say this because I'm not at all convinced that all presidents will have the same view about money that Ronald Reagan has. Certainly, not all previous presidents have. Now, that is in contrast with the whole question of an administration that's elected by the people. They've presented their case. They would not be the administration if they hadn't won. So, how do you do a good job of getting the kind of monetary policy that's consistent with the administration's overall policy objectives? I view the middle ground as maintaining a high degree of independence but achieving as well better cooperation and coordination.[18]

In the end, concern over interest rates abated to the point where the controversy over the relationship between Treasury and the Fed subsided. Nonetheless, the office of monetary affairs vigorously pursued informal contracts with the Fed that went beyond meetings between the secretary and the chairman. About every six weeks, it convened a meeting of administration economic advisers just short of the principals' level with corresponding members of the Fed. Almost weekly, senior staff analysts from both sides met to exchange views on the coordination of fiscal and monetary policies.

The Office of the Assistant Secretary for International Affairs (OASIA). This office contains four main policy units headed by deputy assistant secretaries. Referred to as "deputates," these offices are concerned with international monetary affairs, trade and investment policy, commodities and natural resources, and developing nations. International monetary affairs, as we have seen, maintains a strong relationship with the undersecretary for monetary affairs going beyond its immediate responsibilities within the OASIA. In most administrations, this dual responsibility gives the deputate added clout within Treasury. Two conditions circumscribed its standing during Reagan's first term. As already discussed, the administration and the undersecretary placed less emphasis on international monetary affairs than domestic matters. In addition, the Reagan administration departed from recent practice by appointing a lawyer, Marc E. Leland, as assistant secretary for international affairs. Leland was primarily interested in negotiations concerning trade and investment or debt crises in Third World countries. His training and favored activities left little room for participation in the more global aspects of monetary affairs.

At the beginning of the administration, the OASIA took a very aggressive stance toward the review of U.S. contributions to multilateral development banks. This move coincided with the first indications that major defaults on loans by developing countries deeply in debt could shake the world economy. In a real sense, OASIA packaged for export the stringent fiscal policies pressed by David Stockman. That is, the administration wanted Treasury to stanch the flow of funds being sent to the multilateral development banks with a view to getting more economic growth for less money.

Referred to as "conditionality," the new approach based U.S. support of the lending programs run by organizations such as the International Monetary Fund on the degree to which negotiations over loans led borrowing nations to adopt fiscal policies more consistent with their means. The parallel between this tack on foreign aid and U.S. budgetary policy did not end with stringency in economic aid programs. In bilateral aid, the State Department and the Department of Defense coaxed the administration into the same profligacy toward military programs in sympathethic developing countries that it had succumbed to at home. In other words, the administration's exceptionally strong emphasis on security issues produced a bureaucratic environment in which Treasury found it doubly hard to express its reservations about military aid programs.

The Office of the Assistant Secretary for Domestic Finance (OASDF). As with the OASIA, the OASDF was formally under the direction of the undersecretary for monetary affairs during Reagan's first term. This fact, along with Beryl Sprinkel's primary interest in relations with the Federal Reserve, meant that the assistant secretary for domestic finance reported most matters directly to the secretary. The deputates that came under his jurisdiction included "federal finance"—taking in government financial arrangements, market analysis and agency finance, "financial institutions and capital markets," and "state and local finance."

Of these units, the Office of Financial Institutions and Capital Markets had assumed the heaviest work load during Reagan's first term. That is, it developed the legislation surrounding the deregulation of savings and loan companies that now allows these organizations to compete in capital markets more on the same footing as banks. The Office of Federal Finance, on the other hand, had completed its tour de force under the Carter administration when a long-term project, the creation of the Federal Financing Bank, consolidated agencies' financing of programs into a centralized system of government securities. Finally, the Office of State and Local Finance also experienced a busier period under the Carter administration, which saw a heightened consideration of intergovernmental matters in virtually every department. Under Reagan, a bold set of proposals for the reform of intergovernmental financial arrangements met such intense resistance from state and local governments that the administration abandoned its plans by fall 1982.

The Office of the Fiscal Assistant Secretary (OFAS). The fiscal assistant secretary manages the day-to-day financial operations of the federal government. His work, which relates to that of the OASDF more than to any other part of Treasury, focuses on relatively technical matters connected with the federal government's collection and disbursement of funds. For instance, the OFAS currently tries to develop ways to bring Treasury further into the computer era by increasing its reliance on electronic rather than paper transactions. As well, the office developed under Carter a system whereby the the federal government began to collect interest on its deposits in commercial banks. It might all sound pretty technical. However, the fact that hundreds of billions of dollars pass through the Treasury each year should alert us to the massive task involved in managing this cash flow efficiently.

The Office of the Assistant Secretary for Economic Policy (OASEP). We saw previously that the OASEP formed part of the ill-fated arrangement early in the Reagan administration whereby an undersecretary for tax and economic affairs straddled both the revenue generating and analytic sides of fiscal policy. As well, we have already examined the office's part in the troika "2" and "3" levels of discussions between Treasury, the Council of Economic Advisers and the Office of Management and Budget. Here the assistant secretary serves as the Treasury representative on T2. On this body, the deputies of the three agencies attempt to achieve a consensus on political considerations as related to the annual economic report and the budget before the reference to the principals and, eventually, the president. As well, OASEP career economists represent Treasury on the more technically oriented T3.

The assistant secretary under Carter, Daniel Brill, gained a very high profile within the administration even though his efforts to consolidate all Treasury economic analysis under one roof failed. Brill effectively used his chairmanship of three to four weekly meetings of the Economic Policy Group's deputies' committee to secure his position as the main conduit of macroeconomic advice to the secretary and the wider fiscal policy community within the executive. On matters of analysis, thus, the OASEP held a position of primacy in relation to the Office of the Assistant Secretary for Tax Policy. As put by a political appointee in that office under Carter:

> To some extent, the responsibility for pure fiscal policy rests more with Dan Brill.... With respect to macroeconomic issues, he has probably greater input than me, but I have some input. Once a decision is made to increase or decrease taxes and how much, it becomes a question of "which taxes and how?"—that is the responsibility of Office of Tax Policy.[19]

The advent of supply-siders in Reagan's Treasury altered the concordat between Economic Policy and Tax Policy on analytic domains. The political masters of the former, in fact, proved to be the mainstays of the supply-side view in Treasury. As one appointee noted, their incentive-oriented macroeconomic approach to taxation deliberately suspended the revenue-focused analysis that provided Tax Policy's bread and butter:

> Tax Policy has always been the office fulfilling Treasury's traditonal role of preserving revenue. In this administration, tax policy has been interpreted from the point of view of incentives more than preserving revenues . . . trying to pursue tax-rate reduction to enhance production incentives and labor-supply incentives. We really are loose with Treasury purse strings because we are more concerned with macroeconomy.[20]

This change of emphasis went beyond the previous primacy of OASEP in reviewing the macroeconomics behind the tax part of the fiscal framework. It tended to make irrelevant much of Tax Policy's microeconomic analysis. One career official in OASEP strained to put a charitable light on his heightened role in tax analysis by implying that his political masters were simply eliminating the middleman: "I guess in some cases they felt that Tax Policy either took too long or sandbagged or stonewalled or didn't do the work that they really wanted to get done."[21] Not mincing words, an OASEP political appointee asserted that, in fact, the entire microeconomic bent of the Tax Policy Office provided very little of use to the supply-side venture:

The way taxes affected the Gross National Product, in the old way of thinking, was how big were they—not on what did they fall, or what was the likely public reaction or labor's or employers' response. You just looked at how big were the taxes. The theory was that if you tax money away from the economy, that depresses activity. But if you spend money, that expands activity. It doesn't matter how much you tax as long as you spend it. . . . The correct way of looking at how taxes affect the economy has nothing to do with the dollar amount. Rather, it is what did the tax cause the person to do or how did it change his thinking? And that is a different type of computation, which they have been somewhat slow to gear up to. . . . They do the micro and the thousand and one legal questions involved with the tax code as opposed to the economic ones.[22]

The Office of the Assistant Secretary for Tax Policy (OASTP). This office takes in the deputates concerned with tax analysis and legislation. Over thirty economists work in the analysis unit, with half assessing the distribution effects of taxes and the others estimating revenues under various assumptions. The former activity includes examining the relative burdens of tax provisions on different segments of society. The latter extends to longer-range inquiries aimed at improving Treasury's understanding of the implications of various elements of tax law for the economic behavior of individuals and corporations.

The legislation deputate operates with over twenty tax lawyers who, unlike their colleagues on the analysis side, have mostly interrupted careers in the private sector to serve relatively short terms in government. While the legislation unit must spend a great deal of time drafting measures proposed by the administration of the day, it also concentrates considerable effort in responding to anomalies and defects in the tax code indentified by the Internal Revenue Service. In their efforts on behalf of the administration and in response to issues raised by the IRS, the officials working on legislation bring to their work personal agendas. These derive from their study in and practice of tax law.

The efforts of both deputates under the Carter administration met with considerable frustration. The administration's comprehensive tax reform package fit the dual concerns in the OASTP at that time for plugging tax loopholes and improving the progressiveness of various provisions. Progressive tax policy connotes redistributing tax loads from the less well off to the more affluent. As well, the proposals put forward by Carter sought to include tax "expenditures"—deductions and credits given to stimulate specific sectors of the economy—more directly in the budget figures. By 1978, it became clear that the president's legislative wish list exceeded Congress's desire for reforms. During the rest of the administration, a series of tax "crises" brought a mass of ad hoc busywork to OASTP. For instance, in early 1979 it staffed administration schemes for stemming inflationary wage increases through the tax system, none of which came to fruition. From spring 1979 to the end of his term, Carter's groping for energy tax measures that would help him out of OPEC-induced economic crises found the OASTP almost totally given to "what if" exercises emanating from a nearly desperate White House.

The macroeconomic strategy adopted for his first term by Reagan neatly skirted the pitfalls encountered by reformers under Carter. By stressing dramatic tax reductions rather than reforms of the tax code, the supply-siders presented a legislative program that left little room for congressional whittling on behalf of special pleaders. As well, the strength of the Reagan mandate for tax reductions, combined with the freshness of the same signal given U.S. lawmakers in the 1980 election, counseled quick action. In fact, the OASTP played a limited part even in technical preparation of the legislation which passed Congress in August 1981. Much as had occurred with David Stockman's budget in OMB, the administration had worked its plan out in detail before taking office. It left very little room for contributions from Treasury.

Immediately after passage of this tax measure, it became clear that the Reagan administration was going to face much larger deficits than it had projected. A search for additional revenue soon ensued. Even here, the OASTP had only a muted word. The administration liked to generate its own ideas about how to raise revenues. In the words of one OASTP official:

> In Fall 1981 it became clear that they hadn't been able to cut outlays by a magnitude that would, in fact, produce a manageable long-run deficit. . . . They again departed from procedure by not asking at that point, "What can we do to improve the system and pick up some revenue without damaging incentives generally?" Instead, they gave us a whole list of crackpot schemes that we were supposed to provide revenue estimates for.[23]

Consistent with its macro approach, the proposals put forth by the administration tended toward broad brush strokes, placing a premium on aggregate revenue generation with little attention to programmatic detail. The latter would normally be the approach taken by OASTP in any search for new revenues to offset components of the deficit brought on by spending beyond an administration's objectives for various economic sectors. The official continued: "There's another way to go. That is to say, "Since we weren't able to, for instance, cut the Department of Energy's subsidies for synthetic fuels, . . . maybe what we can do is reduce the industry tax preferences at the margin in such a way that we don't affect incentives to invest."[24]

The Search for Coordinative Machinery

The preceding section probably suggests to the reader that harmony among the disparate elements of economic policy making does not come easily. Between parts of the Executive Office of the President, the strengths of agencies' mandates with reference to the constellation of issues bearing down on an administration greatly affects their influence relative to one another. The broad strategic preferences of an administration also shape the array and importance of issues to which agencies will find themselves admitted. As well, personalities—especially those of the key appointees—will greatly affect whether the agencies can capitalize on the combination of jurisdictional advantage and their political masters' interests that each administration presents. With respect to the Treasury, internal organizational difficulties—many with historic roots—exacerbate obstacles to coordination resulting from conflicts in agency mandates, the preferences of an administration, and the proclivities of appointees.

Roger Porter has served Presidents Ford and Reagan in White House secretariats attempting to bring greater coherence among agencies controlling the administration's economic policies. He notes, as succinctly as anyone else, the compelling reasons for more elaborate coordinative machinery within the economic policy sector.[25] That is, the fragmentation of the process, along with the extraordinarily intense economic pressures since the early 1970s, have left little more margin for inadequate machinery than exists in the national security field. Porter then sets the parameters for cabinet-level bodies attempting improved integration of the administration's economic stance: they would include all cabinet-rank officials who have a legitimate interest in major economic issues and who share "collective responsibility" for advising the president.[26]

As reasonable as Porter's assertions might seem, presidential acknowledgment of these points has come very slowly and sporadically. Eisenhower was the first to use collective consultation extensively in making economic policy. However, his approach tended to replicate the fragmentation already present in the process. For example, a National Security Council body called the Energy Resources Council operated by statute; the Advisory Board on Economic Growth and Stability and the Economic Policy Board functioned according to executive order; and the Council on Economic Policy, the Agricultural Policy Committee, the Council on Foreign Economic Policy and the Committee on Export Expansion worked from less formal mandates.[27] Adding to these more or less regularized committees, a host of ad hoc and/or relatively specialized groups took shape under Eisenhower.

Kennedy did not disguise his deep antipathy toward Eisenhower's passion for coordinative machinery. Thus, he dismantled his predecessor's elaborate economic policy committee system.[28] Although he relied for the most part on ad hoc groups, Kennedy did relent in some key areas. Most notably, he struck the first formal "troika." As we saw above, this body brings together the principals of the Treasury, CEA, and OMB to coordinate development of the fiscal framework. Johnson mostly followed Kennedy's relatively ad hoc system.

Nixon started off by strongly affirming the concept of formalized collective consultation in major policy sectors. He created cabinet-level committees entitled Economic Policy and International Economic Policy, to which all secretaries and senior White House aides with strong interests in these areas belonged. These panels soon lapsed into disuse. During the remainder of his administration, Nixon first relied upon the forcefulness of John Connally, treasury secretary during 1970–72, to knock heads together on economic policy. Then George Shultz, secretary from 1972 to 1974, cajoled colleagues through private consultation.

In the event, only Ford among the presidents between Eisenhower and Carter made a sustained effort to regularize the cabinet-level integration of economic policies. Here Ford's treasury secretary, William Simon, enjoyed the status of first among equals amid economic agency heads.[29] He chaired the Economic Policy Board whose executive met almost every day—roughly one out of four times with the president. This core group at first included only the heads of Treasury, CEA, and OMB. Eventually it took in the secretaries of state, commerce, and labor as well. Its executive director, William Seidman, participated fully in its proceedings. He also coordinated the activities of an elaborate network of permanent and ad hoc subcabinet committees which prepared issues for submission to the EPB. This arrangement avoided Eisenhower's pitfall. That is, the system of specialized subcommittees provided for a high degree of issue articulation while assuring, at the end of the day, that work was submitted to an umbrella committee with the fullest possible authority.

The Carter Administration

In keeping with its unstructured view of cabinet government, the Carter administration initially formed an inclusive body for deliberation in economic issues. Styled the Economic Policy Group, this committee was accessible to virtually every interested agency head and White House aide. In fact, someone had to fetch an additional chair when the vice-president appeared a few minutes late for EPG's first meeting. Such an unwieldly body soon became a nominal entity. Two successive committees took up the task of integrating departmental and agency stances before reference to the president. The first, the EPG "executive committee," consisted of the treasury, commerce, and labor secretaries, along with the heads of the CEA and OMB, and the assistants to the president for domestic affairs and policy, Stuart E. Eizenstat, and national security affairs, Zbigniew Brzezinski. The vice-president and a senior appointee from the State Department frequently joined the executive committee, which met about once a week.

Midway through the administration even the executive committee proved too bulky. Thus, the EPG "steering committee" emerged as the effective senior interdepartmental council on economic policy. This body tried to limit participation to the heads of the three central economic agencies—namely, Treasury, CEA, and OMB—and the vice-president, along with Eizenstat and Brzezinski. It also operated informally. That is, weekly meetings took place at breakfast in the treasury secretary's dining room. The treasury secretary chaired the steering committee. However, Michael Blumenthal's frequent falls from grace with the White House hampered his effectiveness as chief economic spokesman for the administration. The committee did not work from formal agendas complete with supporting briefing books. Follow-through left a great deal to be desired. Career respondents complained that requests for information emanating from steering group sessions often would come from several agencies whose principals had arrived that morning from an EPG breakfast with different versions of the type of analysis that the committee had agreed upon.

The relatively unstructured nature of EPG, combined with Blumenthal's tentative position, brought chaos to major economic policy decisions. Respondents identified two major problems. Inadequate coordinative machinery made it very difficult even to track the progress of major initiatives through interdepartmental discussions and the White House. One career official, who allowed that the Nixon and Ford administrations had probably gone overboard, saw clear advantages to having at least some structure in the Economic Policy Group.

It was probably overstructured during the Nixon and Ford administrations. This wasn't bad for a bureaucracy. After a while, you got to know whom to call when you wanted to know where a paper was and to get some feedback. Now it is chaotic. It is much more difficult for people at our level to find out what's going on.[30]

Second, several respondents observed that Stuart Eizenstat's involvement in EPG as a virtual principal belied any claim he or members of the Domestic Policy Staff could make to neutral, process-management roles. As one political appointee put it, Eizenstat's approach contrasted sharply with that of William Seidman, to the detriment of interagency coordination under Carter:

Something that Ford had, that in retrospect doesn't seem like a bad idea, would be to have a truly neutral broker. This would be someone who was a collator of other people's ideas rather than a player. He would put diverse views down in one memo whose form satisfied the major players. This would reduce the multiplicity of paper going in. Under the current EPG structure, everyone has a policy—a really active position. Thus, the memos that go to the president presumably reflecting the views of all the economic advisers actually state the views of the authors somewhat better. This fact leads to the proliferation of cover memos and counter memos. . . . So what you really want is someone who is trusted by the president. However, he doesn't really take a view. He understands the arguments but doesn't present positions of his own.[31]

As with domestic economic issues, structure did not become the order of the day in the Carter administration's handling of international monetary, financial, and trade issues. With respect to the former two areas, Treasury chaired the International Monetary Group, which rarely met. Since it controls the actual levers for international monetary affairs, the department operated from the premise that it should not square its policies with others unless absolutely necessary. Regarding trade, the Trade Policy Committee, if anything, came into its own under Carter. While the elaborative coordinative structure was already in place, Carter's giving very high priority to the Multilateral Trade Negotiations in Geneva and appointing one of his most prominent cabinet secretaries, Robert Strauss, to head the STR gave heightened legitimacy and force to the TPC process.

Several Treasury officials took strong issue with what appeared to them as an erosion under Carter of their department's primacy in international economic affairs. In the process, they cited Eizenstat's various interventions. As well, they noted that Charles Schultze had obtained for CEA a near lead role in formulating the 1979 package for defense of the dollar. They also registered concern that preparation of the president for annual economic summits of the seven leading Western nations rested with Henry Owen of the National Security Council staff. The situation prompted one career official to assert that the treasury secretary could not operate effectively with his counterparts in foreign countries. These all recognized that the Carter adminsitration did not speak through one economic authority in the same way they do:

There is a great deal of sense in institutionalizing the role of the treasury secretary as the chief economic spokesman. That's very important because of the weakness of Blumenthal last year had its implications for the whole monetary system, on the dollar and so forth. . . . One can argue very logically that, in a world in which we are increasingly interdependent economically, in which most of the other top economic spokesmen are finance ministers who want to consult with and negotiate with

their counterparts who have equal authority, the U.S. government is not really geared up to participate in that process.[32]

As understandable as such Treasury frustration might seem, too
much blame should not be thrust upon the very concept of executive office involvement in major international economic issues. As
one Treasury respondent acknowledged, the other participants in
economic summits have moved increasingly toward assigning the
preparation for these meetings to officials reporting directly to
their chief executive. More generally, the intractability of the international economy has made issues arising in this sector standard
fare for the central advisory staffs of presidents and prime ministers
alike. However, the Treasury respondents' concerns do stem from
two factors in the executive branch that make life even more difficult for any American "finance minister." First, the U.S. cabinet
has a very weak collective esprit. This means that agency heads
who go public in their disputes with the treasury secretary usually
escape penalization so long as the president agrees with them and/
or does not become concerned about the image of fragmentation
that such appeals evoke. Second, the underdevloped U.S. machinery for executive-branch coordination coughs up a disporprotionate
number of poorly prepared issues, thereby guaranteeing intensely
bitter dispute between competing parties.

The Reagan Administration

In sharp contrast to Jimmy Carter, Ronald Reagan came to office as
a strong believer in institutionalized cabinet consultation. In fact,
he employed during his first term cabinet-level "councils" in the
economic policy sector much more extensively than had any of his
predecessors. Here the Cabinet Council on Economic Affairs
dominated domestic economic policy, while three other committees—the Cabinet Council on Commerce and Trade, the Trade
Policy Committee, and the National Security Council Senior Interagency Group on International Economic Policy—contended for
the more disputed turf upon which international economic policy
is developed.

The Cabinet Council on Economic Affairs (CCEA). This committee consisted of the secretaries of treasury, state, commerce,
labor, and transportation, as well as the director of the Office of
Management and Budget, the U.S. trade representative, and the

chairman of the Council of Economic Advisers. While the president retained the chairmanship of the CCEA, he in fact only attended one out of every four or five meetings. In the president's absence, the treasury secretary served as chairman pro tem. The entire council met two to three times every week. On average, some fifteen CCEA working groups would be preparing issues for discussion in council meetings. Normally, an assistant secretary from the department pressing a specific policy decision would chair these subcommittees. Other appointees concerned with the issue would represent their agencies on working groups.

CCEA meetings chaired by the president took place in the Cabinet Room, while all others occurred in the Roosevelt Room, which is also in the West Wing of the White House. The assistant secretary responsible for presenting the results of a working group would sit behind his cabinet secretary. Other high-level departmental appointees would take seats along the wall of the meeting room. Normally, they would not intervene unless requested to do so by a CCEA member.

Such dynamics more sharply distinguished principals from others present at CCEA than did those of the Economic Policy Group under Carter. However, many lapses occurred in the cabinet council system due to the tendency for agency secretaries to send deputies to meetings not chaired by the president. CCEA's importance mitigated the frequency of deputization. Nonetheless, respondents reported very spotty attendance on the part of some members. For instance, one official could not recall a single occasion upon which Alexander Haig attended a CCEA not chaired by the president. Meetings that the president chaired became command performances. One top political appointee gave us a peek inside:

> The secretary presents the points he wants to make. He's been briefed to the eyeballs. We sit there and hope that he will be able to do and say all the things that he's supposed to. The atmosphere is a bit charged.... The president is a good-humored and relaxed man. He has a little joke here and there and he's self-effacing—that type of thing. But, they're all kind of sitting around there. They all want to have something to say about the proposition so they can look knowledgeable about it. It is potentially disastrous.... All you need to do is have somebody say something that throws you off track and you can end up 100 miles from where you started. ... So, I have gone to

those things with great trepidation; . . . we shouldn't go unless we abolsutely have to.[33]

The same respondent provided an insight to the changed dynamics of the CCEA sessions not chaired by the president. Here cabinet secretaries or their deputies would view the committee more as a forum for public notice unless, of course, the officials reporting on a working group showed signs of indecisiveness. In this respect, subcabinet officials presenting working group results played a crucial role:

There isn't a lot of continuity to these council sessions. Not the same people come all the time. . . . My sense of the whole thing was that most of them did not really feel that my issue was a responsibility of theirs. . . . It is like an information clearinghouse or a vehicle for record notice. . . . Everybody likes to be in the process; . . . they'd say they'd been to those meetings and they'd heard those things. . . . You've got to be an SOB. I said to myself, I am not going to let any one of these cabinet guys throw a pregnant question on the table that I'm not going to take on directly. . . . I always went in and said, "No, it's like this." But you have to do it in a nice way. . . . It was almost as if I was this bright young man that they had commissioned to go out and study this question and whose judgment they should respect.[34]

Not even Reagan appointees uniformly granted the CCEA rave notices. Most respondents gave it considerable credit for bringing greater order to U.S. economic policymaking. In fact, many career officials offered that the CCEA compared very favorably to the machinery in place under Carter. As one said,

Through it the administration has captured a good deal of the White House and OMB domains. In the last administration they functioned separately. . . . Every time you got something done each one had to rethink it. You had the associate director of OMB for this or that area and the Domestic Policy Staff guy both thinking they were equals of the deputy secretary of the Treasury. So, you had all these equals who had to decide something. Since the administration fundamentally didn't seem to want to do anything anyway and all of these people were uncoordinated, you never got anything done. . . . But, by putting it into a cabinet council where all of them come into the same room, . . . they've had their say all along and they're all on board.[35]

The voices, career or appointee, that dissented from the generally positive assessment of CCEA mostly focused on frustrations regarding turf. Usually this involved opening up analytic patches, where respondents had normally taken the lead, to participants lacking both expertise and interest. Here critics asserted that the CCEA process raised issues extraneous to the straightforward task of finding the best policies in specialized areas such as taxation. One career official in Treasury put his case emphatically:

> It's only in the Treasury and the Internal Revenue Service that you find anybody in government that has a comprehension of the tax laws . . . the most sensible way for them to proceed is in fact to request the secretary of the treasury to prepare a set of options having simply said, "We'd like to raise a certain amount of revenue and we would like not to interfere with the investment incentives we enacted. Prepare a set of options."[36]

Such criticisms perhaps beg the important point that cabinet councils attempt to formulate and legitimize policies that go beyond the narrow precincts of departmental mandates. Finding a way to reconcile the administration's tax reductions with the pressures for added revenues brought on by massive deficits would, it appears, elevate tax law to a high plane. OMB and CEA, regardless of their analytic grasp of the vagaries of tax economics, will quite naturally demand access to such issues.

The principals of Treasury, OMB, and CEA—normally joined by the secretary of state and the assistant to the president for policy development—met almost every Tuesday morning to identify matters to be referred to the CCEA. Indeed, they decided which issues should bypass this apparatus entirely. This would not have come as a surprise to a seasoned participant in executive-bureaucratic politics at the highest level. In the words of one Treasury appointee, the really difficult decisions for the administration eventually ended up going to top White House aides before presentation to the president anyway:

> Major tough decisions get talked about in cabinet councils. But we all know that they go to the Legislative Strategy Group or to Meese's office. You really start to get final decisions up there. . . . The tough decisions that go to cabinet council get

there because they are difficult ones that are not going to be elevated all the way to the president. They are not tough in that sense. But, everybody wanted to be able to say, "Well, we discussed it within the administration and that's why we went this way or said this thing."[37]

The CCEA owed much of its relative success with the issues it did handle to a small staff in the Office of Policy Development which coordinated its meetings and the activities of its working groups. The OPD director, Roger Porter, served as the executive secretary for CCEA. Porter, who worked in the Ford administration under the executive director of the Economic Policy Board, brought to his work a mix of partisan political credentials and the extensive experience with interdepartmental bureaucracy rarely found among appointees in White House policy shops. He guided the complex array of working groups that prepared issues for CCEA agendas. According to the administration's initial design, he chaired a "secretariat" consisting of assistant secretary–level officials responsible for policy coordination in the departments and agencies that belonged to CCEA. However, the overlap in the membership of working groups and the frequency with which one or the other convened would make formal secretariat meetings somewhat redundant.

In part, Porter could thank his strong relationship with Donald Regan, the treasury secretary during his first term, for his success with CCEA. However, he did appear, in our respondents' eyes, to epitomize the neutral broker role both in his grasp of the bureaucratic processes and his insistence that as many major issues as possible pass through the CCEA. One appointee put it very directly:

> Roger Porter has been very imperialistic in terms of the role of the CCEA. He has drawn an increasing number of issues into his orbit. He's also very good at making sure that the papers that go before the group are well prepared and distributed ahead of time. He watches that the process works quite fluently. He has a very close relationship to Don Regan. The other cabinet councils do not work with anywhere near that efficiency.[38]

Of course, neutral brokerage carried the day only in matters suited to relatively wide interdepartmental consultation. The most sensitive administration issues might call for a much firmer hand. Here the OPD staff recognized the limits on working groups. When chaired by an agency with an especially strong stake in an extremely contentious dispute, such bodies might leave the administration floundering. In other words, some circumstances call for the White House to take the lead in preparing issues for presidential decisions. One official reported:

> There's one that happens to be a hot one right now. We've got to move it. So we're calling the meetings and we will essentially run them. We'll be responsible for producing the briefing material for it although on paper it will look like someone else's doing. That's fine. It just happens to be on a fast track. It also happens to be a very important issue. We don't have enough time. We've got to get it done in three weeks. We looked over the situation and decided there wasn't anybody else who was going to be able to do it in that amount of time the way we wanted it done.[39]

The International Economic Affairs Committees. Three cabinet-level committees operated in this policy sector during Reagan's first term. The Senior Interagency Group–International Economic Policy (SIG-IEP) emerged in summer 1982 as a result of conflicts between administration advocates and opponents over the sale of Western pipeline technology to the Soviet Union. As part of the National Security Council committee system, SIG-IEP included the assistant to the president for national security affairs along with the secretaries of state and defense, and the director of the Central Intelligence Agency and the chairman of the Joint Chiefs of Staff. By way of exception, the treasury secretary—who normally would not involve himself in NSC processes–chaired SIG-IEP largely on the grounds that he serves as the administration's chief economic spokesman. This arrangement permitted the treasury secretary to assume a more explicit responsibility toward meshing international economic issues with national security concerns. It did not have a parallel in other administrations.

The SIG-IEP maintained a fairly high level of activity, with meetings every two weeks or so. However, the committee did not always draw representation from participating departments at the principals level. By way of example, the assistant to the president for national security affairs attended about one in four SIG-IEPs. As with all other SIGs, the chairman could invite representation from any department that expressed an interest in a subject being considered by SIG-IEP. This provision gave both the commerce secretary and the U.S. trade representative regular access to NSC processes that previously they rarely obtained.

The two remaining committees involved themselves in international economic issues mostly through their responsibilities toward trade policy. The Cabinet Council on Commerce and Trade formed part of the cabinet council system that operated on the domestic policy side. Its chairman pro tem, Commerce Secretary Malcolm Baldridge, took extremely seriously his department's operational responsibilities for trade policy. He, therefore, elevated many trade issues which the Carter administration resolved in the statutory Trade Policy Committee to matters that had to be resolved by the president. In this respect a procedural wrinkle connected with the cabinet council system gave the commerce secretary an advantage over the U.S. trade representative. When the former lacked a consensus in his committee he could send a decision memo giving the president a choice. Indeed, he could organize a decision session at which the president would actually preside. The CCCT met once a week on average and the president actually chaired the council about once a month.

On the other hand, the TPC, though statutory, did not operate under the halo effect of presidential chair. When the U.S. trade representative failed to achieve a consensus in his group, the contending parties quite naturally came to view the CCCT as the senior and therefore appellate body. The STR found that direct appeals to the president were the only way around this process. Obviously, it had to avoid using this tack too often. When it actually decided to go directly to the president, it would have to make sure that it held the issue very closely within STR. One senior appointee gave an example of STR efforts in 1982 to assure that the president approved the long-term trade agreement with the Soviets:

> There are other channels of communication in the administration. We decided this when seeking the president's approval of the long-term trade agreement with the Soviets. The issue was very hot. We believed that our views had to be heard directly by the president. If we would have let it pass through the conventional process, it would have somehow been leaked to the press or people would have taken pot shots at it. This would have prevented us from getting the type of provisions we were seeking. So, we went directly to James Baker over in

the White House and explained the issue and the advice being given to the president.[40]

While the enhanced role of the commerce secretary, working through the vehicle of CCCT, made life more difficult for the STR, Treasury had learned to cope with a heightened involvement of the NSC staff in its affairs. For the most part, Treasury does not face much competition from other agencies in matters falling clearly within its jurisdiction. One appointee noted this applied in areas such as U.S. policies toward the International Monetary Fund and the World Bank: "Other agencies would have a different perspective on the issues that are of concern to them. But the SIG-IEP is not going to tell us anything about IMF policy or about the World Bank. Issues are presented to them for ratification. But the nature of the membership of the SIG is such that no one is going to challenge Treasury's views in those areas."[41]

Such a sanguine analysis does not apply to matters with U.S. security ramifications. Before creation of SIG-IEP, Treasury found itself actually presented with fait accomplis emanating from the NSC process. That is, NSC decisions to which Treasury had no regularized access denied the department a role in the gestation of national security programs with major economic components. As one respondent noted regarding the Caribbean Basin Initiative:

> Treasury is not a member of the NSC. That has always been a problem. With an administration getting into so many policy areas, there are economic implications. Usually the secretary gets invited. But, there have been occasions when he ought to have been there but wasn't invited. The Caribbean Basin Initiative was one of these. The CBI was approved by the NSC in November 1981. To my knowledge, the Treasury didn't even know about it until January 1982. It turned up as $350 million in our budget.[42]

The creation of SIG-IEP remedied this situation at least insofar as the treasury secretary's chairmanship of the new body assured his access to security matters with international economic significance. As well, the NSC senior director for international economic affairs, in his capacity as executive secretary of the SIG, reported to the treasury secretary in addition to the assistant to the president for national security affairs.

Conclusion

This chapter has examined, through a survey of the central-agency units that develop U.S. economic policy, the effects of the Carter and Reagan administrations on their operation. With respect to those organizations clustered within the Executive Office of the President, we noted that each owes its existence to a crisis period that led the administration of the time to conclude that the president required more immediate sources of advice and staff support with economic affairs. That is, executive office agencies supposedly approach issues in ways that go beyond the efforts of Treasury and/or operational departments concerned with economic affairs.

In assessing the operations of executive office units under Carter and Reagan, three factors emerge as key. Clearly, the missions of the various agencies have played a part. OMB claims a say regarding macroeconomic forecasts beyond its actual analytic capacity by virtue of its stewardship over the expenditure budget. The CEA calls upon its exceptional brain power—thanks to its practice of relying largely on academics brought in for two-year-or-so stints—to take the lead in executive office economic analysis. Unfortunately, administrations often would rather base forecasts on political expedients than state-of-the-art models. The STR benefits from its responsibility for a statutory committee process through which trade issues must pass before reaching the president's desk.

To be sure, the policy preferences of each administration can enhance or diminish the effectiveness with which each agency fulfills its mandate. Under Carter, OMB played a subdued role in forecasting, largely because CEA was allowed to use its analytic capacity to the fullest. The administration, in other words, gave much deference to the integrity of forecasting. During Reagan's first term, OMB's macro approach to expenditure budget put it in league with Treasury supply-siders in departing from economic strategies that focused more on Keynesian categories such as the economic impact of the deficit. In those more conventional terms, CEA found itself a voice in the wilderness. The STR encountered even more frustration. First, by instituting an elaborate system of cabinet councils designed to achieve greater interdepartmental coordination in key policy areas, the administration created one body, the Cabinet Council on Commerce and Trade, whose status exceeded that of the Trade Policy Committees even though the latter works from a statutory base. Second, the administration's anti-Soviet enthusiasms led early in the first term to a number of National Security Council interventions in trade policy issues. Intense conflict in this field surfaced in 1982 with the embargo of pipeline technology going to the Soviet Union. At that point, the president took the moderates' counsel and established a Senior Interagency Group, under the NSC system and chaired by the treasury secretary, to facilitate a more measured integration of trade policy and security issues.

Finally, personalities have contributed to the success or failure of the executive office units. Under Carter, OMB did not find much help in the lack of stature of its two directors—Bert Lance and James McIntyre—in economic affairs. Meanwhile, the prominence of Charles Schultze and Robert Strauss in the Washington policy arena helped considerably their respective agencies—the CEA and STR—in getting their positions heard. Under Reagan, the combined resourcefulness of David Stockman and his first associate director for economic policy, Lawrence Kudlow, gave OMB a strong presence in all administration dialogues over the forecast and the fiscal framework. On the other hand, William Brock's very low profile in the administration fit the reduced clout of STR's Trade Policy Committee process all too well.

The organization of the Treasury, we found, raises issues about its capacity for internal coordination. Indeed, both Michael Blumenthal and William Miller took insufficient cognizance of the difficulties of integrating their department's positions and activities. Donald Regan displayed somewhat more talent at mediating conflicts within his massive department. Despite the obvious inadequacy of current arrangements, efforts to bring greater coherence to Treasury's organization have met with sparse success. Of three major attempts to consolidate authority, only Beryl Sprinkel's widened authority for the undersecretary of monetary affairs worked reasonably well—largely because Sprinkel gave units that interested him less than others a very long leash.

Under Reagan, Treasury has suffered less from its relatively poor internal coordination than it did under Carter. This appears to be ironic as the political appointees in the current administration have held radical views of the economy that do not always coincide. Yet, the Reaganites have demonstrated a high capacity for keeping their disputes within the family. In fact, they very often work out their differences without reference to career officials. The latter often find themselves relegated to staffing out "what if" exercises without participating in any meaningful way in the development and elimination of policy options. Here the Office of the Assistant Secretary for Tax Policy appears to have suffered the most. When macroeconomics does not look for an empirical base in detailed analysis of the effects of taxation, tax analysts find it difficult to gain access to discussions over fiscal policy.

With respect to improving U.S. coordinative machinery, the Carter administration marked a nadir for developments in economic policy. Carter failed to build on the Economic Policy Board process that had achieved considerable success under the Ford administration. He did not limit membership to the EPB's successor, the Economic Policy Group. Even when the EPG was reduced in size to include only the most vital economic policy advisers and agency heads, it met too infrequently and structured its proceedings and follow-through inadequately. As well, EPG lacked a secretariat with convincing neutrality. The assistant to the president for domestic affairs and policy, Stuart E. Eizenstat, had not cultivated within the Domestic Policy Staff a knack for process management. Recurrent White House frustration with the views of Treasury Secretary W. Michael Blumenthal led all too frequently to Eizenstat's short-circuiting interdepartmental efforts to resolve conflicts over administration economic policies. That is, Blumenthal was not allowed to function as first among equals in the economic policy community. In fact, he all too often found his authority and that of his department undermined by the White House.

To say that the Carter administration represents a low point for the coordination of U.S. economic policy does not ignore the fact that such dynamics do not fit easily into the wider context of the presidency. The relatively low level of collective responsibility in U.S. cabinets preordains that agency heads will take conflicting public stances much more than would ever occur in the United Kingdom. What is more, issues reach cabinet-level panels, and eventually, the Oval Office, less well developed than in an executive-bureaucratic environment such as Britain's. There staffs working under the prime minister place a very strong premium on central management of interdepartmental consultation. However, within the limits of the existing system, presidents can resort a great deal more to mechanisms that will enhance the coherence of their economic policies. The relative success of the Reagan administration with cabinet councils appears to validate this point.

During the first term, the Cabinet Council on Economic Affairs achieved the greatest success among the committees operating within the economic policy field. The regularity of its meetings, it appears, established a particularly strong bond among its members. The frequency with which the president actually chaired sessions encouraged direct participation by all principals. Many observers have noted that meetings chaired by the president can become set pieces. Such sessions, nonetheless, expose the president to face-to-face encounters with advisers not always given access to the Oval Office. For their part, agency heads may obtain from these meetings an understanding of the president's mind on key issues and how better to organize and communicate their positions. On the staff level, the Office of Policy Development's small unit working in support of the CCEA excelled. This was largely owing to the experience under the Ford administration and restrained style of Roger Porter. Porter's success suggests that greater use of aides who have already worked extensively in organizations such as OPD would improve the executive office's capacity for neutral brokerage.

Any assessment of the Reagan efforts to enhance interdepartmental coordination through more regularized cabinet-level consultation must certainly recognize the limits to this process. As one observer noted, we should imagine a ten-point scale. Here issues whose difficulty with respect to interdepartmental coordination fall below "six" probably can be worked out by agencies pretty much without detailed references to cabinet councils. On the other hand, matters exceeding "seven" will likely require a very firm guidance from the White House even if they receive considerable development from a cabinet council. In fact, some issues will be so fraught with interdepartmental conflict and/or so politically sensitive that open-ended cabinet-level discussions might well prevent decisive administration action.

Under such circumstances an administration might choose to draw into consultations a few crucial agency heads. It might even mandate an agency to act unilaterally. Such options are open to British prime ministers as well. Thus, the concentration of executive authority in the presidency does not explain the exceptions to the round-table norm that occur even in a relatively collective administration such as Reagan's. The fact remains that CCEA's effective jurisdiction over economic affairs tended to cluster in issues of moderately high importance, whereas comparable panels in the United Kingdom extend their authority into many of the exceedingly difficult matters facing a government.

Even more fundamentally, Reagan's first-term format did not work as well in relation to international economic issues as it did with regard to domestic ones. Initially, the dysfunctions resulted largely from conflicts between the jurisdictions of the statutory Trade Policy Committee and the somewhat redundant Cabinet Council on Commerce and Trade. The latter emerged in 1981 as a key element of Reagan's cabinet committee system. For the most part, the TPC lost considerable standing during the first term. The president chaired the CCCT. This fact alone brought about a serious truncation of TPC's highly formalized interdepartmental machinery long used for the resolution of trade issues. Later in the administration, serious tensions arose when the National Security Council staff and the Pentagon increasingly flagged trade issues with security implications as ones that must pass through the NSC process. After summer 1982's ill-fated embargo against the sale of pipeline technology to the Soviets, Reagan appointed the treasury secretary, Donald Regan, as chairman of a new NSC senior interagency group for international economic affairs (SIG-IEP). This move lessened the tension between agencies immediately responsible for trade matters and the national security community. Of course, the CCCT was disbanded at the beginning of the second term. As well, the CCEA's successor, the Economic Policy Council, has inherited the defunct SIG-IEP's jurisdiction over international economics issues with national security ramifications. These two developments have dispelled a great deal of the former confusion over trade issues.

6. Coping with Cyclical Forces
Affecting the Budget and Management

We have just examined how central the development and integration of economic and fiscal policies are to any administration. Along the way, the reader probably has concluded that economic fiscal policies take in a host of interrelated issues. Many of these penetrate deeper than simply the question of how aggregate revenue and expenditure policies might advance the macroeconomic goals of an administration. Presidents often must rise to expectations concerning the impact of specific policies on different sectors of the economy and sociodemographic groups. Indeed, presidents must watch that they pursue policies sufficiently responsive to various segments of industry and society to maintain key elements of their electoral support.

The budgetary process calls upon a delicate balance between the fiscal policies deemed optimal for the achievement of the president's macroeconomic objectives and all of the special claims for spending pressed both from within and outside government. Administrations normally attempt to go beyond a simple "first-by-the-post-with-the-most-clout" method of sorting various appeals for initiation, continuation or elimination of programs. In other words, they usually make efforts to ground their allocation of human and physical resources on assessments of the actual or projected effectiveness of desired expenditures. They try, therefore, to adduce data that evaluate the actual or forecasted costs and benefits of programs. These analyses often simply provide rationales for what an administration intends to seek anyway. However, rigorous assessments might bump program proposals up or down several notches in the hierarchy of policy priorities when administrations actually take merit criteria seriously.

Relatedly, administrations usually must respond to the pervasive belief among the general public that no matter what government attempts, it does so much less efficiently than the private sector. A paradox operates here. Everyone expects from government greater value for money. Yet specific efforts at increasing government efficiency seldom retain the concentrated attention of the public. They stir resounding approval even more rarely. Nonetheless, new presidents launch almost by reflex into efforts that at least make it appear that they have addressed the efficiency issue.

Budget and management policies cover four general areas. These include stances regarding departments' and agencies' expenditure budgets; evaluation and improvement of the effectiveness of programs; management techniques that will improve government efficiency; and personnel policies—especially those relating to senior executives. For the most part, these various functions fall within the compass of the Office of Management and Budget (OMB). In addition, the Office of Personnel Management (OPM), created under Carter in 1979, operates under a director reporting to the president who speaks for the administration on many key elements of personnel policy.

What Does Budgeting Emphasize?—A Movable Feast

Aaron Wildavsky, in the second edition of his classic work on budgetary politics, pointed up the changes in the functions of OMB and its predecessor, the Bureau of the Budget (BOB), since the 1950s.[1] He stressed here the crucial role played by what exactly a president wants from his budget office. For instance, Richard Nixon's move to create superdepartments raised the specter of grossly unwieldly jurisdictional chunks under each cabinet secretary. If the Nixon reforms had come to fruition, OMB simply would have had to abandon its tradition of detailed budget examination. In the process, it might have become "a technical management agency devoted to small efficiencies and divorced from top leadership."

Of course, the economic turmoil of the mid- and late 1970s radically diminished the feasibility of OMB's traditional role. Wildavsky had urged that OMB focus more on the big picture in order to cope better with the vast growth in government spending.[2] However, deficits beyond anyone's wildest fears have replaced the sheer size of government as the central budgetary concern during the Reagan era. Wildavsky never was a great believer in the amenability of budgeting to finely honed approaches. In one of his most recent works, he comes very close to asserting that only blunt instruments such as cash ceilings could achieve the spending regimens called for by the stringency-minded in our own era. That is, analytic approaches like "performance," "program," and "zero-base" budgeting only whittle away at the fringes of expenditure control:

> I have argued that to the extent that governments are serious about limiting spending . . . they will become concerned about overall spending limits; . . . countries that desire to keep spending from growing to a greater proportion of national product than it already is will move toward some mechanism for imposing limits. Where the budgetary reforms to which we are accustomed are concerned with the quality of spending, the new wave will emphasize quantity. . . . Where PPB and ZBB and the rest were avowedly apolitical, drawing on economic or management science for legitimacy, spending limits will be openly political, resting on explicit choices about total spending and its major subdivisions.[3]

Pressures toward stringency have unquestionably altered the relevance of OMB's analysis-based examination to the development of an administration's expenditure budgets. However, OMB watchers point as well to institutional factors that further weaken the agency's role. Writing at the end of the Carter administration, Allen Schick posited an ebb and flow between two extremes in presidents' use of the budget agency. In times of constraint, they tend to employ OMB as a "decisional" instrument for linking programmatic choices to budgetary imperatives.[4] In expansionary times, presidents quickly conclude that giving OMB its analytic reins will simply delay pivotal initiatives. By reflex, the agency's officials feel most at home with nay-saying. As well, they tend to focus on efficiency and effectiveness issues that do not lend themselves to the narrow time frames of presidents anxious to radically enhance governmental activitiy within specific sectors.

Schick goes beyond a treatment of the waxing and waning in OMB's institutional contribution to the budget process. He asserts that a serious erosion has taken place in OMB's ability to maintain the integrity of the budgetary process. The major assaults came through the impatience of Kennedy and Johnson for change. This overrode the highly routinized nature of review established under Eisenhower. Richard Nixon deepened the trend by installing political appointees, styled "associate directors," between OMB's director and the career heads of budget examination divisions. The new layer, Schick believes, accelerated the process whereby OMB became less a decisional and more an "accounting" agency. That is, Schick asserts that OMB has become increasingly oriented to providing technical support for what presidents intend to do regardless of analysis.

The contrast between OMB under Carter and Reagan suggests that the agency's success with respect to expenditure control differs even under stringency-minded presidents. As Richard Nathan has observed, both presidents sought to impose severe constraints on spending.[5] Carter's efforts foundered due to inadequate discipline in the "formulation, enactment and execution" of budgets. Reagan, according to Nathan, effectively utilized the budget to achieve his policy objectives.

Nathan seems to pin his analysis excessively on Reagan's success in employing the budget toward cutting back social programs. He therefore passes up an opportunity to note that, even under the same president, the budget process might operate differently with respect to various policy sectors. Nathan's analysis seems, in fact, to overlook Reagan's promotion of profligate spending in the Pentagon. This has helped balloon the deficit far beyond limits associated even remotely with stringency. In the words of one OMB career official reflecting halfway through Reagan's first term:

> We were quite disappointed in the first year. There was no big assessment of defense. It was like they just didn't want to do it. They just wanted to add dollars, which they did. Our advice to the administration when they came in was . . . add a few billion bucks—from five to ten, depending on how far you want to go—then do a big study and decide how to allocate. . . . But they didn't follow that advice. They just added twenty-six or so billion. This was beyond our wildest imagination. It probably was even beyond the wildest expectations of the defense establishment. . . . There was no substantial new initiative. It was just a lot more of the same.[6]

Figure 4 further develops Schick's approach to allow for additional refinement. It suggests that shifts in how presidents have engaged OMB in the budget process follow cyclical trends associated with the state of the economy. Periods of accelerating growth tend to conjure up for departments visions of "candy stores" of possibilities for fresh and enhanced expenditure programs. The sharper the economic recovery, the greater the expectations. In time, doubts arise over the durability of the expansionary period. Growing deficits brought on by an administration's lack of expenditure restraint and/ or a marked dip in revenues connected with slower growth eventually turn its attention to the need for a period of consolidation. Yet, administrations will tend to look simply for ways to pare expenditures. They will focus more on whether programs can operate with lower funding than whether they should continue at all. That is, they will concentrate on efficiency rather than effectiveness.

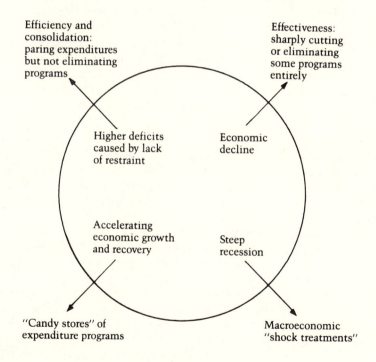

Efficiency and consolidation: paring expenditures but not eliminating programs

Effectiveness: sharply cutting or eliminating some programs entirely

Higher deficits caused by lack of restraint

Economic decline

Accelerating economic growth and recovery

Steep recession

"Candy stores" of expenditure programs

Macroeconomic "shock treatments"

Figure 4. The Relationship between Budgetary Policy and Cyclical Developments in the National Economy

Only when the economy stalls or slips into decline will administrations begin to ask whether a wide array of programs might be sharply curtailed or eliminated altogether. However, overtures toward analysis will continue until, by all appearances, a recession takes on the traits of a tailspin. Then the need for broader macroeconomic strokes gains the widest currency. Before the bouts with stagflation during the 1970s and early 1980s, administrations tended in these periods to choose stimulative deficits involving a mix of increased spending and tax reductions. When faced with simultaneous high inflation and unemployment during periods of recession, recent administrations have spoken more of the need for balanced budgets and tight control of the money supply. The deeper the recession, the more likely presidents will be to propose macroeconomic shock treatments. These leave virtually no room for fine tuning of spending cuts according to analytic criteria.

Figure 4 helps us keep a weather eye for what the state of the economy tells us about an administration's preferred approach to expenditure budgeting. However, we should not lose sight of the fact that a president's style of operation—as discussed in chapter 4—does not always correspond to the requirements of the times. For instance, the capacity of a priorities and planning style to sort through conflicting departmental claims without stifling restorative programmatic innovation suggests that it best fits an administration that hopes to stem an economic decline with creative remedies. But few U.S. presidents have carried off with aplomb a priorities and planning style even in auspicious economic times. Further, the fragmentation of the American executive branch—not to mention that of the policy arena more generally—makes the hope of even routine meshing of departmental initiatives with overarching administration goals very elusive.

There was an incongruity between the president's approach to the budget and economic conditions during both the Carter and Reagan administrations. By midterm, Carter—facing a clear weakening of the world economy—avoided applying disciplined priorities and planning to budgetary issues, notwithstanding the need on several fronts for a very hard-nosed curtailment of departmental wish lists. On the other hand, Reagan's survival politics approach to cutting domestic spending exacerbated both the depth of the 1980–82 recession and its effects upon those dependent on social welfare programs. Paradoxically, as already noted, he approached defense expenditure as if economic forecasts were rosier than his sunny dispo-

sition. During the first two years of the administration, he stalwartly protected the Pentagon even from a broker politics–style
trimming of expenditures.

An Institutional Legacy

No president starts with a tabula rasa when trying to bring a particular emphasis to budget and management policy. He must work
with the institutional aparatus he inherits. Overwhelmingly, he
will find this in the Office of Management and Budget. After briefly
outlining the role of OPM, this section will assess in detail elements of OMB's organizational structure and civil service culture
that appear to have withstood the test of time.

Even after seven years, it is not clear that the Office of Personnel
Management has earned its spurs as a central agency. The office is
one of three new organizations that emerged from the splitting up
of the former Civil Service Commission under Carter's Executive
Branch Reorganization Plan of 1978. Unlike the CSC, OPM functions under a partisan director rather than a bipartisan commission. With its head reporting directly to the president, the new
agency was designed to enhance administrative control over policies governing personnel management throughout government.
Thus Carter moved to the direct compass of presidential authority
several functions clearly associated with "positive" personnel management. He construed these to include training, assessments of
productivity, examinations, pay and benefits, and relating personnel policies to other management issues.

Under Carter, OPM's relatively wide scope served as a justification for its aggressively assuming responsibilities connected with
the development and management of the senior executive service
and the conduct of labor relations. However, stewardship over the
ultimate levers in steering departments toward service wide standards for personnel management remained in the hands of OMB.
That is, the director of OMB still recommends to the president the
actual funding and staff-complement levels within which departments and agencies manage their personnel.

With respect to OMB, pressures for a separate budget office had
consolidated by the 1910s.[7] Successive deficits, deepened by the
enormous fiscal requirements of World War I, had convinced Congress of the need for a central, executive-branch agency responsible
for submitting administration estimates. In 1921, Congress created

the Bureau of the Budget. In order to break an impasse over whether BOB should report to the treasury secretary or work directly under the auspices of the president, Congress struck a compromise. Although the director would report to the president, his agency would reside in the Department of the Treasury.

The early 1920s saw the emergence of the view that greater economy and efficiency in government would reap huge savings in public expenditure. As early as 1900, Frank J. Goodnow had identified administration as a sector of government that should be as autonomous as possible from politics.[8] In their turn, Woodrow Wilson and Luther Gulick pressed the imperative of finding broader applications of managerial science in public administration.[9] In the words of Wilson, only a sharp distinction between management and politics would assure that the apparatus of state ran efficiently and economically: "The field of administration is a field of business. It is removed from the hurry and strife of politics. . . . It is part of political life only as the methods of the counting-house are a part of the life of society; only as machinery is part of the manufactured product."[10]

Such sentiments became resoundingly incarnate in the early BOB. Its first director rendered his responsibility toward the president in terms that strongly echoed Wilson's: "No Cabinet officer in the bridge with the President advising as to what direction the ship of state should sail . . . will properly serve the captain of the ship or its passengers, the public, if he resents the call of the director of the budget from the stoke-hole, put there by the captain to see that coal is not wasted."[11] For the most part, the pre-Roosevelt BOB fit into the executive-bureaucratic politics of the time. It essentially sought better ways of helping departmental managers administer. Its role was an evangelical one of spreading the economy-efficiency word. It did not greatly influence the development of fiscal policy even insofar as that was a demarcated function of government.

Roosevelt simply bypassed BOB during the installation of the key elements of the New Deal in his first term.[12] The radical initiatives designed to end the Depression would not allow for dithering interventions from the custodians of managerial prudence. With Roosevelt's second term, however, thinking in the tightest circles of the administration turned increasingly to BOB's potential role in coordination of various policy objectives. This flew in the face of traditionalists who viewed budgeting as a subdivision of the administration of money. These even argued that BOB should strengthen its links with Treasury units responsible for the handling of the nation's finances.[13] The ultimate transfer of BOB to the Executive Office of the President under an activist director, Harold Smith, dramatically widened the compass of budget examination. BOB would now consider as a matter of course how secretaries' policy and expenditure proposals fit the president's legislative program and fiscal priorities.[14] Significantly, Smith undertook to revamp the expertise of BOB staff by seeking recruits with broad training in the social sciences and strongly oriented toward planning approaches to public policy.

During the 1940s and 1950s, BOB assumed a pivotal role in the monitoring of policy and expenditure proposals from the standpoint of the president's interests. With varying degrees of success, its leadership sought all along to maintain a distinction between BOB's safeguarding of the president's "institutional" interests and the White House's minding of the partisan-political agendas of each administration. Some believed this to be as untenable a distinction as the early policy-administration dichotomy. For instance, in 1947, Elmer Staats faulted the agency's traditional approach to advising the president as contributing to its failure in providing long-term coordination for the executive branch.[15] Indeed, the innate conservatism of the Eisenhower administration seemed to many to foster an excessive emphasis on BOB's institutional role. BOB's view of budget examination so fit Eisenhower's modest policy agendas that Democrats began to associate the agency with the unimaginative and shortsighted nature of the administration.

The Eisenhower regimen even applied to defense expenditure where ceilings kept the forces' individual shares of the national security budget at specific percentages and the aggregate price tag between 9 and 10 percent of GNP from 1955 to 1960.[16] Allen Schick views the Kennedy administration as the point where BOB began to find it difficult to wield the budget as a policy instrument. That is, its capacity to link administrations' programmatic decisions to budget considerations began to wane. However, the historical record presents us with a more complicated picture. Even under Eisenhower, BOB's routinized approach linked program and budget considerations only insofar as aggregate spending within and among the services was capped. As Robert McNamara, Kennedy's secretary of defense, observed regarding Pentagon spending:

We found that the three military departments had been establishing their requirements independently of each other. I think
the results can fairly be described as chaotic: the army planning . . . was based on a long war of attrition, . . . the air force . . .
on a short war of nuclear bombardment. Consequently, the
army was stating a requirement for stocking months of fighting
supplies against the event of a sizable conventional conflict
while the air force stock requirements for such a war had to be
measured in days, and not very many days at that.[17]

Of course, McNamara ushered in the era of the planning-program-
ming-budgeting system (PPBS) whereby the Pentagon would centralize planning while allowing operational elements relative autonomy
in how they actually met various programmatic objectives. The approach became the cornerstone of budgetary reform throughout the
U.S. government. As well, it legitimized the belief under Johnson—
eventually to be adopted in the Heineman Report—that BOB should
assume the lead in improving the programmatic effectiveness of the
Great Society.[18]

The Heineman concept carried over to the Nixon administration.
Notwithstanding the Republicans' commitment to shrinking the
size and degree of centralization of government, Nixon continued
the quest for a budget office that could improve the effectiveness of
programs undertaken by the federal government. He banked very
heavily on the capacity of managerial reform to bring about the
desired changes. The administration restyled BOB as the Office of
Management and Budget and introduced its "Management by Objectives" program.

Both moves stressed the need for clarification of the specific results anticipated from programs. A focus on objectives would help
managers achieve the level of effectiveness that had proved so elusive under budgeting methods focused too strongly on dollar
amounts.[19] Nixon's building antagonism toward the permanent bureaucracy along with the fatal reality of Watergate preordained the
foundering of these initiatives. Yet they added to the legacy of the
budget office. They gave impetus to OMB's interest in management policy. That is, the agency made a new effort to go beyond
the budget examiners' tendency to dismiss management issues as
having relatively marginal effects on aggregate expenditure levels.

Nixon's emphasis on the budget office's potential role in improving government management harked back to the original thrust behind the creation of BOB in 1921 as a separate Treasury bureau reporting to the president. That is, the administration's efforts stemmed from the belief that a strongly management-oriented central agency would press departments to find economies that both cut expenditure and improved cost benefits.

Two broad schools of thought have coexisted over the years both in BOB and OMB. The first, called the "management side," has preferred proselytization to coercion. It assumes that right-minded administrators will adopt improved management techiques when they see the operational benefits to new approaches. The second, known as the "budget side," holds that management policy only touches upon a relatively small proportion of the aggregate budget. A budget office, according to the second perspective, will always stress issues such as whether a program should continue at all and how much it should receive next year. Questions as to whether a program can be managed more effectively and efficiently will always take a back seat to expenditure issues.

Even on the budget side, examiners do adjust their approaches to economic conditions and stylistic preference of an administration. Under some circumstances, they will adduce mounds of analysis to back up their recommendations about spending levels. In others, they will confine their efforts more to enforcing the implications of aggregate targets for departments' and agencies' spending plans than fine-tuning according to the vagaries of individual programs.

The Budget Side

A look at OMB's organizational chart reveals an institution encompassing numerous offices and divisions. Some of these—for instance, Operations and Communications, Counsel's Office and the Office of Economics and Planning—perform functions that however important to OMB's institutional interests, rarely relate directly to the detailed development of the administration's expenditure budget. Another constellation of offices—during Reagan's first term, Management, Information and Regulatory Affairs, Management Reform Task Force, Federal Procurement Policy–focus on management policy matters that normally serve as only secondary concerns in the budget examination process. This leaves us with Legislative Reference, the Budget Review Division, eight budget examination divisions and four special divisions as the units working under the executive associate director for budget and legislation.

Officials working in the eight examination divisions serve as the oarsmen of the budget process. Organizationally, the divisions pair up under four political appointees: International Affairs and National Security come under the associate director for "national security and international affairs"; Transportation, Commerce and Housing, and Justice, Treasury and General Services under "economics and government"; Labor, Veterans and Education, and Health and Income Maintenance under "human resources, veterans and labor"; and Natural Resources, and Energy and Science under "natural resources, energy and science." Each of the PADs—political associate directors—also claims his own special studies division. These units mainly assess issues that overlap examination divisions and/or the authority of the individual PADs.

While there are close to 700 professional and clerical staff members in OMB, under 300 of these work within the budget examination or special studies divisions. However, the units make up for their relatively lean staffing in two ways. First, all of the division heads enjoy the highest rank available for career members of the Senior Executive Service. This situation even contrasts with that in the Department of Treasury whereby office directors usually attain only the second highest rating for the career elements of the SES. The full rating of the career officials at the top of divisions tends to pull the ranks of their staff upward as well. OMB budget examiners thus bring to their relations with their career counterparts in operational departments a valuable "brass" factor that adds to their authority. In this regard, examiners also make astute use of their status as members of the Executive Office of the President. They even display in their offices such symbols of authority as U.S. flags and presidential seals.

Second, budget examiners bring a great deal more to their work than simply "clout." They draw upon immense experience as well. The divisions tend to cultivate a "best and brightest" tradition. They administer very stringent recruitment criteria for new officials. They also maintain virtual "tenure stream." Those who gain entry and prove themselves early can look forward to secure careers in budget examination.

The budget division's staffing practices provide the foundation for two precious institutional characteristics. These are a vast reserve of expertise on the vagaries of departmental expenditures and an esprit de corps centering largely on a fierce protectiveness about the interests of the presidency in the unfolding of the budget process. One PAD put especially well the budget side's immense knowledge base:

> There are no wiser people inside this Executive Office fence . . . than the career OMB staff. Nobody like me who walks off the street knows what the budget examiners know. They know where all the skeletons are buried, everything that has been tried in the last twenty years, why it worked, why it didn't work, who likes it on the Hill, who doesn't like it on the Hill. That tremendous wealth of institutional knowledge is extremely valuable when you start asking . . . about budgets.[20]

By the same token, one long-standing career member of OMB explained in clear terms his agency's primary orientation to serving the presidency independent of the coloration of an administration:

> We always talk in this institution first about accountability to the president. We work for him. We are all fed with stories about the beginning of this institution when the first director asserted that if the president said you have to shovel garbage on the front steps of the White House you do it. . . . what we're trying to do is give the president the best information possible . . . to keep the president out of trouble. We are supposed to be a career service which provides . . . a continuity of government.[21]

How much of this is bravado? Allan Schick has asserted that the integrity of the budget process has faced assaults by every administration since Eisenhower. In fact, he cites the literature evaluating the Truman and Eisenhower administrations to press the view that both presidents' regard for BOB routines gave the agency an autonomy that it subsequently has lost.[22] Thus, more than Richard Nixon's insertion of PADs between the director and career officials has eroded the sway of examiners over the budget. The spotty adherence to institutionalized examination on the part of the recent administrations has also weakened the capacity of career officials to bring their expert knowledge and dedication to the presidency to bear adequately on the budget process. David Stockman's leadership style, as we will see later in this chapter, certainly provides an apt illustration of Schick's point.

Notwithstanding the obvious slippage, budget examiners still think very much in terms of set procedures for handling their annual cycle. Further, as demonstrated under the Carter administration, they do not hesitate to exploit available openings for getting their procedures back on track. Fiscal years begin on October 1. For example, a broad review of budget issues for 1987–88 would have taken place in spring 1986. This stage in the process would try to identify contentious issues likely to become "presidential." As well, it would begin to anticipate the budgetary consequences of central items likely to be embodied in his State of the Union address in January 1987 as part of the administration's legislative program.

After the spring review, the budget director sends letters to each department outlining the dollar levels within which departments should keep their expenditure plans for 1987–88. A fall review centers on the numerous outstanding issues between the administration's budget regimen and departments' pleading of special-case considerations. Much of this phase takes place in informal contacts between examiners and officials in operational departments. However, OMB does call structured hearings in the New Executive Office Building in which office directors and bureau chiefs, usually accompanied by their assistant secretaries, present their cases before the budget examiners reviewing their expenditure proposals and the OMB branch chief responsible for their agency.

If a department fails to win the day in hearings and still believes it cannot live within OMB levels, it can ride the review escalator further. Here departmental political appointees would take the matter to their administration colleagues in OMB. The points of contact, assistant secretaries with PADs on up to secretaries with the director, depend on the circumstances. A strong "No" from career budget examiners will probably enjoy the backing of the PAD. Thus, circumvention will probably require discussions among the highest ranking appointees. On the other hand, limits in political credit and the time available to press appeals dictate that departmental appointees exercise restraint in riding the review escalator to another tier.

Part of OMB's institutional obligation toward the presidency involves severely limiting departments' engagement of the appeals apparatus. Budget officers around the world recognize that exceptions provide the raw material for deficits. Thus, examiners instinctively try to head appeals off at the pass to preserve the integrity of the budget process. Yet, the concentration of ultimate responsibility for U.S. administrations' budgets in the hands of the president makes OMB's task much more difficult than that of corresponding agencies in more collective executive branches. In many cabinet systems of government, the fact that all ministers share authority over expenditure plans can make the budget agency's restriction of appeals to the prime minister almost preemptive in character. That is, spending ministers find soon in their careers that successful back-door appeals will so rankle cabinet colleagues that, next time around, offended ministers likely will invoke their prerogatives with a vengeance.

In some respects, OMB does not seek to protect the president from budget issues. In fact, the more time he gives to OMB, the greater the likelihood that examiners will establish the value of their craft firmly in the president's mind and in the consciousness of his White House aides. One PAD saw this process work under Carter when the president frequently undertook detailed review sessions that included career officials from OMB:

> The director will just turn around and say: "Joe here knows everything in the world about that, Mr. President, ask him." That has been very useful to us. . . . The White House staff . . . began to appreciate the resources that are here in OMB. They have developed relationships with career people such that . . . they have access to data and perspectives on issues that they wouldn't have if they didn't know OMB was there.[23]

Career OMB officials thrive then when *they* gain entry to the highest counsels of an administration—even direct exposure to the president. Yet, an administration with an open-door attitude toward budget examiners likely will extend this approach to operational departments unhappy with their lot. Institutionally, OMB can draw upon an arsenal of devices designed to keep issues away from the president. To begin, it can choose to camouflage the policy guidance followed by budget divisions. For example, examiners usually channel formal correspondence with departments through the relatively juridical Legislative Reference Division. This helps make OMB's verdict on an expenditure issue appear to comply with the technical requirements of the administration's budget guidelines. At the neck of the process—where special pleaders try to get to the president, the institutional bias of OMB prefers directors who take the view that only rare cases should be appealed beyond them.

Legislative Reference's presence on the budget side contributes greatly to the centrality of budget examination to OMB's role. Legislative Reference must clear the legislative proposals of agencies' appointees, congressional testimony, official statements, and public speeches. It seeks, thus, to assure that the administration speaks with one voice. Its limited resources, however, force Legislative Reference to consult elsewhere in OMB and the Executive Office of the President when it identifies apparent violations of presidential stances and directives. From the standpoint of budget examiners, Legislative Reference provides an indispensable early warning system for spotting attempts by administration officials to promote initiatives with major expenditure implications without first obtaining OMB approval.

The Budget Review Division maintains very strong links with the examination divisions by virtue of its "ringmaster" responsibility for keeping consistent and centralized budget figures. At the end of Reagan's first term, its branches included Budget Preparation, Fiscal Analysis Resource Systems, and Federal Program Information. A great deal of the division's work centers on relatively technical matters associated with developing guidelines for departmental budget submissions, tracing actual outlays during the current fiscal year—with special emphasis on identifying systematic under- or overspending, relating economic forecasts to expectations for spending levels, and day-to-day monitoring of the implications of administration and congressional decisions for the aggregate budget objectives.

The Management Side

BOB emerged during an era in which the burgeoning of modern administrative science in the private sector was propelling American business methods into paramountcy throughout the world. Those behind the creation of BOB believed that the application of private-sector management techniques to the public sector would greatly improve the economy and efficiency of government. However, this orientation fell by the wayside as BOB began to enjoy the authority resulting from its strengthened association with the president. As the budget became a key device for executive-bureaucratic leadership, review of expenditure proposals became a craft in its own right. Its practitioners plied their trade much more according to the tenets of bureaucratic politics and policy analysis than those of public administration and organizational theory.

Since the rise of budget examination, BOB/OMB officials concerned with management policy have found it difficult to focus their agency's attention on effectiveness and efficiency issues. In good times, their reservations about programs and organizations appear overly detailed. In bad times, their expertise really can only influence the margins of massive pressures to cut expenditure. During intervening periods, officials on the management side often find more sympathetic listeners among budget examiners. Even in these instances, however, BOB and OMB have grappled with an internal organizational problem. Should management analysis run essentially as a free-standing consultancy that budget examiners can draw upon as required? Or should management experts work in tandem with examiners in the budget divisions?

Institutionally, the budget agency has vacillated on this issue at least since the 1950s. One venerable career official hinted strongly that how the "M" side should mesh with the "B" side posed a genuine conundrum:

> I have seen it tried in various ways. The first reorganization I went through was 1952. They split up the old estimates division into the budget divisions. They decreased the size of the administrative management division by putting a lot of management analysts in the budget divisions. Within two years, the management analysts had all become good budget examiners. . . . There were many mutations over the years. When Fred Malek became deputy director of OMB in 1973, he decided to put a management division along with the budget divisions under each PAD. As you know, we now call those special studies divisions.[24]

The move under Nixon that the above respondent refers to formed part of the most concerted effort in years to reinstitutionalize the budget office's management function. As we saw above, the administration had changed BOB's name to the Office of Management and Budget in 1970. Under Malek's direction, it launched into the management by objectives program in 1973. The approach charged budget examiners with the task of assuring that departments evaluate their programs systematically according to cost-benefit criteria.[25]

The surviving "special studies" divisions have pretty much taken on the ethos of budget examination. However, their officials—largely through the auspices of their cross-cutting approach to issues—retain the strongest capacity in OMB for encouraging examiners and departments alike to evaluate the effectiveness of programs. Each of four special studies divisions consists of around five professionals largely trained in economics, systems analysis, and operational research. Major assessments under Carter of the performance of the all-volunteer armed forces, future housing needs and nuclear nonproliferation, and examinations under Reagan of the domestic spinoffs of the U.S. defense buildup, the effectiveness of using army reserve units to reinforce active divisions and maritime policy serve as examples of the types of studies in which the divisions have involved themselves during the last two adminstrations.

As their lean complements suggest, the special units must be selective about the studies they undertake. If they have established a strong relationship with their PAD, much of their work will reflect the preoccupations of OMB appointees across Pennsylvania Avenue in the Old Executive Office Building. PADs lack personal staffs. Some, however, have developed such strong relations with their special studies divisions that they have entrusted them with inquiries cutting at the very heart of what the administration seeks by way of critical assessment of existing and proposed programs.

The special studies units ply a precarious course between maintaining their autonomy and working effectively with the much larger examination divisions. To be sure, when a division is presented with a possible project, it must first judge whether the proposal meets relatively demanding internal criteria:[26] Are decision makers likely to actually decide the issue on analytic grounds? Will it be relatively easy to tap sufficient data? Should the division actually conduct the study or should it request agencies to conduct most of the research? Would the entire study work just as well if agencies were simply encouraged to undertake the project on their own?

In any event, officials in special studies must keep in mind the fact that they need the support of examination divisions in two ways. First, budget examiners are the most likely consumers of their analysis. Second, a project probably stands little chance of success without budget examiners' cooperation in assembling data. One respondent provides a particularly apt description of in-house OMB constraints on special studies:

There are advantages and disadvantages to having separate little groups that do special studies. . . . The biggest advantage

is that you are not tied down to day-to-day responsibilities. . . .
But you have to make sure that the selected issue is worth that
kind of intensive review. . . . So, it really requires that we work
closely with the budget divisions. . . . They are a tremendous
source of information. . . . They control certain key approval
chains in the executive branch. . . . We have to be close-in
enough so that we are working on issues of use. We don't want
to get so close that we get swamped.[27]

Special studies divisions focus on management issues only insofar as organizational considerations emanate from in-depth inquiries into existing or proposed programs. However, OMB houses
divisions that concentrate explicitly in various areas of management policy. The deputy director of OMB normally centers his
energies on the "M" side of OMB's responsibilities. Thus, the divisions working on management issues must adjust their approaches
to the preoccupations of deputy directors who, on average, turn
over every two years. As well, an associate director for management guides the day-to-day operations of management divisions.
This fact alone leaves the "M" side at a disadvantage. The budget
side's executive associate director and four PADs clearly lend a
great deal more "brass" to budget examiners' claims than that enjoyed by officials in the management divisions.

Under Carter, five divisions came under the associate director for
management and regulatory policy. These covered management improvement and evaluation, personnel policy, regulatory policy and
reports management, information systems policy, and intergovernmental affairs. This arrangement pretty much continued the resource
levels and emphases of the management side under the Ford administration.[28] Ford's OMB had departed from Nixon's in that it placed
only one administration official, instead of five political appointees,
over the management divisions. The Reagan administration thus
further rolled back the associate director for management's domain
when it collapsed two divisions under an "Office of Information and
Regulatory Affairs" directed by a separate OMB administrator, and
abolished the personnel policy and intergovernmental affairs divisions. It did, however, move one division, "financial management"
from the aegis of Budget Review to the Office of Management. The
core activities of the office consisted by the end of the first term
simply of "management reform" and "finance accounting."

The Presidential Touch

Earlier, in figure 4, I proposed an analytic framework for assessing whether a president's stylistic approach to the budget process fits the economic times. In the best of all worlds, presidents would strive for a priorities and planning style. This approach provides for consistency between overarching administration stances on expenditure and responsiveness to the special requirements of various policy sectors. Executive-branch politics in the United States, however, makes adoption of the priorities and planning style very difficult. It is more likely to emerge as a pious aspiration once a decline in economic circumstances convinces administration officials that they should have made tougher decisions earlier on. That is, they realize that a lot of what they are doing or plan to undertake simply does not meet the requirements of programmatic effectiveness.

Broker politics usually presents itself as the most realistic stylistic approach for presidents. Rather than seeking to "cover the waterfront," broker politics focuses attention on the truly contentious issues between key elements of the administration. For the ordinary run of the budgetary matters, it will simply keep a weather eye for lapses in governmental efficiency. Too many of these can discredit an administration or segments of the apparatus of state. If economic times are auspicious, even presidents who stake out the relatively realistic broker politics approach will actually lean toward administrative politics with reference to budgetary issues. The pressures from departments and agencies to reap the benefits of an expansionary period mute concerns about efficiency, let alone programmatic effectiveness. Thus administrative politics fosters a great deal of expenditure that would not withstand careful analysis.

On the other side of the coin, severe economic conditions will tend to force presidents into survival politics. In our post-Keynesian era, this calls for broad-stroke approaches in the form of sharp expenditure cuts. Here, as with administration politics, little attention is given to analysis of efficiency and effectiveness. This would simply forestall the imperative of the day, namely, ruthless stringency. Survival politics often errs on the side of overly restricting some programs that should be encouraged in order to foster recovery or ease the impact of a recession on the poor.

Jimmy Carter

As noted in chapter 4, Jimmy Carter never reconciled his personal working style and the organization of his administration. Regarding the latter, his strong emphasis on the "spokes-in-a-wheel" format introduced—in theory—one of the purest forms of administrative politics in the recent history of the presidency. However, Carter actually indulged an exceptionally strong penchant for programmatic detail. That is, he operated as if he were following a priorities and planning approach. The resulting disparity between the organization of the Carter administration and the president's personal style certainly contributed to the malaise that had, by summer 1979, plunged the administration into survival politics.

When inaugurated, Carter faced a slowing of the recovery from the 1974 recession. By the end of 1976, growth—which had reached an annual rate of 9.2 percent in the first quarter—had slumped to less than 3 percent.[29] More distressing, although it had fallen, unemployment still remained at 7.9 percent. As a candidate, Carter had presented as one of the central planks of his platform the goal of a balanced budget by 1981. As president, he chose a circuitous route to this objective—which, of course, the public largely identified as the hallmark of the new administration's domestic program. He rejected most of Gerald Ford's package of budget cuts for fiscal year 1977, and advocated a modest package of stimulative tax cuts and spending increases.

Carter's eventual predicament points up the price often paid for unrealistic campaign promises. The balanced budget proposal served its purpose as a campaign gambit responsive to the electorate's deepening concern over the size of government. It did not, however, fit the objective economic conditions. The desire to prolong a recovery and distribute its benefits more widely simply would not support the type of radical treatment that convincing first steps toward a balanced budget would require. Without a clear economic rationale, the electoral strategem eventually fell by the wayside. Yet Carter had so associated himself with the balanced budget that voters would continue to judge his performance accordingly. In fact, the president imposed upon departments the rubrics of "zero-base" budgeting. Carter had introduced the method for the first time at the state level in the United States while governor of Georgia. It attempts to encourage decision makers who wish to

fund new programs or enhance existing ones to prioritize departmental expenditures so as to identify those which might be substantially reduced or curtailed altogether.[30]

As noted by Laurence E. Lynn and David deF. Whitman in their
assessment of the abortive administration effort to reform the welfare system, zero-base budgeting fit entirely Carter's analytic approach to decision making. However, Carter failed to distinguish
between the analytic and normative relevance of zero-base assumptions.[31] If the technique becomes a decree to be applied woodenly,
it loses its capacity to encourage departments toward more creative
expenditure review.

This became clear during the welfare reform. Carter required that
competing cabinet secretaries fashion proposals that followed zero-
cost planning. That is, he wanted them to find improvements and
economies while assuming that the entire new basket of programs
would not cost any more than the old one. However, as the analysis
dragged on, the heuristic element to the process waned. It became
apparent that the president actually wanted to keep the reform
within a real-world zero-cost framework. Thus, the participants in
the exercise became extremely reluctant to point to possible economies on their part and quick to attack the ineffectivenes of others'
programs. As the conflicts deepened, its analytic intricacy became
byzantine and the president became weighed down by options.[32]

Trying to Get the Budget to Steer Policy Details. As already
noted, my interviews during the Carter administration took in
both appointees and career officials. These sessions thus provide
numerous perspectives on Carter's approach to the budget and use
of OMB. On the level of the president's strategy, many respondents
on both the political and career sides saw the potential benefits to
zero-base budgeting. Two years into the administration, several
even praised the technique's capacity to ease the president's decision load by making secretaries arrange their own priorities.[33]

As might be expected, departments learned to obfuscate the zero-
base process. One very senior OMB appointee underscored this fact
even while he reflected favorably on the administration's implementation of the approach:

> Its real value is the priorities it forces the agencies to adopt.
> We can trade these off better. It enables us to do cross-agency
> comparisons. . . . We then pose our rankings against the agen-
> cy's and try to make our decisions in terms of priorities also.

Then an agency submits an appeal. They suddenly rank their 467th priority first! We can force a question as to "why . . . what changed?" . . . but zero-base budgeting does not let one hide from the political realities of life. . . . It hasn't been as important to me as the *priorities* and the forcing of people to put a fair amount of analytic rigor into what the minimal level is.[34]

While zero-base budgeting had not proved to be a panacea, our respondent at least thought it played an important role in raising the level of discourse as OMB and departments locked horns on expenditure issues. This perspective coexisted with another one that enjoyed especially wide currency among appointees. This highlighted the degree to which Carter consciously chose to place strong emphasis on the budget. The president, the appointees maintained, had decided that the budget provided the best vehicle for determining the contours of departmental policies.

One appointee, who had worked in nonpartisan positions both in the Nixon and Ford administrations, put a very fine point on his preference for Carter's more analytic approach. He believed that it gave the administration more control of policies:

OMB is a lot more challenging place in which to work under Jimmy Carter; . . . he relies on the institution more than either Nixon or Ford did. That is, on a day-to-day basis—as an input and a source of analysis and judgement on a whole range of issues. . . . One measure, although it may be a perverted one, is the frequency with which the president comes back to us and says, "Here is something else I would like your advice on before I make up my mind."[35]

Many career officials expressed a revisionist view of the Carter years when I reinterviewed those still in OMB during Reagan's first term. In fact, one respondent lent a sardonic element to his estimation of Carter's approach: "In this administration, OMB really doesn't have any institutional interest in program detail. In the last administration, *when Carter was budget director,* we did."[36] He also made the point that the Reagan administration revealed nowhere near the interest in honed OMB analysis that the previous one had.

Along the same lines, another career respondent allowed that Carter's interest in the budget waned during the last two years of the administration. The president had become overloaded with foreign affairs issues and believed that all the attention he had given to the budget had not paid off:

> The interest declined rapidly when he realized that he didn't have the opportunities to make the kinds of efficiency savings that he'd been able to make as governor of Georgia. It involved difficult . . . decisions—taking away from one program he favored to benefit another. He recognized the agony of budget making and lost interest in it. He didn't spend much time on the last budget at all.[37]

During his salad days, Carter's interest in the budget had led to an unprecedented surge in OMB morale. In the first year, review sessions between the president and top OMB appointees added an entirely new wrinkle. They admitted career officials and allowed them to speak to the vagaries of various programs. The anecdotes still abound. One GS-16 official—three levels down into the career ranks—emphasized the exceptional nature of Carter's approach. He recounted an argument he had with the president: "Staff guys *have* been at meetings with the president and *have* entered into the dialogue. . . . I have had the opportunity to have the president say he didn't like to disagree with people but he disagreed with me. . . . I decided the discussion was over at that point. I stopped pressing the argument I was trying to make."[38]

Even the flagging of the president's direct interest in their budgetary areas by midterm had not daunted many appointees' fervor for the concept that decisions over expenditure provided a crucial mechanism for steering the administration. One associate director put it most effusively. The respondent, in pointing to Bert Lance's spotty performance, also gave substance to the cynical view expressed above that the president served essentially as his own budget director during the first two years of his term:

> We saw the president a lot and we didn't see Bert Lance very much. . . . So, we felt very much personally accountable to the president in the first year. . . . And that hasn't gone away—despite the fact that I see him considerably less now than I did then. He manages to forge very personal loyalties because of the way he deals with his staff. I have spent enough time with him, and watching him discuss things, ask questions and make decisions. I have enough sense of what he wants to know be-

fore he makes a decision; . . . I must say it's really neat. It's a very helpful way to start out a job.[39]

The above passage reflects an incongruity that had emerged on the domestic side by midterm. Most political appointees held steadfastly to the belief that analysis was driving the budgetary process which, in turn, was maintaining consistency between administration policies. In practice, disarray in Stuart Eizenstat's Domestic Policy Staff and poor leadership from the OMB director, first Bert Lance and then James McIntyre, had simply exacerbated the tendency for tough decisions to bottle up in the Executive Office of the President.

Regarding Lance, Lynn and Whitman quote Sue Woolsey, an associate director for much of the administration, who drove home the point that the first budget director remained exceptionally chary of skirmishes with cabinet secretaries: "He didn't want to be bothered with the program details, and he had staff which felt that program details are the program, so I found it very difficult to get my whale to fight with the other whales."[40] As for McIntyre, several career officials noted that Carter's selection of the highly cautious Georgian as budget director suggested that he wanted to accommodate the conservative side to his own personality. Eizenstat—so the analogy went—was the surrogate for the president's progressive side. In the words of one career respondent: "Eizenstat and McIntyre represented the two facets of Carter. He wanted to be a program liberal, but he definitely was a fiscal conservative as well. And it was hard to make these two things meet. He had two people sometimes going down opposite directions—both with his approval."[41]

The resulting tensions between the two approaches to budgetary issues contributed greatly to the paralysis that seized many key domestic policy sectors. In the words of a budget examiner heavily involved in health cost issues, the administration was at a loss as to how to coordinate any major examination of policy involving tough choices:

It's not clear that Carter forms these groups of advisers who work together and provide a consensus opinion about what he ought to do. . . . There has been a lot of paper flying around. As a matter of fact, at one meeting he began with a gruff comment that he'd received a memo from everyone in the room that day.

He clearly was not pleased about it. . . . There are no simple solutions. . . . And, now you're down to . . . two different ideas about how you should solve the problem and these are often diametrically opposed.[42]

The final year of the administration, of course, saw a dramatic worsening of economic conditions. As well, fiscal conservatives were working the public into a lather over the size of government. We might have expected that such circumstances might have concentrated conflicting administration minds. Carter might at this point have brought an end to the drift by casting aside the analytic rhetoric and imposing a program of stringent controls. In fact, his July 1979 shakeup of the administration suggested a tough new approach to dithering among his advisers over programmatic priorities. Yet, Democratic presidents find themselves at a distinct disadvantage in situations such as Carter was in by mid-1979. A draconian fiscal framework would not sit well with much of the party's bedrock support. In the end, as already noted by a respondent cited above, Carter's resolve to act decisively on domestic budgetary issues was never really tested out. The Iranian hostage crisis and other foreign affairs preoccupations began to consume virtually all of the president's time.

"PRP"—A Pure Carterism. No assessment of budgeting and management policy during the Carter years would be complete without a treatment of his ambitious President's Reorganization Project. Carter firmly believed that comprehensive reorganization of government would greatly improve the effectiveness and efficiency of program delivery. He did not stint in assigning resources to the task. In sheer terms of personnel, the PRP greatly augmented OMB's complement with career officials from other departments and political appointees. At its height, the project took in five divisions.

Peter Szanton, an associate director under the project, has edited a volume which reviews in detail PRP's approach and record.[43] Generally, the project set forth three goals: (1) reorganization of public service management; (2) regulatory reform and reduction of paperwork; and (3) improved coordination of governmental programs through creation of new departments and rationalization of the functions of existing agencies. The first initiative culminated in 1979 with the emergence of the Office of Personnel Management as a freestanding agency reporting directly to the president.

The second coincided neatly with the widespread interest elsewhere in the Executive Office of the President with deregulation of sectors such as the airline and trucking industries. It yielded considerable fruit.[44]

Unfortunately, the efforts toward comprehensive reorganization of government proved to be far too ambitious. Carter eventually did create two departments, namely, Energy and Education. Notwithstanding the Reagan administration's designs for their disbandment, both agencies have survived long enough to suggest that they have become permanent features in the executive-bureaucratic landscape. However, several key efforts gobbled up huge resources and immense quantities of the president's time without producing tangible results. These initiatives included moves to revamp the integration of domestic economic development policies, to create a Department of Natural Resources, and to improve coordination of trade policymaking. Carter invested about half his time, over a two-week period, on the first initiative. At the end, he had little to show for his efforts. When he became similarly bogged down in the second project, he decided to cut his losses so precipitately that key members of the working group were caught totally by surprise. Of course, the quest for better coordination in the trade policy field has confounded even the relatively disciplined Reagan administration.

If Carter had staked out for himself a relatively modest set of goals to accomplish with the PRP, we probably would now rate the project a success. However, the comprehensive nature of his approach planted the seeds for the sense of failure that seized the PRP by 1979. To be sure, the project had tried to avoid a top-to-bottom approach that focused too much on the organizational requirements of the modern presidency. As one appointee put it, the PRP attempted to work upward, from the programmatic level, to find better ways of coordinating between departments: "We are looking at the government from the bottom up in a fairly pragmatic way. Not trying to redesign the whole . . . but redesigning the pieces from the perspective of the better functioning of the programs and the services of the constituencies of the agencies involved."[45] To remain faithful to its avowed approach, the project would have had to restrain itself ruthlessly in selecting its initiatives.

A career OMB official provided an assessment of the PRP that makes several compelling points. The respondent has had perhaps more experience with the vagaries of reorganization than anyone inside or outside government. First, he noted, a simple fact of political life in Washington seemed to have escaped the framers of the PRP. That is, even fairly minor reform efforts run up against the sheer intractability of many pockets of the executive branch and Congress: "It always amazes me in hindsight how much it takes at the front end to get such a little thing out of the back end; . . . that isn't only true of the Carter thing. It's been true of everything I've been associated with. You have to put tremendous force at the front to get anything out of the back just because the system screens are so complex."[46] Second, such a sweeping reform project runs into the phenomenon whereby support for change and the educability of interested parties varies dramatically between programs. The Carter approach did not adequately account for these factors: "Carter—it's even more doubtful now that I look back at it—began with the *a priori* that the government needs sorting out. . . . He started with the assumption that we had to sort out the boxes and reorganize them. There probably wasn't that much pent-up demand. Most good consultants will tell you that when they come into a firm or a government agency, they take the ideas that are on the drawing boards of the staff and then implement them. They act as a catalyst." Finally, the principal appointees in the project placed far too much trust in the capacity of brute staffing to override the inherent constraints upon reorganization: "There was the assumption that it was labor-intensive analysis that would help. Absolutely wrong! It's not a matter of putting a lot of analysis on the problem. It is the wisdom of the analysis that is important. . . . They would have been better off with a small group—lowering the noise level dramatically and thinking carefully about what could and should be done."

A crucial factor in the failure of PRP was overstaffing. Several respondents noted the degree to which the complement for the project exceeded the limits of the law of diminishing returns. One PRP member, a career official on loan from an operational department, presented the argument as follows:

PRP . . . is kind of a "fly-by-night" organization. The authority that Congress gave the president was three years. . . . A lot of the people who have come in are bright, eager, young people with idealistic concepts on how to shake this government up . . . to simplify government, cut the red tape of bureaucracy and bring in a breath of fresh air. . . . And the old-timers are saying, "Look, we've seen task forces come and go.". . . . That's the bureaucratic problem. Everybody says, "This too shall pass—we'll still be around after you guys come and go."[47]

The administration simply supplied cannon fodder to dismissive OMB pros when it brought into the PRP too many appointees and detailees with right-minded views on reorganization but little or no experience in central agencies.

OPM: A PRP Success Story? The establishment of the Office of Personnel Management differed markedly from other PRP reforms, including the creation of the departments of Energy and Education. It held out the hope for revitalizing a dimension of administration that affects all of government. The management of the civil service poses some of the greatest difficulties in the operation of modern bureaucracies. When agency administrators manage their personnel better, government becomes more effective and efficient.

Carter won a great deal from Congress when he gained approval of OPM. The enabling legislation did more than set up a new office reporting directly to the president. It enshrined, as well, the principle that a central agency can most effectively establish the broad contours for positive personnel management within operational departments. It also provided specific programs—such as the Senior Executive Service—through which OPM could work toward accomplishing its overarching objectives.

The various provisions of the enabling legislation, the Civil Service Reform Act (1978), had not come without very astute executive-bureaucratic gamesmanship on the part of its advocates. Allan K. ("Scotty") Campbell provided the entrepreneurial skill necessary to transform his agency, the Civil Service Commission, into a presidential office with teeth. At crucial moments, sympathetic OMB players on the career side such as Edward Preston and Howard Messner knew how to sell the plan to skeptical colleagues. On the political side in OMB, the likes of Wayne Granquist—who even used Hamilton Jordan's college roomate to approach Carter's most trusted aide and, therefore, the Oval Office—adeptly negotiated the White House labyrinth.[48]

Spirits were upbeat in OPM as old CSC hands, joined by an influx of recruits from other agencies, set up the new office. OPM's mandates from the Civil Service Reform Act to undertake independent evaluations of work force effectiveness and manage the Senior Executive Service seemed to give it two especially potent devices for cajoling departments toward improved personnel management.

Correspondingly, Campbell set up an agency relations group. This consisted of four units that—though much smaller—sought to shadow the policy sectors headed by PADs on the budget side of OMB. Added leverage with OMB over such issues as staff productivity, and creation and allocation of SES positions theoretically would enable OPM to link its personnel policy guidance with budgetary directives.

Even under Carter, this plan floundered. The budget side of OMB stalwartly held that expenditure concerns take precedence over all management issues. Thus, OMB never acknowledged OPM's overtures for a special synapsis between the budget and personnel management. Internally, OPM faced a peculiar twist of fate. The Carter administration began to invoke pressures for budgetary restraint to justify damaging delays in the staffing up of the OPM unit that was supposed to spearhead the agency's plans for enhancing productivity measurement throughout government. Thus, several elaborate programs never went beyond the drawing board stage. Similarly, the administration and Congress reneged on financial elements of the SES crucial to its design. Of course, OPM has fared even less well under Reagan. However, that tale awaits the section which follows.

Ronald Reagan

George Bush, the ever adulatory vice-president, styled Ronald Reagan's plans for fiscal policy "voodoo economics" while a candidate for the Republican nomination in 1980. Indeed, any rudimentary knowledge of economics would suggest that the essential elements of Reagan's fiscal proposals were deeply contradictory. Reagan, like Carter, made a balanced budget the centerpiece of his avowed program. Of course, this goal had proven entirely elusive under Carter. Reagan pledged himself to doubling the effort by undertaking very severe cuts in domestic expenditure. Yet, the two other pillars to Reaganomics—tax cuts and increases in defense expenditures—would cancel out any strides taken toward a balanced budget through dramatic reductions of domestic spending.[49]

A supply-side nostrum held that dramatic tax cuts would largely pay their own way by stimulating economic growth.[50] Theoretically, the resulting increases in the tax base would maintain aggregate revenues at close to pre-cut levels. In fact, the 1981–82 recession triggered sharp revenue shortfalls which, even early in Reagan's second term, still required correction. The president's simultaneous pursuit of immense increases in defense expenditure further reversed engines in his fiscal framework. Rather than shrinking toward the balanced-budget objective, the deficit expanded into an unseemly bulge.

Budgeting on Automatic Pilot. Reagan has refused throughout his presidency to alter his contradictory domestic and defense spending policies. This fact highlights the degree to which macro-level policies have dominated the approach to budgeting under Reagan. Once settling upon aggregate budget figures, the administration pretty much has applied across-the-board cuts to domestic spending and increases to defense spending. This has meant a great deal less detailed expenditure analysis than occurred under the Carter administration. It also has spelled relatively minimal direct presidential involvement in budgetary details.

Seasoned observers have not dismissed Reagan's aloofness out of hand. As one OMB veteran offered, examiners at least operate with a clearer idea of where the president stands on the principal issues than under Carter: "The total emphasis . . . was on the budget . . . and the new economic program that President Reagan was pushing, to the exclusion of almost everything else in terms of priority setting. This approach was very singleminded and, from their point of view, very successful."[51]

One OMB respondent had attended an especially large number of budget sessions with Carter. He thus cited his own case to underline how remote career officials were from the Reagan administration's penultimate and final decision-making bodies in his policy area. These are the Pentagon's Defense Resources Board, taking in the department's top appointees, and the Budget Review Board, consisting of David Stockman and top White House aides:

> This administration hasn't brought the civil servants in. . . . I used to go to meetings with Carter where all the details were considered. Now, just about everything gets resolved before it goes to the president. . . . The Budget Review Board . . . reviewed all the issues before they went to the president. I don't even get to go to Defense Resources Board meetings, unless my PAD happens to be out of town. They're very strict about that.[52]

Of course, the administration took great care at the outset to screen political appointees for ideological purity. This paid off in the form of exceptionally strong discipline among cabinet secretaries. In the words of one career official: "This administration reminds me somewhat of Nixon's in expecting a very high degree of political loyalty. People are very carefully screened. They don't want holdovers or Democrats or just Republicans. They have to have true-blue Reaganites."[53]

Yet, many OMB budget examiners noted a unique element to the Reagan—as against the Nixon—administration's discipline. Consistent with the "round-tabling" norm which, as we have seen, operates at the core of the Reagan advisory system, many career officials stressed the effects of the administration's teamwork. As well, they made strong associations between the collegial relations of top appointees and the group dynamics promoted by the Budget Review Board and cabinet councils. As one respondent put it: "It's been a process aimed at building teams in various functional areas . . . to keep everybody's consciousness focused on the fact that what may be good for their particular agency may not fit in with the broader policy set that is being worked out for all similar areas. . . . These forums tend to discourage logrolling."[54]

Of course, David Stockman's contribution to establishing and maintaining fiscal discipline in the cabinet secretary ranks enters the equation here. Ideological compatibility and group dynamics did not do all the work. Stockman's mental agility and forceful personality provided the dynamo for the arduous and intricate task of implementing the administration's expenditure plans. From the very beginning, Stockman displayed to all involved his mastery of what, as construed by those closest to the president, was required of departments. Stockman maximized his legitimacy through working in tandem with James Baker, Edwin Meese, and Reagan's first assistant to the president for policy development, Martin Anderson. One OMB appointee explained:

> We had a group of people which consisted of Meese, Baker, Anderson and Stockman. We sat them down at one end of the table. We had the cabinet appointees-to-be paraded in with whomever they wanted to bring and sat them at the other side of the table. And we handed them a list of things we wanted to do and suggested that they give at the office. . . . They had not seen their natives yet. And, we were extraordinarily successful in our track record of appeals in that particular venue.[55]

One career official corroborated these remarks. He also gave a fly-on-the-wall account of the solid front Stockman et al. presented to neophyte secretaries:

I sat in on a session involving the secretary of housing and urban development. He wasn't too familiar with his programs. Some people there on his behalf were trying to say, "We've gone too far." They just got dumped on. Not just by Stockman, but by a number of other key people in the White House. They sat around the table saying, "This is what we're going to do— figure out how to do it."[56]

Notwithstanding the tremendous thrust behind Stockman's approach to the budget, the mystique surrounding the former budget director does warrant probing. Many respondents on the political side of OMB attributed almost superhuman qualities to Stockman's grasp of detail. For instance, one appointee took exception to the view that the president did not involve himself in the intricacies of the budget. Stockman, the official argued, had all the details of the budget in his head. Reagan, thus, could certainly derive as much knowledge about programs from private sessions with top aides and his genius of a budget director as Carter did from review sessions including OMB budget examiners: "They didn't have a budget director either who sits down with 99 percent of it in his head and goes through it with the president. . . . He does the selling to the president himself and he does the presenting; . . . the president's not getting any less of a chance to make decisions."[57]

Career officials took a dimmer view of Stockman's aplomb with the budget. They grant that he had worked out a comprehensive plan and had devised many detailed ways in which to implement it. However, he demonstrated little interest even in budget analysis that would reveal better ways of achieving the administration's programmatic objectives. One budget examiner made this point as follows:

It was more than the back of an envelope, but less than a fully worked-out plan. . . . It wasn't clear that they had really figured out how they were going to execute it or whether their amounts made sense. . . . They didn't want analysis. They pretty much knew what they wanted to do. So, an analytic piece which either said, "Yes, you're right, go ahead" or "No, you're wrong, this is going to create havoc" wasn't the kind of thing they needed. They didn't want to hear if it was wrong. And, if it was right, it was a waste of time to do the analysis.[58]

Of course, Stockman's budgetary discipline declined the further he got into the first term. Through a process of attrition, OMB began bartering cuts in some areas with the understanding that cooperative secretaries would protect cherished programs from further restraint. Once letting out these IOUs, the budget office had to negotiate around sacred cows while searching for cuts that would significantly reduce the deficit. The process constrained appreciably Stockman's practice of the art of the possible.

Nonetheless, a politics of consensus—centered on the Budget Review Board—helped to contain disputes between secretaries and OMB *and* to maintain the administration's harmonious image. As one appointee noted, this phenomenon took especially strong hold in discussions during 1982 concerning fiscal year 1984. It stemmed from the fact that the president's top White House aides and his principal economic advisers had gotten from him, directly and early on, specific guidance on many outstanding issues:

> This year for the first time we did a very top-down process. We met with the president and worked through a wide range of different categories of the budget. . . . We got his rough guidance for seventy-four different budget categories and subcategories. We then translated these into an OMB passback to the agencies. As a result, we fought it out at that level to some degree. One or two agencies, notably Health and Human Services, came back and appealed the whole thing. As for the rest of them, I was getting the feeling that they knew what was going on. Thus, none of the appeals went to the president simply because we knew what the president was going to buy and not going to buy. We knew what to fight and what to quit on.[59]

Through all of this, budget examiners, while busy enough, have felt especially remote from their political masters. As for the PADs, they frequently submit their own material to the Budget Review Board without seeking guidance from their divisions.[60] Early in the administration, career officials lowered their sights to the "what-iffer" as the highest analytic art form to which they could aspire. One respondent presented the flavor especially well:

> Last year, we were incredibly involved in all sorts of what-iffers. . . . Stockman would be up on the Hill and we'd get an indirect call saying, "What if we have to give back some money in this program; what implications does it have?" And in the entitlements area . . . he had a lot of questions about what happens if we change the formula slightly in this direc-

tion or that. There were huge exercises gone through by staffs around here to cope with the fact that our bosses were running discussions on the Hill with key leaders.[61]

This was life in the greenwood. By midterm, the administration's bipartisan task force with the congressional leadership—called the Gang of Seventeen—sharply cut the diffuseness of budget negotiations. As well, "what-iffers" had filled many gaps in Stockman's grasp of budget complexities. Officials began to receive detailed rather than exploratory guidance about the types of figures the administration needed. Budget examination became for many a take-home examination. Some queries would even come to officials' desks in outlines scratched in Stockman's own hand on yellow legal sheets: Here are the cuts I want you to display, this is where you should find the funds, these are the outlay impacts I want over time, these are the program implications you should illustrate. One career OMB official presented the transition into the midterm phase as follows:

> Last year almost literally every day there would be some kind of exercise from the director's office. He needed some numbers or a crosscut or something. This year, that's been far less frequent. . . . We had a long period of top-level negotiations. He needed information for the major categories that they were arguing over. But he didn't need at that time all the kind of detailed data on a program-by-program basis that he used before.[62]

As viewed from the career side of OMB, budgeting under Reagan is clearly done on "automatic pilot." However, the coordinates are different for domestic and defense spending. Of course, the order of the day for domestic programs has been cuts. Some examiners in domestic policy divisions enjoyed the frantic activity at the beginning of the administration. Indeed, they found that the "what-iffers" provided welcome opportunities to identify programs on their personal lists of questionable expenditures. On the other hand, examiners dealing with defense expenditure stood by helplessly as the administration threw money at programs without concern for the merits of various arms systems. By midterm, the political leadership was so entrenched in its indifference to analysis of defense issues that OMB's national security division had lost nearly a third of its examiners.

Under the circumstances, even Stockman enthusiasts among career OMB officials registered the sinking feeling that their agency was losing its soul in the process of simply responding to data exercises. One respondent put it in a nutshell:

> David Stockman makes budgets through policy decisions or stating preferences and asking someone else to fill out the charts and the schedules necessary to accomplish that. On the other hand, the best work of OMB in the past has emerged when people—even at the junior level—develop ideas, strategies, issue papers and proposals, when directors choose among alternatives in the formal review process. This involved the spring and fall reviews. That process is in a shambles now. This year we renamed the spring review the spring/summer review. Very few sessions actually took place. The director gets the books. He then makes a set of decisions from these or holds a very perfunctory review session. Sometimes he doesn't even show up. Or he leaves the room while the meeting is in progress. . . . He's an absolutely brilliant operative in terms of taking the policy directions of the president and putting them into place. . . . But that takes a toll on staff creativity.[63]

Stockman's approach consistently overrode the traditional schedules of the spring and fall reviews. As well, guidance had become a one-way street. It allowed for little or no exercise of OMB's institutional vigilance over the long-term interests of the presidency.

The Waste Busters. One finds strong parallels between the Reagan administration's emphasis on broad-stroke budgeting to the detriment of programmatic evaluation and the Thatcher government's stress on aggregate spending levels as against policies based on quantitative assessment of effectiveness and efficiency in the United Kingdom.[64] Under both regimes, the ideological consensus starts with the assumption that government has grown like Topsy and deserves to be mercilessly cut. Analysis would only postpone or, worse, obscure that necessity.

Such a macro approach to budgeting can drastically curtail the marketability of expertise in management policy in central agencies. What happened to Britain's Civil Service Department (CSD) in 1981, two years into the Thatcher government, would, in fact, serve as a harbinger of the fate of OMB's management side and the Office of Personnel Management. The United Kingdom's CSD had since its creation in 1968 enjoyed a "sign off" power whereby it could refuse to approve spending directly connected to management and personnel. This authority gave CSD greater leverage when trying to impose new regulations regarding management and personnel or encouraging departments to voluntarily improve their administrative practices.

By 1981, Mrs. Thatcher had concluded that the CSD was simply a pack of poachers turned gamekeepers. In her view, the department's management specialists offered too many defenses of existing civil service practices on the grounds that "after all, government is an entirely different thing from business." As well, CSD's personnel policy experts had cited, one time too often, the deleterious effects of draconian cuts in staffing and severe constraints on salaries on civil service morale and performance. Mrs. Thatcher thus split the CSD department by returning its parts concerned with administrative costs, staffing, and compensation to the aegis of Her Majesty's Treasury. This move left the management and personnel policy analysts with their "department" degraded to an "office" and no real leverage.

Of course, the management function in OMB has always had to coexist in the same central agency with budget examination. Thus, it had no "sign off" to lose under a macro-oriented administration such as Ronald Reagan's. However, Mrs. Thatcher's one enduring crusade on the management side tips us off to a clear similarity with the Reagan administration. This common thread, indeed, appears to manifest itself especially in governments and administrations dedicated to the fervent belief that the civil service service is far too big. The assertion that sizable savings in government spending will accrue if departments will only conduct their affairs on a businesslike basis normally accompanies avowals of the dangers of big government.

Under Thatcher, the businesslike nostrum took shape in a series of "scrutinies" of the costs of various administrative functions. Conducted under the direction of Sir Derek Rayner—a special adviser to the prime minister who remained vice-chairman of the retail chain of Marks and Spencer while working in No. 10 Downing Street—the scrutinies sought a demonstration effect. That is, they would make ripples beyond documenting inefficient practices in selected functions. They would also illustrate how managers responsible for comparable activities throughout government might make considerable savings. In 1982, Sir Derek's approach became formalized in a Financial Management Initiative (FMI) whereby permanent civil servants and ministers alike began, theoretically, to shoulder more explicit responsibility for efficient management.

Significantly, and by way of contrast with similar efforts during the Reagan administration, those spearheading Mrs. Thatcher's campaigns against waste have maintained a relative sense of proportion about how much can be saved through more efficient management. First, they have usually acknowledged that expenses directly associated with government administration constitute only about 10 percent of the expenditure budgets. Outlays for goods and services make up the overwhelming bulk of government spending. Even Mrs. Thatcher's reducing the size of the civil service by 14 percent only cut the total cost of government by less than .5 percent. Second, the scrutinies and the FMI have kept their claims of credit for specific savings at modest levels. For instance, Sir Derek, after fully 135 scrutinies between 1979 and 1982, identified savings once and for all: he envisioned annual savings of only 37 million, and potential savings of only 300 million, from total government expenditures amounting to approximately 114 billion pounds.[65]

At the outset, the Reagan administration advocated bold efforts to simplify the administrative apparatus of the U.S. government. Most notably, it planned to dismantle the departments of Energy and Education, both of which had been created by Jimmy Carter; to consolidate all functions associated with trade in a Department of Industry and Trade; and to merge the Bureau of Reclamation and the Army Corps of Engineers, two vast bureaucracies whose jurisdictions overlap, into one agency. Although the administration has floated these proposals through the cabinet council system several times, it has yet to expend the time and political capital to actually bring about a single alteration of such magnitude. When we consider the relatively meager results from Carter's comprehensive effort to reorganize government, we can hardly fault the Reagan administration for half-hearted pursuit of its various proposals. Especially during the first term, the "pragmatic" side to the White House saw that even the optimal organizational arrangment for cabinet might not yield benefits that would cover the costs of knocking secretaries' heads together and winning the support of effected interest groups and their patrons in Congress.

Two large Reagan administration projects have actually gained the limelight in the management field. Like Rayner scrutinies and the Financial Management Initiative in the United Kingdom, they both focus on ways in which government administration might be improved. However, neither has exercised restraint in its claims for the savings that would result from its recommendations. As a result, the projects have lacked credibility.

The first project, dubbed "Reform '88" by 1982, took initial shape in some twenty special projects on waste, fraud, and abuse in government. These were conducted by departmental inspectors-general under the aegis of a presidential council titled "Integrity and Efficiency." The deputy head of OMB, who covers the bulk of management issues on behalf of the director, chaired the council. As well, the projects drew upon staunch support from Edwin Meese, the former counselor to the president. He maintained a strong interest in management issues throughout the first term of the Reagan administration.

The upgrading of the special projects into a comprehensive reform initiative occurred as the administration became aware of a deeper issue than inefficient and illegal use of resources. As they assessed departments' cash management, audit follow-up, debt collection, internal control, and efforts toward modernization of accounting systems, officials began to conclude that the governmental apparatus had become exremely antiquated. One respondent recalled how he had presented the problem to the president when reporting on the status of the waste, fraud, and abuse projects: "But, Mr. President, that is not how we really save money. . . . We have to go in and make fundamental changes . . . in the gutsy, grimy business that's down on the basement floors of these departments . . . that basically provide cabinet secretaries information on how well they're doing at reducing costs."[66] The same official offered some flagrant examples of just how basic some of these problems are:

> We've got 325 primary financial and accounting systems that are basically incompatible; . . . we have 350 payroll personnel systems; . . . we do most of our auditing manually. . . . Computer cross-checking has been in the private sector for ten or fifteen years. We don't have one automated collection station in the entire federal government. . . . Macy's in Kansas City had one in 1971. . . . So, I'm not talking about highly sophisticated, on-line, state-of-the-art. I'm talking about what was available in the private sector ten years ago.[67]

Reform '88, thus, emerged from these more fundamental concerns. It also dovetailed with the administration's need for OMB-based implementation of the recommendations from the President's Private Sector Survey on Cost Control headed by J. Peter Grace, the chairman of W. R. Grace and Co. This vast project took in some thirty-six task forces and tapped over 2,000 private-sector executives. It undertook detailed studies of waste, system failures, personnel mismanagement, and structural deficiencies throughout the U.S. government. It drew considerable fire at its inception. The fact that, in numerous instances, executives received assignments to task forces studying agencies with which their corporations dealt on a regular basis posed serious conflict-of-interest concerns. Procedures whereby the studies gave investigators privileged access to government information exacerbated dangers of abuse.

By fall 1982, the administration underlined its seriousness about Reform '88 by establishing a Cabinet Council on Management and Administration. Edwin Meese assumed chairmanship of the new committee and responsibility for maintaining momentum for over twenty major projects. These all cut across departments and, therefore, required coordination between cabinet secretaries. Mostly through officials loaned from other agencies, OMB set up the Presidential Task Force on Management Reform which consisted of over thirty senior civil servants working essentially as the secretariat for Reform '88.

Notwithstanding its boldness, the midterm strengthening of the administration's commitment to management reform eventually obtained a dubious track record. At the heart of the difficulties rests a simple fact. Often it is better to execute under central-agency auspices only a few demonstration projects. Modesty in scale fosters genuine creativity and provides straightforward examples of ways in which departments might benefit from more efficient practices. As we saw above, Mrs. Thatcher's attempts to improve management in government have generally held to this limited compass. One OMB career official asserted that the Reagan administration lost sight of the strictures of scale. For instance, he held that the Grace Commission manifested roughly the same grandiose character as the President's Reorganization Project (PRP) under Carter:

> Again, you will have the same thing you had with the PRP, which is people describing different components of the elephant—the tail, the nose, the tusk, the eyeball. Some of it will be brilliantly done. Some of it will be scholarly done. And,

some of it will be successful. But, all of it will be random. It's just impossible to orchestrate something that large and complex and that quickly. . . . Again, we're caught up with this impatience. They want the stuff fixed now. And they are so convinced that the nature of the problem is opposition. . . . They are very much less inclined to listen to us until it's very late in the process.[68]

Management reformers who carve out more than they can handle frequently fall into the trap of inflating their claims to success. In order to maintain the support of top administration officials and attentive publics, they have to show some return from their projects. Both Reform '88 and the Grace Commission undermined their credibility by failing to adequately negotiate this potential pitfall. Joseph R. Wright, the deputy director of OMB who set up Reform '88, faced the acute embarrassment of having his boss, David Stockman, publicly challenge the validity of the alleged $31 billion in savings identified by inspectors general in a 1984 report. As it turned out, much of the amount came from "cost avoidances." For example, Stockman raised doubts about $5 billion of a total of $12.5 billion supposedly recovered through improved debt collection. The funds in question actually had accrued from crop loans that farmers had repaid when, in the regular course of business, market conditions for grain had improved. Similarly, the Grace Commission, reporting in January 1984, weighed in by projecting that $424 billion supposedly would be saved upon acceptance of its recommendations over a three-year period. By citing a figure so patently beyond the amounts to be saved by even the most thoroughgoing cuts in administrative costs, the commission strained the credulity of all but the most sanguine believers in the superiority of commercial management practices over those in government.

The Gutting of OPM. I noted in an earlier section that Jimmy Carter's creation of the Office of Personnel Management constituted what was potentially the most significant accomplishment of his "President's Reform Project." In 1979, OPM officials banked heavily on their presidential mandate for a more positive form of personnel management throughout the U.S. government. That is, they planned to utilize new instruments such as work-force effectiveness studies and the Senior Executive Service to guide departments to more creative stewardship of human resources.

Such aspirations only elicit pained howls from those who believe that a good civil service is one which has submitted to sharp reductions in force and tight ceilings on compensation. In Britain, for instance, Mrs. Thatcher stripped the Civil Service Department of its "sign off" over staffing and compensation after its more positively oriented personal policy experts had bleated once too often about the effects of her staff cuts and pay limits on civil service morale. As did the Thatcher government, the Reagan administration took a decidedly skeptical view of positive personnel policies. It even assigned to OPM a director, Donald Devine, who consistently registered public criticisms of central elements of his agency's approach to personnel management. As one official observed, Devine's appointment sealed a fundamental reversal of the tack OPM had taken under Carter: "The director came in and rather early stated publicly and within the agency that his approach to personnel management was so-called bedrock personnel management. He was going to do the traditional old personnel things and not a lot of this expensive, esoteric jazz like productivity and quality of work life."[69]

Several OPM respondents remarked upon the fact that the administration's designation of Devine as director simply underscored OPM's institutional vulnerability. That is, whether a director opts for positive measures and maintains the active interest of the White House likely will determine OPM officials' leverage much more than any fresh powers gained through Carter's reforms. Along this vein, one respondent contrasted OPM's lot under the more expansive Allan K. Campbell during the Carter administration with how it had fared under Devine:

> The previous director and his deputy were into many things that were beyond the realm of traditional personnel management. Their attitude toward running OPM was very much one of openness to new ideas and initiatives. . . . It was kind of "Let a thousand flowers bloom" . . . . They were building what they called the "managers' network." . . . They, indeed, consciously defined OPM's clientele as, first, the line managers of government and, second, as the personnel people. Devine came in, looked at all of that, and said "We are going to concentrate on 'bedrock' personnel management. We are going to cut ourselves back to concerns with pay, benefits, recruiting, hiring, firing, discipline, and other traditional personnel management areas."[70]

As a result of the Reagan administration's emphasis, OPM has become an enforcing agency—leaving its positive functions to atrophy. Regarding the Senior Executive Service, the administration has systematically undermined such integral provisions as bonus and award systems, has maintained pay caps substantially out of line with comparable compensation in the private sector, has essentially abdicated a cental administrative role regarding creation and granting of SES positions, and has actually permitted considerable loss of ground in developmental assignments such as transfers between departments, secondments to the private sector, and sabbaticals.[71]

With respect to work force effectiveness, the administration has farmed out assessments entirely to departments under the rubric of "performance measurement." In theory, the system would link meritorious performance with compensaton. In practice, the assessments were paper phenomena. Even an appointee intimately involved with the system's implementation tips us to the fact that it was put in place with no real intention of substantive implementation: "We had until October 1981 to make sure that everyone was covered under the system. We made the deadline. We have now gone to the next step, that is, trying to improve the system—make it work, make it simpler, make it useable and make it meaningful in terms of assessing performance of employees."[72] Indeed, one OMB respondent gave a damning assessment of OPM's actual involvement in performance appraisals:

> OPM did not play an active part in it, amazingly. They've not really used the tools of the civil service reform in a very aggressive way. They have really left the field on that matter to OMB. We aren't directing the agencies as to what critical elements to include. We're only explaining the philosophy and central parts to performance appraisal. They have to decide. . . . We knew that if we didn't get some of the things we wanted in there, agencies would fill in the sheet with things they were interested in and forget about priorities.[73]

Conclusion

This chapter has focused on the dimension of central coordination and control in which the connection between macroeconomic policies and specific government programs comes to the fore. The

1960s and 1970s saw an explosion in analytic approaches to sifting through various demands upon finite budget sums. We might thus expect that the U.S. government enjoys now, in comparison to the 1950s, a much greater ability to hone resource commitments according to assessments of the effectiveness and efficiency of various programs. To the contrary, frustration during Jimmy Carter's presidency indicated that efforts to fine-tune resource allocations after establishing the broader fiscal framework might immobilize an administration. As well, Ronald Reagan's aloofness from budgetary detail has preordained a serious bifurcation of budget policy. On the one hand, severe cuts in domestic programs, have—even according to some central players among Reagan's advisory team—posed very serious question of fairness. On the other, the Pentagon continues to win most of its budget battles, notwithstanding the many horror stories indicating that much of what it takes on it does with scant regard for costs and benefits.

Within this wider frame, many students of the Office of Management and Budget have registered concerns about the agency's capacity for fulfilling its mandate. That is, they worry that OMB no longer provides an analytic base for the president's resource decisions. Nor does it adequately maintain a vigil for the long-term interests of the executive branch. Some observers, such as Aaron Wildavsky, even ask stoically whether the federal government has simply grown too big for fine-tuning. Pointing to the relative success of automatic budgetary decision regimens such as Britain's "cash ceilings," those stressing the size issue wonder if these techniques might have supplanted detailed assessments of programs on their merits as the most realistic functional aspiration for a budget office. While acknowledging the gradual decline in OMB's analytic sway over budget decisions, other scholars—Allan Schick, for example—grant an ebb and flow whereby the agency does more or less well, depending upon the stylistic preferences of various presidents.

I have attempted to temper these bleak views of OMB. I have argued that the nature of an economic epoch works as a separate influence from the magnitude of aggregate expenditure on the relevance of budget analysis. This effect will ameliorate or exacerbate any long-term slippage in the prestige of an agency or declines associated with the various approaches of different presidents. Our current era is one in which much of the relation between macroeconomic policy and allocation of resources to programs has operated within the constraints presented by the economics of decline.

Thus, agencies responsible for expenditure budgets have, in most advanced liberal democracies, found the market for their analytic skills sharply curtailed.

Along with the above, we should keep in mind that the budget and management "sides" to the agency rarely operate in complementary balance. In fact, the early Bureau of the Budget styled its task as bringing management science to bear on bureaucracy to such a degree that policy-oriented and analytic budgeting was not fully established as an agency goal until the late 1930s. Since then, the budget office has undergone internal strains between proponents of these two emphases. For the most part, those stressing budget analysis have maintained hegemony. The Nixon administration initiatives favoring their side, did, however, give OMB's management experts a brief period in which they enjoyed rough parity with budget examiners.

The Carter and Reagan administrations provide contrasting experiences with using OMB in attempts to give central guidance to the executive branch without violating the integrity of its institutional mandate. If OMB best fulfills its mission by keeping a weather eye for long-term issues and developing analysis-based options for the president, the agency reached its apogee during the first two years of Carter's term. Eventually, it became increasingly clear that Carter had grossly overloaded himself and his closest advisers. He had taken on far too many issues and pursued virtually all of them in detail. By midterm, OMB began to see its role truncated. An excess of analysis had given the administration chronic indigestion. The bad turn in the economy by 1979 presented a potential role for OMB in establishing a more stringent fiscal regime. By then, however, international preoccupations had seized Carter. He could scarcely find time for domestic issues at all, let alone make tougher budget decisions.

Through all of this, the management side of OMB fared reasonably well. It had astutely kept itself cordoned off from the secondment-based President's Reorganization Project, also housed in OMB. Yet, it did engage selectively in reform efforts congruent with its goals. Principal among instances of such strategic involvement in the PRP was the management side's civil service reform.

The Reagan administration's approach has greatly damaged both the fiber of OMB and its utility as the watchdog for the interests of the presidency. The president's relative detachment from budgetary detail has badly harmed morale in OMB. It has offered precious few opportunities for officials to believe that analytic assessments would even be grasped by the president if, indeed, they ever reached him. The personal style of David Stockman, however, assured that the vast majority of matters never reached the president. The administration's strong internal discipline has meant that appeals from cabinet secretaries of cuts on the domestic side have remained extraordinarily faint. And, even in the relatively rare instances of conflict, Stockman denied his agency so much as a brokerage role. He provided career officials such detailed guidance that they found virtually no opening for conducting, not to mention serving up, analytic assessments of options on the basis of merit.

Of course, the president's unflagging commitment to increasing Pentagon resources ran the budgetary engines full speed ahead in defense expenditure. As a result, Stockman lost most of his battles with Caspar Weinberger. The Pentagon's unchecked spending spree has deeply concerned OMB officials trained to examine the long-range benefits of defense programs. More worrisome, staff cuts have accompanied slumping morale to the point where career officials wonder if, assuming a more receptive administration, they have not lost their core capacity for analysis. The management side has lost a great deal of ground under Reagan, too. While trumpeting—often inflating—its accomplishments in pursuit of waste, fraud, and abuse, the administration has undermined OMB's credibility for fostering positive management practices in departments. However, OMB officials working on the management side can always take solace in the fact that they are not in the Office of Personnel Management. For four years, that agency labored under a director who took great pride in having returned his agency to "bedrock"—read "antediluvian"—functions.

7. Structure and Two Different Mixes
of Three Bureaucratic Cultures

The search for a governmental approach that suits the institutional development of the presidency, the political environment of the day, and the stylistic approach of an administration at a given point in history involves more than getting the organization of the executive branch correct. Insofar as they characterize an administration, executive harmony and policy competence rely heavily upon the men and women who make the machinery work. Most of these never attract significant public attention. In fact, those on the "career side" find the very prospect of publicity abhorrent. This book has focused on the officials working in central agencies. This chapter will look behind the scenes to provide a detailed view of the role orientations and work worlds of the officials most responsible for assisting the president in providing, at the center, coordination and control of the executive branch for his administration. It will also examine in detail these officials' orientations toward public service and their career and sociodemographic backgrounds.

If we undertook this examination in the United Kingdom, we would be studying a relatively homogeneous group of officials. Most would belong to the permanent civil service. That is, they would have entered the bureaucracy fairly soon after graduating from university. Throughout their careers, they would have eschewed any tendency toward specialization. Instead, they would have moved through several areas of their department with a view to honing their "generalist" ability to manage various policy sectors. Many would have joined their central agencies on loan from operational departments. In the transaction, the central agencies would have gained the advisory acuity of people who have worked at the "sharp end" of government, while the operational departments would have allowed their officials to experience firsthand how policies are meshed at the center. Of course, Whitehall's norm of obedience to the government of the day would have maintained every assurance of job security even for our migratory officials. Its neutrality, thus, places the U.K. permanent civil service in a position whereby its ways of operating remain relatively immune to changes in the political leadership.

Central agencies in the United States present a much more varied picture. We can identify, however, three broad groups of officials. Two of these make up the cohort of political appointees. First, "politicos" have gained their positions by functioning as operatives within successful political campaigns. Many bring to their work significant experience in Washington under previous administrations. Yet their standing in the campaign preordained their actually obtaining a significant post under the incoming president. Consequently, politicos gravitate toward shaping the administration's overall political strategy. Their direct involvement in substantive policy issues tends to focus on building the coalitions—between other political appointees, and with Congress and the various attentive publics and interest groups—necessary for the success of major administration initiatives.

Members of the second group, "amphibians," need not to have distinguished themselves as political operatives to have won their appointments. They almost always display the correct political coloration and frequently have worked in campaigns. However, they all claim an expertise within a substantive policy field. This plays the most significant role in their landing a job in an administration. When they do call upon prior experience in Washington, this normally has involved work in policy-oriented shops either in central agencies or operational departments. Amphibians tend to subdivide into those who advocate specific policy proposals and those who emphasize neutral brokerage of conflicting agency stances. Those with the widest experience in Washington's bureaucratic labyrinth will likely demonstrate the strongest bias toward the latter focus.

Career officials stand to the side within the executive-bureaucratic milieu of central agencies. In fact, some observers might overlook them entirely. Virtually all professional-level officials operating out of the White House Office are political appointees. In all of the various units within the Executive Office of the President (EOP), the Department of Treasury, and the Office of Personnel Management, appointees occupy the uppermost policy positions. Yet, career officials remain the oarsmen of every agency except the White House Office and a few parts of the EOP. They serve as the repositories of institutional memory at the very center of government. They know how to get the policy process working in an administration's favor and how their political masters might avoid certain failure. Unlike their opposite numbers in Britain, they normally have received academic or professional degrees beyond their bachelor's. Since entering government, many have stayed within cognate fields. Indeed, they have frequently spent a disproportionate segment of their career working in their current subdivision of an agency. Thus, U.S. central agents on the career side constitute a hybrid culture. They are formed of one part bureaucratic acumen and another part strong expertise in and commitment to a specialized policy field.

Finding the optimal mix of the politico, amphibian, and career cultures has become the center of considerable discussion in the literature on the presidency. Regarding politicos, the proliferation of positions suited for operatives, especially in the White House, assures that there is no dearth of appointees fitting into this category. Problems arise, however, when administrations choose politicos who—whatever their performance in election campaigns—lack experience in Washington. Career officials "you have always with you." The question remains just where they should fit within the central agency complex. From the standpoint of numbers, OMB, Treasury, and OPM are overwhelmingly staffed by career people. Even in these organizations, however, debates arise as to how many layers of appointees should operate above the career officials. As well, some observers maintain that policy secretariats in the Executive Office of the President should make greater use of career officials. In fact, the National Security Council staff has followed a tradition whereby some of its members come on loan either from the permanent civil service or the military.

The emergence of the amphibians poses the greatest number of questions as to their proper place in central agencies. In 1959, Richard Fenno noted that the expansion of the Executive Office of the President adversely reflects on the ability of cabinet secretaries to cope with coordination on their own.[1] To a degree, the meetings during the Eisenhower administration in which departmental offi-

cials worked together to prepare issues for cabinet-level deliberations recognized the need for more systematic treatment of policy
coordination.[2] Indeed, Fenno suggested that a "policy staff" reporting directly to the president would best guide such processes.[3]

In practice, administrations have found it extremely difficult to
arrive at politically acceptable and managerially effective ways of
providing staff support for interdepartmental coordination. In a
sense, the task comes down to finding the best mix between staff
members who owe their first loyalty to the president and those
dedicated above all else to making the state apparatus work.[4] Even
in the former case, officials prove most effective when they have so
structured their careers that they have obtained some command of
the intricacies of substantive policy issues. To a degree, they must
have become policy professionals. Regarding the second group,
members of a policy secretariat view themselves partially as facilitators of the governmental decision process rather than simply custodians of narrow clusters of interests associated with their governmental experience and subject-matter expertise.

Observers have increasingly recognized that administrations
should dip into two pools when recruiting for secretariats. That is,
they want to draw upon career civil servants as well as policy
professionals with bona fide partisan credentials. A 1980 report of
the Presidential Management Panel of the National Academy of
Public Administration even suggested that the Senior Executive
Service might function as a key source for "professional generalists" who balance their substantive grasp of issue areas with governmental experience that has fostered "temperaments better
suited to the facilitative role."[5]

Although they reveal no preference for career officials over appointees, one of the most articulate spokesmen for cabinet secretariats on the domestic side, Roger Porter, and one of the most
noted authorities on national security coordination, I. M. Destler,
stress the need for developing in the Executive Office of the President units that will maintain low profiles.[6] Both authors promote
the view that cultivating neutral competence and severely restricting the size of secretariats offer the surest route to effectiveness.

This chapter will probe in detail the politico, amphibian, and
career groups as found within the White House, the Executive
Office of the President, the Department of the Treasury, and the
Office of Personnel Management. As already noted, this book is
based on in-depth interviews with 192 respondents. In previous

chapters, numerous quotations from verbatim transcripts of these sessions give a sense of the "flavor" of life in central agencies. The coding of our officials' responses for computer analysis affords an opportunity for a more quantitative approach in this chapter.

The tables in the following sections provide the percentages of career officials, amphibians, and politicos under Carter and amphibians and politicos under Reagan who gave the relevant responses. In numerous places, I will point up especially strong differences—for instance, in the answers given by amphibians under Carter and Reagan or between amphibians and politicos under Reagan—by noting in a superscript the statistical significance of the finding. The letter "a" will stand for a .001 probability of the difference occurring by chance, "b" for .01, and "c" for .05.

In the case of career officials, this chapter will not draw upon comparable data between the Carter and Reagan administrations. Rather than seeking complete interviews with an entirely new batch of career respondents, in 1982 I simply held update sessions with thirty-seven surviving officials whom I had seen during the Carter administration. I provide detailed information on the methodological dimensions to the quantitative data in appendix 1.

Role Perceptions

In recognition of the salience of officials' views of their personal roles, this section first examines our respondents' reports of their involvement in the three central-agency core functions considered in this book. These include development of an administration's strategic plan and the review of specific policy proposals in light of it, integration of economic and fiscal policies, and the allocation and management of physical and human resources. We will then examine how respondents characterize their operational style. To what degree do they see themselves as involved in policymaking, management and implementation, or communication?

After focusing on respondents' reports of their personal roles, we will move to a treatment of their perceptions of their agencies' functions. Here, the analysis will focus on their assessments of which core functions their agency emphasizes, the points in the policy process where it makes its presence felt, how it relates to sources of political authority, and how it compares to other agencies in the pursuit of its mandate.

Views of Personal Roles

With respect to respondents' perceptions of their own responsibilities, Table 2 summarizes those data relating to central-agency core functions. Even under the Carter administration, the findings suggest considerable unevenness in what career officials, amphibians, and politicos stressed in reporting their roles. While amphibians tended somewhat more to claim involvement in overall strategic planning for the administration than did career officials, politicos greatly outstripped both groups in orientations toward the role.[a] Over 30 percent of all groups saw themselves as helping to assure that substantive policy decisions actually adhered to the administration's strategic plan. Yet, 84 percent of politicos associated

Table 2

Respondents' Perceptions of Their Responsibilities Regarding Central Agency Core Functions (in percent)	Setting priorities and making substantive policy
	Strategic planning
	Substantive policy decisions
	Intergovernmental affairs
	Integrating economic and fiscal policy
	Tax policy
	Fiscal policy
	Macroeconomic policy
	Sectoral economic policy
	International economic policy
	Resource allocation and management
	Expenditure budgeting
	Organizational Structure
	Evaluation of effectiveness and efficiency
	Personnel policy
	Senior executive policy
	Administrative policy

themselves with this function, which was exactly double the comparable figure (42 percent) for amphibians.[a] Conversely, politicos apparently engaged themselves less than the others under Carter in shaping economic and fiscal policies[b] and allocating and managing resources.

Across administrations, the starkest differences appear regarding respondents' involvement in "strategic planning" and making "substantive policy decisions." Reagan appointees overwhelmingly revealed greater concern with the administration's political strategy and policy priorities than was registered by their counterparts under Carter.[a] However, they tended less than the Carter appointees to describe their direct involvement with efforts to assure that specific policy decisions take place in accordance with their admin-

Career N=69	Carter			Reagan		
	Amphibians N=38	Politicos N=25	All Appointees N=63	Amphibians N=29	Politicos N=31	All Appointees N=60
39	50	92	67	45	84	65
6	11	36	21	38	68	53
32	42	84	59	21	58	40
7	8	8	8	7	16	12
46	47	8	32	59	32	45
7	13	0	8	28	10	18
20	8	8	8	21	7	13
17	21	4	14	38	16	27
3	16	0	10	28	13	20
22	11	4	8	28	10	18
57	42	36	40	35	52	43
33	13	12	13	10	19	15
10	16	12	14	7	7	7
29	34	12	25	28	19	23
15	5	0	3	17	16	17
3	8	12	10	17	13	15
1	0	0	0	7	16	12

istration's overarching plans.[c] Interestingly, in view of the supply-
side and monetarist thrusts of his first term, Reagan's politicos
tended more than Carter's to claim some role in shaping economic
and fiscal policy.[c]

Table 3 presents our officials' responses to questions concerning
their stylistic approaches to their work. Before examining these
data, we should call upon a useful theoretical framework provided
by Joel D. Aberbach, Robert D. Putnam, and Bert A. Rockman.[7]
These authors maintain that four images might guide any attempt
to clarify government officials' views of how they operate in fulfillment of their functions. In each case, the images distinguish between the stylistic self-characterizations likely to emerge from
political appointees and permanent civil servants. A traditional,
turn-of-the-century image draws a sharp distinction between the
appointees and bureaucrats by asserting that the former make policy and the latter only administer it. Image I continues to hold
sway among some practitioners. However, it obscures the fact that
permanent officials exert immense discretion both in how they
carry out policies and the advice they give to their "masters."

Image II gained currency in the middle part of this century. It
appeared to provide a more accurate delineation of the roles of appointees and career civil servants. Although both partake in policy
decisions, the former seek simply to impart facts and knowledge

Table 3

Respondents' Descriptions of Their Approaches to Their Work (in percent)	
	Policy formation
	Policymaker
	Policy facilitator
	Policy adviser
	Management/implementation of policy
	Manager
	Implementor
	Communication
	Within government
	Outside government

while the latter stress the need to accommodate the conflicting values of diverse interests. Yet, as Aberbach, Putnam, and Rockman point up and as we will see later in this chapter, modern political appointees frequently bring to their work scholastic training and professional expertise rivaling those of permanent bureaucrats. This is especially the case with amphibians. As well, empirical research on career civil servants' actual involvement in the executive-bureaucratic arena indicates clearly that they scarcely shy away from mobilizing and mediating between various governmental and societal interests.

Aberbach, Putnam, and Rockman thus offer two additional images for the analysis of the roles of appointees and career bureaucrats. The first of these admits that the latter engage freely in politics. However, these permanent officials tend to mediate narrower bands of concerns than do appointees. As well, they normally eschew passionate and ideological commitments.

Image IV casts a shadow of doubt over even this modest amount of differentiation between the two groups. Citing *The Superbureaucrats* by Colin Campbell and George J. Szablowski, the authors maintain that two circumstances in advanced bureaucracies might cause career officials' stylistic approaches to merge with those of political appointees.[8] These conditions develop most readily in executive-bureaucratic arenas in which career officials work colle-

	Carter			Reagan		
Career N=69	Amphibians N=38	Politicos N=25	All Appointees N=63	Amphibians N=29	Politicos N=31	All Appointees N=60
97	95	96	95	93	87	90
6	16	20	18	21	26	23
38	34	56	43	62	58	60
75	82	64	75	72	45	58
36	40	28	35	52	29	40
32	26	16	22	41	19	30
6	16	12	14	21	13	17
23	34	48	40	31	61	47
17	18	18	18	28	61	45
12	24	44	32	7	36	22

gially with "outsiders" and "irregulars" and in central agencies involved in integrative tasks that cover the entire compass of government. Regarding the latter, Aberbach, Putnam, and Rockman make some points that bear upon any examination of career officials in highly developed central agencies:

> The staff members of these central agencies differ from more traditional civil servants in the broader, more flexible authority they enjoy; in their greater social representativeness and substantive innovativeness; and in their recognition of the legitimacy of politics—not merely in the sense of responsiveness to clientele interests, but in the broader sense that Image III ascribes to politicians alone.[9]

Table 3 summarizes our respondents' descriptions of their approaches to their work. The first of these centers on the nature of our officials' tasks. To what degree do these involve making policy, policy management and implementation, and communication? Virtually every member of all the major groups reported some functions related to policy. The very small proportion (6 percent) of career officials under Carter who attributed "policymaker" status to themselves fell far short of the comparable figures for amphibians and politicos, 16 and 20 percent, respectively. It is thus clear that all three Carter groups felt much more comfortable with styling themselves as "facilitators" and "advisers" than as policymakers per se. However, amphibians clustered closer to career officials than to politicos. In fact, the 34 percent of amphibians who saw themselves as facilitators fell just short of career officials and fully 22 points behind politicos who associated themselves with the approach (56 percent). Amphibians yielded the highest proportion among the Carter groups aligned in some way with policy management and implementation functions. As well, they came out more like career officials than politicos in their self-reports of involvement as communicators.

Such findings suggest a considerable convergence during the Carter administration between career officials' and amphibians' stylistic approaches. That is, both groups appear to fall between Images III and IV. While they revealed little ambivalence toward obligations within policy development, respondents eschewed giving expansive descriptions of their involvement. Their characterizations of their style employed language fitting more neutral images such as advising on policy, managing, and furthering communication within government. Scholars who have searched for a nascent culture of neutral brokers within the U.S. public service should take heart from such results.[10]

A counterindication of a trend toward convergence presents itself when we look at the Reagan appointees' stylistic preferences. Both amphibians and politicos under the current administration tended more than their opposite numbers during Carter to view their style at least partially with reference to policymaking. Relatedly, both Reagan groups yielded greater proportions claiming involvement in facilitation and smaller percentages styling themselves as policy advisers. In addition, Reagan amphibians espoused relatively strong interest in management functions. On the other hand, Reagan politicos demonstrated a much stronger orientation toward communication within government than did their equivalents under Carter[a] or their amphibian colleagues.[b] With respect to communication with Congress, interest groups, and attentive publics, Reagan amphibians stand out as far less consultative than both their Carter counterparts and politico associates.[b]

In a recent article, Donald Naulls and I report comparative research on the adoption of operational styles among central agents in the United States, the United Kingdom, and Canada. We found that where respondents locate themselves upon the policy-role ladder relates strongly to where they position themselves in relation to their policy arena's most formidable networks. In this respect, Canadian central agents provide the extreme case: "The clearest beneficiaries of insertion in policy networks ... walk along the most sharply delineated policy-maker path. That is, they tend not to interact with elements of the policy arena not rated as 'movers and shakers.' "[11]

We have seen in previous chapters the degree to which Reagan appointees tend to "roundtable" issues among themselves. As well, they maintain a sharp line of demarcation between themselves and career officials. Many of the latter believed that Reagan appointees had created for themselves a superbureaucratic sphere based on exclusion and conquest rather than convergence and consensus. The fact that Reagan amphibians made scant mention of communication outside of the executive branch perhaps provides us the first evidence of such an insular mentality.

Characterizations of Agency Roles

A crucial element to our respondents' views of their individual roles is their status as members of central agencies. These organizations shoulder specific responsibilities related to coordination and control of the operational units of government. Thus, how our officials describe the roles of these agencies tells us a great deal. The core function stressed by career officials, amphibians, or politicos might reflect differences in the positioning of the respective groups. Or the stylistic orientations of the Carter or Reagan administrations might work a separate effect. As well, group and administration influences might appear in relation to respondents' views of their agency's main approach to the policy process, reports of interactions with various administration leaders, and conceptions of which other central organizations wield influence within their general sphere of activity.

Regarding core roles (table 4), Carter politicos demonstrate a

Table 4

Respondents' Views of the Roles of Central Agencies (in percent)	Agency's role in relation to core functions
	Priority-setting, reviewing substantive decisions
	Economic/fiscal role
	Allocation/management role
	Agency's role in policy process
	Initiation
	Coordination
	Implementation
	Political leaders toward whom agency has special responsibilities
	President
	Cabinet members
	Agency head
	Deputy agency head
	Congressmen and senators

marked tendency to view their agency as oriented at least partially toward setting administration priorities and assessing policy initiatives in relation to these. Whereas only 46 and 55 percent of career officials and amphibians saw their agency in this light, fully 88 percent of politicos touched substantially on this core area.[b] This strong emphasis on priority-setting and substantive decision-making roles accompanied relatively low proportions of Carter politicos who construed their agency as involved in developing economic and fiscal policies[b] and/or guiding the allocation and management of government resources. Although they too give considerable weight to the priorities/substantive sector, the Reagan politicos cited the other roles somewhat more than did their counterparts under Carter.

Table 4 next summarizes respondents' characterizations of their organization's mode of operating within the policy process. Substantial shifts appear between the two administrations in politicos' perceptions of agency approaches. The three Carter groups all gave

Career N=69	Carter			Reagan		
	Amphibians N=38	Politicos N=25	All Appointees N=63	Amphibians N=29	Politicos N=31	All Appointees N=60
46	53	88	67	41	84	63
46	37	8	25	62	29	45
55	40	40	40	35	55	45
70	79	60	71	48	42	45
62	61	56	59	72	84	78
25	21	36	27	21	16	19
80	84	100	90	48	77	63
7	5	8	6	17	39	28
45	50	20	38	83	42	62
3	0	0	0	24	3	13
22	24	28	25	0	0	0

first billing to policy initiation (60 to 79 percent) and then extended fairly strong recognition to coordinative functions (56 to 62 percent and, finally, allowed relatively modest attention to implementation (21 to 36 percent). Here Carter politicos put forth the most even portrayals with 60, 56, and 36 percent mentioning initiation, coordination, and implementation, respectively. The Reagan appointees present a different picture. They give the nod to initiation[b] and implementation considerably less than do their counterparts under Carter. Moreover, they assign an exceptionally high profile to coordinative functions[b]

Similar patterns emerge with respect to respondents' references to various sources of political authority in describing their agency's roles. All Carter politicos made at least some mention of the president while rendering what their agency is supposed to do. The two other Carter groups both registered over 80 percent who accorded president-oriented roles to their agency. Less than 8 percent of each Carter group dwelt at all on agency functions in support of collective cabinet processes. While fairly substantial proportions of Carter career officials and amphibians mentioned their agency's head in describing its work (45 and 50 percent, respectively), only 20 percent of politicos did so.[c] Finally, much more even figures appeared under the attention given by Carter respondents to Congress. Between 22 and 28 percent of each group acknowledged congressional mandates and/or surveillance when outlining their agency's functions.

Along the lines that they followed above, Reagan appointees appear to subscribe to a much more distributed sense of authority *within* the executive branch. Almost equal proportions (63 and 62 percent) identified the president and/or their agency head as the source of their organizations' authority. Fully 28 percent ascribed some importance to responsibilities toward collective decision-making processes between cabinet secretaries. However, this inclusiveness did not extend to Congress. Reagan political appointees ignored Congress entirely in defining the roles of their agencies.

The relatively collective nature of the Reagan administration emerges once again in respondents' characterizations of their organization's role in relation to that of other agencies operating within its sphere. Table 5 presents the findings. The first heading displays the breakdowns of respondents' mentions of other agencies while outlining their own organization's role. Looking at differences between Carter career officials, amphibians and politicos, the two appointive groups tended more than the permanent officials to cite the White House,[a] OMB, the Treasury Department, and the Office of Personnel Management, and less to flag elements of Executive Office of the President other than OMB.[b]

If we distinguish, in examining references to the White House, between recognition of the "political" and "policy" offices, we discover that all three Carter groups yielded much higher proportions claiming interactions with the latter than with the former. As well, the Carter appointive groups indicated somewhat more than did career officials that their agency worked with the political and/or policy sides of the White House. In light of the Reagan White House's strong track record in the "implementation" of his legislative program, it comes as no surprise that Reagan's politicos gave exactly the same credence to the "political" and "policy" sides of the White House Office when ascribing to them substantial roles within their agency's main fields.

Respondents were asked to characterize their agency's and others' strong suits within the functional areas in which their activities overlap. Their answers touched upon six different approaches. These included neutral brokerage between contesting agencies, representation of clients either within or outside of the executive-bureaucratic complex, managing the policy decision making on the president's behalf, supporting collective processes within the administration, generating alternate views to those emerging from agencies, and providing expressly partisan input to issue assessments. Over 90 percent of both career officials and appointees under Carter believed that the other agencies operating within their organization's main areas gain entry by virtue of their responsibilities toward the president. Between 41 and 48 percent of each assigned some importance to other agencies' activities in the name of neutral brokerage. After that—apart from the 4 percent of career officials who pointed up a significant client orientation in other agencies' approaches—none of the other factors received mention at all. This duotonic pattern revealed itself again in the Carter respondents' characterizations of the strengths of their own agency. However, career officials tended less under this heading to emphasize their agency's activities on behalf of the president while appointees accorded less significance to neutral brokerage.

The Reagan appointees departed substantially from the limited compass adopted by the three groups during the Carter administration. The 77 percent who characterized the other organizations as

Table 5

Respondents' Reports of Their Agencies' Interactions with Other Central Agencies Involved in Their Area of Activity

Other agencies mentioned as overlapping with their own

Treasury Department
Office of Personnel Managemen
Office of Management and Bud
White House:
  Political side
  Policy side
Executive Office of the
  President (excluding OMB)
    Council of Economic Adviser
    Office of the U.S. Trade
      Representative

Characterizations of agencies' strengths in areas of overlapping activity
Other agencies
  Neutral brokerage between
    contestants
  Representation of clients
  Management of policy decisi
    making for the president
  Management of the collectiv
    process in administration
  Generating alternate views
  Adding partisan input to the
    assessment of issues
One's own agency
  Neutral brokerage between
    contestants
  Representation of clients
  Management of policy decisi
    making for the president
  Management of the collectiv
    process in administration
  Generating alternate views
  Adding partisan input to the
    assessment of issues

| | Carter | | | Reagan | | |
Career N=69	Amphibians N=38	Politicos N=25	All Appointees N=63	Amphibians N=29	Politicos N=31	All Appointees N=60
20	40	28	35	24	19	22
9	13	12	13	0	0	0
42	55	64	59	62	52	57
65	76	92	83	79	97	88
12	32	48	38	35	65	50
58	61	88	71	52	65	58
55	47	20	37	45	29	37
38	26	8	19	31	19	25
4	8	4	6	10	10	10
41	45	52	48	55	39	47
4	0	0	0	7	0	3
91	95	96	95	69	84	77
0	0	0	0	59	61	60
0	0	0	0	17	0	8
0	0	0	0	3	3	3
46	29	8	21	62	16	38
1	0	0	0	0	0	0
54	74	96	83	17	29	23
0	0	0	0	41	55	48
0	0	0	0	3	7	5
0	0	0	0	3	0	2

involved in managing matters on behalf of the president fell somewhat short of the 95 percent of Carter appointees giving the same
response.[b] Fully 60 percent of Reagan appointees associated the
other agencies with the collective decision-making process. No
Carter respondents—career or appointed—made such references. Similarly, 48 percent of Reagan appointees—as against no Carter respondents—viewed their own agency's approach to its role in relation to interagency dynamics.[a] Significantly, Reagan amphibians
assigned neutral brokerage between competing parties greater relevance than did both their opposite numbers under Carter[b] and their
politico colleagues.[a] Such findings probably stem from the relatively collective approach to decision making which the Reagan
administration followed during its first term.

Networks, Formal and Informal

Whenever Jimmy Carter and Ronald Reagan invoked the concept
"cabinet government," they tried to express how their administrations would attempt to decentralize presidential power. They sought
thus to correct in advance the tendency whereby virtually every contentious issue ends up in the Oval Office begging for resolution because differences between agencies proved irreconcilable. They also
wished to eschew the image of the imperial presidency evoked by the
Nixon administration when the White House tried to impose discipline by involving itself in the minutiae of departmental affairs.

As we have seen in the preceding chapters, the two presidents
took contrasting approaches to cabinet government. Carter viewed
structure as the bane of efforts toward decentralization. He opted
then for a free-form system. This would encourage cabinet secretaries to decide on their own initiative matters falling clearly within
their jurisdiction. In areas where they encountered the opposition
of colleagues, they would work through informal groups to settle
differences. Although Carter assured agency heads that each would
have equal access to the Oval Office, they were to sharply limit
their use of this court of last resort. In practice, spontaneous and
self-monitoring cabinet government simply did not work. In the
absence of group dynamics, cabinet secretaries never developed a
sense of teamwork. As well, Carter failed egregiously in exerting
the self-discipline necessary to stay out of issues until departmental and interagency gestation had run its course.

Reagan's approach operated from a diametrically different set of assumptions. Chester A. Newland has put these in a nutshell: basing appointments on unquestioned loyalty to the fundamental tenets of the administration; maintaining an overarching focus on broad strategic political strokes; and fostering policy networks within issue areas.[12] The Reagan administration's elaborate system of cabinet councils addressed the latter commitment. It sought self-consciously to build communities of interest between White House aides and administration appointees in the departments and agencies. The communities of interest, in turn, would attempt to settle divisive—though often quotidian—affairs, while at the same time maintaining officials' commitment to Reagan's most fundamental objectives. As Newland has put it:

> A structured but situationally adaptable White House/departmental policy network has been formed which accomplishes three purposes: (1) key departmental and White House officials and staffers are brought together in work on important issues minimizing (but not eliminating) we/they White House/agency divisions which plagued most recent administrations; (2) the cabinet councils, together with other network organizations, take initiatives and facilitate actions on vital second-level policy issues without compelling personal presidential attention to details, thus minimizing two problems of some recent administrations while compensating, in part, for President Reagan's orientation to generalization; and (3) the councils and the policy network help to keep the entire administration focused on the president's general aganda, resulting in unprecedented unity of direction.[13]

We will examine in this section our respondents' reports of policy networks within their sectors of activity. We will look at their perceptions of inner circles within the two administrations, their links with upper-echelon officials in central agencies and operational departments and their exposure to cabinet and interdepartmental committees. In particular, we will keep a weather eye for results which might stem from the different executive styles of the two administrations. Do the Carter soundings—taken in the first half of 1979—reflect the administration's difficulties with and ambivalence toward the spokes-in-a-wheel model? Do the Reagan findings reflect a relatively insular appointive community which bases its internal discipline in large part upon the dynamics of cabinet and subcabinet groups?

Inner Circles

During both administrations, nearly every respondent believed that inner circles dominate the policy process (table 6). In other words, they held that those who fail to win the support of certain key figures simply do not make headway on major issues. Interestingly, Reagan politicos appeared somewhat more likely than even Reagan amphibians to assert that this fact of life applied across the board—independent of issue clusters.[9]

When respondents detailed the qualities that determine membership in inner circles, the various groups gave a more diverse array of answers. Under Carter, between 67 and 68 percent of each group maintained that officials' formal positions substantially affected entry to inner circles. Yet, politicos tended less than career officials or amphibians to cite experience in government and subject-matter expertise (28 versus 48 and 50 percent, respectively).[b] Conversely, politicos gave greater weight than did either career officials or amphibians to the importance of the president's personal trust in attaining status within inner circles (60 versus 35 and 45 percent, respectively).

Other factors drew relatively few responses. These included political ability inside and outside government and personality character-

Table 6

Respondents' Views of Inner Circles and the Characteristics They Attribute to Members (in percent)	
	Are there inner circles?
	Yes: all responses
	Yes: unqualified response
	Yes: qualified response
	What determines membership in an inner circle?
	Formal position
	Experience and expertise
	Trust of the chief executive
	Political ability outside government
	Political ability inside government
	Personality characteristics

istics. With two exceptions, Reagan appointees did not depart dramatically from these patterns. Both of the Reagan groups, especially amphibians,[c] deemphasized the significance of experience and expertise in obtaining membership to inner circles. However, they stressed more than their Carter counterparts the salience of proven political ability outside of the official governmental apparatus.

Interactions

An examination of our respondents' accounts of the levels and frequency of their interactions within the executive-bureaucratic complex fleshes out still more differences between the Carter and Reagan administrations (table 7). With respect to interactions with the president, the Reagan appointive groups, especially politicos,[a] lagged considerably behind their Carter equivalents in exposure to the president. In fact, Reagan amphibians surpassed Carter career officials by only 7 percentage points in reports of interactions with the president. On the other hand, respondents in the three Carter and two Reagan groups demonstrated a remarkable evenness in their accounts of interactions both with their agency principals and deputy heads. This element of uniformity across administrations and

	Carter			Reagan		
Career N=69	Amphibians N=38	Politicos N=25	All Appointees N=63	Amphibians N=29	Politicos N=31	All Appointees N=60
78	92	84	89	86	81	83
32	37	32	35	31	52	42
17	24	24	24	10	19	15
67	68	68	68	66	61	63
48	50	28	41	21	16	18
35	45	60	51	52	52	52
3	3	8	5	7	23	15
4	8	16	11	7	10	8
4	5	4	5	0	7	3

between groups breaks down, however, with respect to interactions with top officials in other agencies. Under Carter, career officials clearly maintained weaker links than did amphibians and politicos with other agency principals[a] and deputies.[a]

With regard to Newland's networking thesis, we might expect that formal meetings took on a special significance as the settings for interactions under the Reagan administration. Actually, fewer Reagan than Carter appointees, especially Reagan politicos,[b] reported that they interacted with the president directly through phone calls, relatively private sessions in the Oval Office, *or* larger meetings. Yet the very small percentages of both groups interacting in the former two settings indicate that larger meetings provided the only occasion for direct exposure to the president for an overwhelming proportion of Reagan appointees.

Committee Work

The greatly enhanced emphasis on cabinet-level committees under Reagan comes through very clearly in table 8. However, Carter's presidency did not run totally without the benefit of such bodies.

Table 7

Respondents' Interactions within the
Executive-Bureaucratic Complex
(in percent)

Interaction

With the president
  Frequency
    At least once a month
    At least once a week
  Form
    Telephone call
    Personal visit
    Official meeting

With own agency head

With heads of other agencies
  or departments

With deputy of one's own agency

With deputies of other agencies
  or departments

On the national security side, Carter's policy review committees and special coordination committees provided fairly regularized cabinet-level forums. Some of our respondents enjoyed access to these. In domestic affairs, the Economic Policy Group—including its executive and steering committees, the forecasting troika, and numerous ad hoc task forces did afford some officials exposure to meetings of cabinet secretaries.

Regarding the density of such involvement among Carter respondents, politicos exceeded amphibians who in turn outstripped career officials both in the number and regularity of their cabinet committee obligations. Clearly, cabinet committees formed a much more important part of the work worlds of Reagan appointees than they did for those of Carter officials. More Reagan appointees than their Carter counterparts attended at least one committee,[b] attended two or more committees,[c] and attended them on a regular basis.[a]

With respect to the policy fields covered, the proportion of all Reagan appointees reporting involvement in cabinet-level bodies concerned with national security, international economics, and domestic economic affairs exceeded 40 percent under all three head-

Career N=69	Carter			Reagan		
	Amphibians N=38	Politicos N=25	All Appointees N=63	Amphibians N=29	Politicos N=31	All Appointees N=60
38	66	96	78	45	48	47
4	32	72	48	38	42	40
1	24	56	37	28	32	30
0	5	20	11	0	10	5
3	18	52	32	14	19	17
35	63	88	73	45	48	47
83	97	80	90	86	84	85
51	79	100	87	79	84	82
68	63	56	60	69	48	58
33	61	64	62	72	68	70

ings. Not reported on table 8—there were no comparable bodies during the Carter administration—were the 28 percent of Reagan appointees who claimed some level of participation in the Cabinet Council on Management and Administration, the 30 percent who said that they attended with some regularity either the Budget Review Board or the Legislative Strategy Group, and the 48 percent who involved themselves often in cabinet councils responsible for domestic issues other than economics. Under all seven headings, the proportion of Reagan politicos reporting involvement with relevant committees exceeded those for amphibians. Yet, even the two groups of Carter appointees registered considerably less direct involvement with cabinet-level bodies than did the Reagan respondents in the areas which were covered by ongoing committees (all comparisons are significant at minimally the .05 level).

In theory, institutionalized cabinet-level consultation advances communication between more than simply the principals involved with policy issues. Regularized bodies operating at the most senior level should improve networking within an administration. This should extend to links among key officials at lower political

Table 8

Respondents' Committee Participation
(in percent)

Cabinet-level field
   National security
   International economics
   Economic affairs

Cabinet-level committee
   attendance
   Number of committees
   One or more
   Two or more
   Frequency of attendance
   Regular
   Periodic

Subcabinet committee
   attendance
   One or more
   Five or more

strata—even those with bases outside the charmed circle of central agencies. Improved networking does not necessarily mean, however, that formal interdepartmental bodies functioning with subcabinet members will take on new life. As Aberbach, Putnam, and Rockman note, officials who gain relatively free access to the most senior councils of the executive branch often will disengage themselves from lower-level bodies.[14]

My comparison of American, British, and Canadian central agents found that the latter functioned under the most complex and routinized system of cabinet-level bodies.[15] As well, Canadian central agents enjoyed by far the easiest access to deliberations at this level. They also rendered much more expansive reports of participation in such bodies. Along the lines developed by Aberbach, Putnam, and Rockman, the Canadians—in every respect—ascribed substantially less importance to subcabinet committees than did American and British central agents. Notwithstanding the plethora of bodies at this level in Ottawa, the Canadian respondents simply exercised relative restraint in engaging themselves personally in such committees.

Career N=69	Carter			Reagan		
	Amphibians N=38	Politicos N=25	All Appointees N=63	Amphibians N=29	Politicos N=31	All Appointees N=60
12	18	16	17	38	48	43
6	3	0	2	41	65	53
6	18	16	17	41	55	48
30	47	68	56	79	81	80
4	24	24	24	35	52	43
10	16	32	22	55	48	52
19	34	36	35	28	32	30
87	90	96	92	90	61	75
15	24	44	32	48	23	35

The Carter administrations' stylistic approach occasioned remarkably equal subcabinet committee participation among the career officials, amphibians, and politicos. Between 87 and 96 percent of the three groups attended at least one committee on a regular basis. However, many more politicos than either career officials or amphibians said that they belonged to five or more committees.[b]

Reagan politicos' reports of their involvement with subcabinet panels appear to fit our expectations based on the comparable data on Canadian central agents. That is, officials with high exposure to cabinet-level bodies will find less time for committees operating without principals. Under Reagan, substantially smaller proportions of politicos than their Carter counterparts[b] or their own amphibian colleagues[c] said that they regularly attend at least one interdepartmental committee. Parallel results emerged with regard to the tendency of Reagan politicos not regularly participating in five or more committees. On the other hand, a more pervasive networking appears to show itself among Reagan amphibians. These proved twice as likely as their Carter equivalents to cite five or more committees which they attended regularly.[c] In several respects, Reagan amphibians viewed interdepartmental committees differently from their politico colleagues as well. They more often reported involvement in one or more committees[c] and five or more bodies.[c]

Getting Beyond the Executive-Bureaucratic Milieu

The assertion that subgovernments—including bureaucrats developing and administering executive-branch programs, their extragovernmental clients, and congressmen and their staff members—emerge within every substantial issue area has become an old saw in American political science.[16] Some of these three-way relationships have taken on such institutionalized form that authors have even styled them "iron triangles." Such executive-legislative-public relationships frequently occur within various policy sectors along extremely open lines—at least for perennial players in an issue area. However, dysfunctions emerge when such networks become so routinized that the perspectives of occasional pleaders and usual outsiders simply do not register. In fact, as Jimmy Carter found, subgovernments often remain impermeable even when the president attempts to promote initiatives nearest and dearest to him.

Table 9 examines two dimensions to the subgovernment issue as it relates to central agents. First, to what degree do respondents under our two administrations interact with senators, members of Congress, and congressional staffers in the course of their work? Second, how extensively do they consult with individuals, groups, and interests outside of the federal government on the various issues that concern them?

At first blush, we might expect that Carter appointees would outstrip both career officials and Reagan amphibians and politicos in contacts with Capitol Hill and involvement with those outside the federal government. It seemed, at least, that the Carter administration largely deserved the image of "special interest politics." Even the residual effects of the public backlash to this approach appeared to have plagued Walter Mondale's drive for the presidency from the primary phase to the bitter end.

A caveat comes to mind here that qualifies the expectation that Carter appointees will prove more active on the congressional front and in public liaison. Clearly, the Reagan approach eschews the type of programmatic detail which would mire its senior officials in protracted negotiations with those outside the federal government. For that matter, the pronounced ideological cohesion of the Reagan appointees has sharply limited the spectrum of views meriting serious consideration in the tightest circles of the administration. On the congressional side, however, the Reagan administration has operated more responsively.

Reagan's sweeping initiatives during his first term did not invite fine-tuning. Nonetheless, the administration chalked up an outstanding "win" record in congressional votes. Admittedly, Reagan's strong electoral victory and sustained public support convinced many moderates in both parties that the president's policies reflected with extreme accuracy the increasingly conservative pulse of the nation. However, Reagan's bonhomie produced optimal results from his numerous direct contacts with wavering legislators. That is, it won congressional hearts into giving assent to what the mind could not embrace. Moreover, the "implementation side" of the White House—headed by James Baker—went beyond the astute use of presidential charm to excellent stage management. It sharply limited Reagan's legislative commitments to those with real prospects of victory. As well, it executed with exceptional intelligence and thoroughness each major effort to win over enough faint congressional hearts for sure victory.

Table 9 reveals that under Carter the two appointive groups registered considerably more involvement with senators and members of Congress than did Carter career officials. Indeed, they were more likely to have interacted at this level at least every month[a] or every week.[a] The figures for relations with congressional staff present a less straightforward picture. Greater proportions of Carter appointees than career officals said that they interacted with staff mem-

Table 9

Respondents' Interactions with Congress and Outside Groups and Interests (in percent)

Frequency of interactions with
    Congress
    With senators
        At least once a month
        At least once a week
    With members of Congress
        At least once a month
        At least once a week
    With congressional staffers
        At least once a month
        At least once a week
    Outside groups consulted
        News media
        Political leaders and party
            workers
        Business leaders
        Union leaders
        Farm group leaders
        Local officials
        State officials
        Religious leaders
        Ethnic groups
            (includes civil rights groups)
        Friends and acquaintances
        Citizens' groups
        Poll takers
        Academics
        Other professionals

bers at least once a week. However, greater percentages of career officials claimed at least some level of interaction with staffers.

An examination of Reagan appointees' interactions with Capitol Hill uncovers one strong theme. Consistent with their stylistic preferences as summarized in table 3, amphibians had much less involvement with Capitol Hill than did politicos. The gap between the two Reagan groups narrows substantially, however, when we

Career N=69	Carter			Reagan		
	Amphibians N=38	Politicos N=25	All Appointees N=63	Amphibians N=29	Politicos N=31	All Appointees N=60
62	82	92	86	59	87	73
22	50	68	57	45	81	63
13	29	64	43	41	74	58
70	82	88	84	59	84	72
22	53	64	57	45	81	63
13	29	60	41	41	74	58
73	58	64	60	38	58	48
51	42	48	44	35	55	45
32	40	44	41	21	45	33
49	55	64	59	45	65	55
4	18	64	37	21	71	47
77	79	68	75	62	81	72
29	53	48	51	38	48	43
10	18	36	25	17	48	33
33	55	56	56	31	52	42
36	55	60	57	31	48	40
13	37	36	37	10	42	27
22	55	60	57	14	45	30
42	53	60	56	48	68	58
35	47	48	48	14	48	32
6	24	36	29	0	29	15
52	50	24	40	48	32	40
46	40	20	32	38	36	37

look at their exposure to congressional staff. In comparison to their Carter counterparts, larger proportions of Reagan politicos stated that they touched base with senators and/or congressmen at least once a week. The same contrast may be seen in the responses of amphibians in each administration: 41 percent of Reagan amphibians tended to say that they had weekly contacts with congressmen and/or senators, compared to 29 percent of Carter amphibians.

Table 9 also summarizes the proportions of the various interview groups saying that they consulted with specific sources of advice and information outside of the federal government. Looking first at the three Carter groups, especially strong differences reveal themselves with reference to nine external sources listed on the table. Such results took in consultation of political leaders and party workers,[a] union leaders,[b] farm group representatives,[b] local officials,[b] state authorities,[b] religious leaders,[b] ethnic and civil rights group representatives, public opinion polls,[a] and academics.[c]

The outside groups cited by all three types of Carter appointees fitted nicely with what we might expect. The 64 percent of politicos who cited political leaders and party workers exceeded by far the comparable figures for the other groups (18 and 4 percent for amphibians and career officials, respectively).[a] Both politicos and amphibians revealed a stronger desire than career officials at least to touch base with a fairly eclectic circle of outside concerns. That is, similarly greater proportions of both groups than found among career officials gave the nod to union officials,[b] religous leaders,[b] ethnic and civil rights groups,[a] citizens' groups, state officials,[b] and local officials.[b]

In yet another important respect, the career and amphibian groups seemed to be parallel. They both appeared to value more than twice as much as did politicos the advice and information they received from academics[c] and other professionals. This finding corresponds well with the fact that a shared regard for expertise serves as the main potential bond between career officials and amphibians. Perhaps most interesting, among all three Carter groups the highest proportion mentioned business leaders among their outside sources of advice and information. All the figures are robust, namely, 77, 79, and 68 percent for the career, amphibian, and politico groups, respectively.

As anticipated, the Reagan respondents reported less inclusive consultation with outside groups than did Carter appointees. Of the fourteen potential outside sources, the figures for Reagan appointees exceeded the Carter ones only in four cases. These included references to political leaders and party workers, farm group leaders, friends and acquaintances, and other professionals. However, the margins between the Carter and Reagan people mostly fell within relatively modest ranges. Only Reagan appointees' hesitance about consultation with ethnic and civil-rights group representatives attained statistical significance.[b] When we compare Carter and Reagan politicos, the ranges became even narrower. In fact, the latter respondents actually produced higher percentages than did the former with respect to eight of the fourteen potential sources.

Under all but two categories, Reagan politicos ascribed more importance to the various sources of advice and information than did their amphibian colleagues. The differences come out as particularly pronounced with reference to consultation of political leaders and party workers,[a] farm group leaders,[c] religious leaders,[b] ethnic and civil rights group representatives,[b] and friends and acquaintances. Although neither margin reached statistical significance, amphibians led politicos in those mentioning academics and other professionals as sources of advice and information. As with all of the Carter groups, business leaders were more often cited by both Reagan amphibians and politicos than was any other source.

Accountability

Traditionally, examinations of officials' accountability involve an assessment of the relative roles of individual and institutional standards of behavior in shaping their goals and activities.[17] Here "subjective" officials would give the strongest weight to moral convictions, professional standards, and views of governance based on individualized—if not idiosyncratic—formulations of accountability. On the other hand, "objective" officials would see their various commitments through institutionalized prisms. For instance, rigorously socialized career officials would balance their obligations in light of fairly constricted notions of public service.

The real-world views of accountability that actually take hold in officials rarely fit neatly into one of these two extreme types. That is, public servants normally combine subjective standards with those learned in the institutional context. These amalgams, in turn, will be influenced by the positions officials hold, the nature of the system of executive leadership within which they operate, and the bureaucratic subculture to which they belong. However, we can certainly envision a cluster of circumstances that would strongly reinforce subjective orientations toward accountability among officials. For instance, senior public servants might hold positions in which they are called upon to tender advice directly to the highest political authorities. Relatedly, the internal politics of their work world might require that they engage fully in executive-bureaucratic gamesmanship.

Table 10 first looks at our central agents' reports regarding the authorities to whom they feel accountable. These fall within four broad categories. The first, authority within a hierarchy, includes bureaucratic superiors, the president, and heads of the agents' departments; the second, collective authority, includes the cabinet and Congress; the third, generalized/external authority, includes the people as a whole and individual segments of the public; and the fourth, individual authority, includes personal conscience and professional standards. Focusing first on Carter respondents: hierarchical authority received the greatest number of mentions from all three groups (90 percent for career officials and 100 percent for both amphibians and politicos). Within this broad category, however, the three groups emphasized different objects. Career officials disproportionately said they were accountable to superiors short of their agency head;[a] politicos, to the president;[b] and amphibians, to their agency head.[c] With the exception of the last, amphibians' responses fell midway between those of career officials and politicos.

All three groups gave the next greatest emphasis to individual sources of accountability. Here the 83 percent of career officials who mentioned either or both personal conscience and professional standards exceeded somewhat the figures for amphibians and politicos (63 and 68 percent, respectively). Personal conscience appears to matter increasingly when we move from career officials through amphibians to politicos. The converse is true for professional standards.[a] With respect to the cluster attracting the third greatest number of mentions, between 40 and 45 percent of all three groups recognized either the general public and/or specific segments of society as the authority to which they felt answerable. However, of the two, the general notion that one should keep the public good in mind far outweighed the other. This leaves us with the least mentioned category, namely, collective authority within the federal government, noted by 20–34 percent of the three groups. (Amphibians yielded the latter figure.) What appears to make a difference here is the 8 percent of amphibians who were prepared to acknowledge their accountability to the cabinet. That is, the groups' references to Congress ranged relatively narrowly between 20 and 26 percent—although amphibians produced the largest figure here as well.

For the Reagan groups, as with Carter appointees, the largest proportion of respondents cited hierarchical and individual sources of accountability. However, the final two clusters, generalized/external authority and collective authority, exchanged places. The Reagan respondents appeared somewhat more inclined than the Carter people to say they were partially accountable to a segment of the population, rather than the public at large. They proved to be one-fourth as likely to give cognizance to the general public as an object of accountability.[a] On the other hand, the Reagan groups assigned just slightly less weight to Congress as an authority than did the Carter respondents. Most significantly—especially in view of their administration's stress on collective dynamics—the 35 percent of Reagan appointees who claimed a sense of accountability to the cabinet exceeded the Carter figure by fully 30 percent.[a] With regard to individual sources of accountability, the Carter and Reagan appointees differed in that the former gave stronger emphasis to personal conscience and the latter placed heavier stress upon professional standards. In fact, the Reagan amphibians mentioned professional standards considerably more than both their Carter counterparts[c] and their politico colleagues.[b]

A theme associated with the designation of their administration's style as following a modified spokes-in-a-wheel pattern suggests itself when we examine the two Reagan groups' perceptions of hierarchical accountability. Both amphibians and politicos yielded close to the same proportions stating that accountability to the president was important. Yet Reagan politicos set off in other directions in two respects. They tended more than twice as much as their Carter counterparts to note that they owed part of their accountability to a hierarchical superior short of an agency head.[c] On the other hand, only 42 percent—as against 76 percent for Carter politicos—said that they held themselves accountable to their agency head.[c] These findings appear to reflect the simple fact that Reagan's administration has employed hierarchical layering, especially within the White House, more extensively than did Carter's.

In addition to ascertaining respondents' objects of accountability, the questions upon which this section is based probed officials'

Table 10

Respondents' Views of Accountability
(in percent)

One is accountable to:
  Authority within a hierarchy
    To one's superior
    To the president
    To one's department head
  Collective authority
    To the cabinet
    To Congress
  Generalized/external authority
    To the people as a whole
    To a segment of the public
  Individual authority
    To one's conscience
    To professional standards

One chooses standards of
  behavior according to:
  Subjective criteria
    Moral convictions
    Professional standards
  Objective criteria
    Requirements of public
      service as a vocation
    Agency's mandates and
      rules
    Responsibilities to
      career superiors
    Responsibilities to
      appointed superiors
  Collective interests among
    agency coworkers
    Desire to develop collegial
      problem-solving skills
    Desire to develop transferable
      skills
    Sensitivity to peer feedback
    Loyalty to colleagues

Career N=69	Carter			Reagan		
	Amphibians N=38	Politicos N=25	All Appointees N=63	Amphibians N=29	Politicos N=31	All Appointees N=60
90	100	100	100	97	94	95
84	68	32	54	79	65	72
58	71	92	79	62	87	75
67	90	76	84	40	42	65
23	34	20	29	48	48	48
0	8	0	5	38	32	35
23	26	20	24	17	23	20
45	40	40	40	14	19	17
45	40	40	40	7	7	7
4	5	12	8	10	23	17
83	63	68	65	83	61	72
36	45	56	39	31	45	38
75	52	36	46	83	45	63
88	79	92	84	93	71	82
25	45	60	51	21	29	25
71	53	36	46	86	52	68
83	74	72	73	82	90	87
49	8	4	6	35	10	22
36	16	16	16	31	13	22
20	11	4	8	14	0	7
45	63	60	62	59	84	72
52	42	28	37	72	68	70
38	34	24	30	31	45	38
20	18	20	19	14	23	18
6	11	12	11	7	3	5
17	11	8	10	38	26	32

answers in an effort to find the rationales for their preferences. These fell within three broad categories. First, officials often discussed subjective motives for selecting one or other object of accountability. Here they dwelt upon moral convictions, professional standards, and/or democratic values. Second, our central agents frequently invoked objective criteria for their choices. These included the requirements of public service as a vocation, the mandates and norms that guide their agency, and/or line responsibilities toward career or appointed superiors. Finally, many respondents went beyond the subjective/objective dichotomy by noting elements of life at their level in the executive-bureaucratic arena that make accountability more than simply finding a balance between two extremes. Such "collective" factors include an interest in improving collegial problem solving, a willingness to develop skills that enhance their mobility between units and agencies, sensitivity to feedback from peers, and loyalty to colleagues.

Among the Carter groups, objective standards fell just short of subjective criteria in their cumulative appeal to respondents. The ranges for those citing objective standards were 72–83 percent, as against 79–92 percent for subjective ones. The collective interests drew considerably less comment. Of career officials and amphibians, 52 and 42 percent cited these factors, while only 28 percent of politicos did so. With respect to the ways in which the various groups sorted through the components of the broad categories, the clearest differences appeared under the subjective headings. Here politicos yielded the largest proportions claiming that moral convictions[b] and/or democratic values[c] undergirded their views of accountability. Career officials, on the other hand, emphasized more than the other groups the role played by professional standards.[b] In the case of all three factors, amphibians occupied the middle ground between the other two groups.

Regarding the objective standards, the responses of career officials were sharply different from those of amphibians. Career officials distinguished themselves in references to their peculiar vocation as public servants,[a] specific mandates and rules,[c] and responsibilities toward other career officials. Amphibians and politicos outstripped career officials in mentioning obligations toward superiors who are appointees by 18 and 15 percentage points, respectively. Insofar as collective criteria for accountability emerged, career officials and then amphibians tended most to acknowledge one or more of the items in this category.

The Reagan appointees were more expansive in citing factors under the three categories of influences on their views of accountability. Among amphibians and politicos, 93 and 71 percent, respectively, cited subjective criteria,[a] and 82 and 90 percent noted objective criteria, while 72 and 68 percent spoke of collective interests. The latter percentages greatly exceeded the comparable figures for the Carter appointees: 42 percent for amphibians,[c] and 28 percent for politicos.[b] Here the Reagan respondents' stronger sense of obligation toward their colleagues in the administration appeared to account for much of the difference both in the case of the amphibians (38 percent as opposed to 11 percent for their Carter counterparts),[b] and politicos (26 percent as opposed to only 8 percent among the Carter group).

Notwithstanding the aggregate frequency of their references to subjective rationales for accountability, Reagan amphibians and politicos gave considerably less weight to moral convictions[c] and democractic values[a] than did their opposite numbers under Carter. In turn, the two Reagan groups favored professional standards more strongly than did the Carter respondents (86 percent for amphibians[b]). Concerning objective criteria, the Reagan groups again appeared to register a stronger espirit de corps than was manifested by appointees under Carter. Here, the amphibians aligned themselves with the vocational dimensions to public service,[b] and mandates and rules more than did their equivalents under Carter. The politicos gave substantially greater attention to perceived responsibilities toward their appointive superior.[c]

Views of Careers and the Paths Followed

In *The Superbureaucrats*, George Szablowski and I asserted at the outset that central agents' views of public service and career paths differ sharply from those that have prevailed within traditional bureaucratic systems.[18] In conventional bureaucracies, officials had to pass rigorously applied merit criteria before winning their positions. These standards normally did not include requirement of advanced academic degrees. Generalist skills, it was believed, best suited government service. In-service training and developmental placement, insofar as these played a part, sought simply to instill in new recruits the folkways of the existing higher-level bureaucratic community. Loyalty, dependability, and length of service determined officials' upward mobility, which usually occurred slowly and deliberately.

Central agents often attain their exceptional standing while breaking many canons guiding traditional bureaucratic careers. Their very entrance into public service might ride on explicitly ascriptive characteristics such as personal dynamism, knowing the right people, or having the desired political coloration. Indeed, representational or affirmative-action criteria might enter into their recruitment and career advancement. In addition, central agents frequently use advanced degrees and subject-matter expertise as their vehicle for admission to and mobility within their public-service cadre. Finally, the process by which they achieve advancement places a premium on imaginativeness and executive-bureaucratic gamesmanship rather than loyalty and seniority.

Many of these points of comparison correspond nicely with the Aberbach, Putnam and Rockman Image IV formulation. That is, they operate at the root of the transformation of bureaucratic cultures whereby officials in the most prized positions, like central agents, begin to view their place within the policy arena as self-consciously political. In fact, in their analysis of younger German officials' relatively strong orientations to political roles, the authors discern a strong connection between career orientations and routes, and Image IV perspectives.

> A rapid generational shift occurred in the period prior to our interviewing, as men who retired were replaced by significantly younger bureaucrats (men in their early fifties) because of the "missing" World War II generation in Germany. And these younger men were more activist and reformist than their predecessors, even allowing for party sympathies.[19]

Table 11 presents the data bearing on career orientations and paths in our current Carter-Reagan comparison. The first set of variables touches on respondents' recollections of why they entered government. As to their motives for entering public service, the three Carter groups rendered contrasting accounts of why they came into government. Career officials gave fairly substantial credit to vocational idealism (32 percent) and scholastic training tailored for public service (33 percent). However, fully 61 percent of the permanent officials straightforwardly admitted that their decision originated at least partially from the attractiveness of a public service career to a youth seeking upward mobility and/or desiring a meaningful outlet for acquired skills. Forty-seven percent of amphibians also cited such motives. This left a large gap, with the 12 percent of politicos giving similar responses.[a] Amphibians set themselves apart when 55 percent—as against 12 percent for each of the other groups—mentioned career experiences garnered before joining government.[a] A much larger proportion of politicos than emerged from the other groups (84 percent versus 4 percent for career officials and 21 percent for amphibians) noted that explicit partisan or political commitments had brought them into government.[a]

The above findings correspond with what we might expect. They provide evidence of the role of the permanent civil service as a creative outlet for highly trained specialists seeking socioeconomic advancement along with career security. As well, they suggest a specialist syndrome among amphibians. These officials trade on detailed knowledge of policy issues and how public and private organizations really operate. Finally, the results concerning politicos reflect the depth of partisanship among appointees who won their spurs through skill in campaign operations and dedication to political causes.

The Reagan appointive groups contrasted with one another and with Carter amphibians and politicos in several interesting ways. Both Reagan groups underscored the salience of their scholastic training to their decision to enter government more than did even career officials under Carter. In fact, a 43 percent margin appeared between mentions of this motive by amphibians under the two administrations.[a] Both Reagan groups were relatively taken by the glamour and excitement of working in government. That is, 41 percent of Reagan as against eight percent of Carter amphibians[b] and 26 percent of Reagan as compared to 12 percent of Carter politicos said that they entered government at least partially because of the psychic stimulus involved with being at the center of an administration.

Reagan politicos tended more than four times as often as their amphibian colleagues to attribute some significance to partisan or political commitments.[b] However, they fell considerably short of Carter politicos in acknowledging this motive.[b] Relatedly, four times as many Reagan politicos as their equivalents under Carter said that entering government provided an opportunity for career advancement.[b] Quite remarkably, only 14 percent of Reagan amphibians—as against 55 percent under Carter—attributed significance to career experience outside of government as an element in their decision to enter public service. In sum, the Reagan appoin-

Table 11

Respondents' Career Orientations and Paths
(in percent)

Reasons for entering
government
  Idealism, desire to serve
  Scholastic training
  Desire to be "where the
    action is"
  Previous career
    experience
  Interest in a specific
    policy sector
  To seek career opportunity
  To express partisan or
    political commitment

When decision was made to
enter federal government
  Before university
  After university,
    military service
  In mid-career

Number of years in federal
government
  1–5
  6–10
  11–20
  21+

Number of years in present
department
  0–3
  4–9
  10+

Number of previous positions
in federal government
  1+
  2+
  3+
  4+

	Carter			Reagan		
Career N=69	Amphibians N=38	Politicos N=25	All Appointees N=63	Amphibians N=29	Politicos N=31	All Appointees N=60
32	18	36	25	10	16	13
33	26	16	22	69	39	53
16	8	12	10	41	26	21
12	55	12	38	14	16	15
6	11	12	11	3	0	2
61	47	12	33	41	48	45
4	21	84	46	10	45	28
13	5	20	11	7	10	8
64	29	44	35	49	45	47
23	66	36	54	45	45	45
10	68	72	70	45	42	43
13	13	16	14	28	29	28
44	11	12	11	7	26	17
33	8	0	5	21	3	12
29	87	100	92	79	100	90
25	11	0	6	10	0	5
46	3	0	2	10	0	5
73	66	64	65	59	84	72
42	40	20	32	31	39	35
19	13	8	11	14	13	13
8	5	8	6	3	7	5

tees, in explaining how they got into government, stressed their educational backgrounds over previous career experience and the desire for career advancement and interesting work over partisan and political commitments.

If our respondents had followed classic career patterns, they would have decided upon public service early, even before attending university, would have enjoyed relatively lengthy service both in government and in their current departments, would have occupied a number of positions in a paced climb up the bureaucratic ladder, and would admit to a dearth of experience in the private sector.[20] Even in more traditional bureaucratic systems, however, central agents frequently follow career paths that short-circuit the canons of classic career development.[21] Here a personal-advancement motive might have taken hold at the outset. That is, many officials select government careers, at the earliest, after completion of their education, and often after some experience in the private sector. Once entering public service, many such recruits become high-fliers, rising rapidly to the top with relatively little regard to length of service in government or specific departments.

We can expect that this examination of U.S. central agents will reveal a less straightforward case of a fluid bureaucratic culture than that prevailing among central agents in some advanced democracies. U.S. career officials tend to remain in the same department for most of their careers.[22] The offices in which they work take on the character of large departments in prestigious universities. Once members have established themselves in a policy shop, they enjoy a relative assurance that they can remain within their chosen specialized area as long as they wish. Leadership of these units tends to go to exactly the types of long-serving and highly regarded individuals who assume the chairmanship of the traditional academic departments. Presumably, the career routes of permanent officials among our central agents will reflect these broader patterns.

The findings in table 11 reveal that few in all five respondent groups aspired to a government career before their university years. In fact, only 20 percent of Carter and 10 percent of Reagan politicos traced their career choice that far back, yet these constituted the largest proportions giving this response under either administration. Under Carter, this leaves career officials with the largest percentage having made their decision after completing a university degree and/or military service.[b] Meanwhile, amphibians tended much more than the other groups to set their choice midway in their work lives.[a] Under Reagan, 10 percent or less of both groups recalled making their decision to enter government early on. However, they divided evenly between those who associated their choice with post-university years and those who said that they made their decision in mid-career.

Two of the above results fit especially well with what we might expect. There is an absence of a strongly vocational public service tradition in the United States. It stands to reason, thus, that career officials would report relatively late decisions to enter government. Carter filled many policy-oriented appointive positions with subject-matter experts lacking governmental experience. This probably operates at the root of the fact that a majority of his amphibians said that they aspired to government service midway through their careers.

Looking at the length of our respondents' tenure both in the federal government and their departments, we find that the career officials logged the most service. They supplied by far the largest proportion of Carter respondents who had spent eleven to twenty[a] or over twenty years[a] in government, and four to nine[b] or over nine years[a] in their department. Fully 70 percent of Carter appointees had worked in government less than six years, over 92 percent had served in their department less than four years. In line with their public image as somewhat more experienced cadres of appointees, substantially fewer Reagan amphibians[b] and politicos[b] admitted to less than six years of experience in government than did their Carter equivalents. However, the two Reagan groups did not significantly outshine Carter amphibians and politicos in service in their department beyond three years.

As we have noted, U.S. permanent officials tend to center their careers within one unit of their department. This pattern emerged clearly in respondents' reports of how many positions they have held while in government. Very few had filled four or more. Career officials among the Carter respondents proved only slightly more likely than amphibians to have passed through two or more (42 versus 40 percent) or three or more previous positions (19 versus 13 percent). The Reagan appointive groups did not differ markedly from their Carter equivalents in the frequency with which they had occupied different posts.

Educational and Social Backgrounds

In advanced Western democracies, high-level bureaucracy has not presented itself as a strong career prospect for those with humble origins. Moreover, some public services have shown a marked preference for recruits who fulfill very specific elite educational criteria. Several studies have uncovered continued evidence of the socioeconomic elitism of senior officialdom in many countries. For instance, Robert D. Putnam has reported that senior officials in Italy, Germany, and Britain continue to come predominantly from the middle and upper classes.[23] As well, Germany and Italy still strongly favor candidates with training in law, while Britain gives a very strong edge to generalists with "Oxbridge" degrees. Ezra N. Suleiman's study of the three corps that supply most senior bureaucrats in France found a number of recruitment biases.[24] For instance, a strong regional favoritism revealed itself in the fact that an overwhelming majority of corps members attended elite Parisian lycées.

Studies of the educational and socioeconomic backgrounds of high-level U.S. officials reveal similar, although less pronounced, biases. Mann, Stanley, and Doig examined the backgrounds of senior U.S. officials from 1933 to 1965.[25] They reported that these came disproportionately from large cities in the East, and tended strongly to be well educated and Protestant. Joel D. Aberbach and Bert A. Rockman, in a later study, compared the backgrounds of senior political appointees and career civil servants.[26] They found that the former grew up in higher-status households and earned their degrees at more prestigious universities than did the latter. They also tended more to have taken law degrees. Larger proportions of career officials, on the other hand, had studied social or management sciences. Nonetheless, both groups could point to strong roots in the Washington–New York axis along the eastern seaboard.

Of course, the rapid growth of bureaucratic establishment in all advanced democracies through the 1960s and 1970s might have led to a more inclusive recruitment of higher civil servants. That is, a new breed of officials with weaker ties to the predominant groups in their respective national elites might have entered government during that period. However, they would not have begun to gain access to the upper echelons of the public service during the late 1960s or early 1970s. As they were conducted during this period, the Putnam, Suleiman, and Aberbach and Rockman studies would have exposed only the first indications of a shift in the accessibility of top bureaucratic positions to a wider range of applicants.

The soundings for this research took place in 1979 and 1982–83. The interval between the interviews for this study and those for Aberbach's and Rockman's survey allowed for almost an entire decade during which a new-breed group might have worked its way into senior central-agency positions. Certainly, the U.S. civil service establishment and central agencies grew rapidly through the 1960s and 1970s. Theoretically, such expansion would have lent itself to an influx of prospective candidates for senior posts who entered government more on the basis of professional ability than having the right connections and bachelor's degrees from the most prestigious universities. In addition, substantial increases in the number of appointive positions in central agencies might have caused administration personnel officers to look beyond Ivy Leaguers and the well connected. Presumably, political appointments hinge increasingly on prospects' proven effectiveness as political operatives or subject-matter experts. If so, politicos and amphibians might have become more heterogeneous both in educational and socioeconomic backgrounds.

Education

More than three-quarters of each Carter group had obtained either a master's degree or a doctorate. (See table 12.) Here amphibians represented the largest proportion of Ph.D.s (42 percent). Forty-eight percent of career officials stopped at the master's level. Yet, a reasonably robust 25 percent went on for doctorates. While fully 72 percent of politicos earned one degree beyond their bachelor's, only a handful (4 percent) became Ph.D.s. Both of the Reagan groups exceeded their opposite numbers in the proportion reporting doctoral degrees. For amphibians, the spread is a relatively modest 8 percent. For politicos, it amounts to 19 percent.

Conventional wisdom would suggest that members of a Republican administration would have graduated from more prestigious universities than would have the appointees of a Democratic president. However, our findings indicate that, if anything, the opposite is the case among Reagan and Carter central agents. Exactly the same percentage of politicos under both Carter and Reagan received their bachelor's degree from an Ivy League university. Even though 21 percent of Reagan amphibians graduated from the Ivy

League, their Carter equivalents bettered this figure by 11 percentage points.

The Reagan appointees' more modest exposure to Ivy League schools becomes even more sharply defined when we examine

Table 12

Respondents' Educational Backgrounds (in percent)

Level of education
  Bachelor's degree
  Master's degree
  Doctorate
Schools attended
  Private secondary school
  Elite college or
  university
    Undergraduate
    Graduate
Undergraduate field of
study
  Liberal Arts
    Classics, humanities
    Social sciences
      Political science
      Economics
  Science, engineering
  Business
Graduate/Professional
Field of Study
  Professional
    Scientific professional
    Liberal professional
      Public administration
      Law
  Academic
  Science
  Humanities
  Social sciences
    Political science
    Economics

where respondents did their graduate work. Carter politicos out-stripped their Reagan counterparts 28 to 19 percent in Ivy League graduate degrees. The comparable gap between Carter and Reagan amphibians was 45 to 17 percent.[c] Surprisingly, the Carter career

Career N=69	Carter			Reagan		
	Amphibians N=38	Politicos N=25	All Appointees N=63	Amphibians N=29	Politicos N=31	All Appointees N=60
23	21	24	22	17	26	22
48	34	72	49	28	36	32
25	42	4	27	48	23	35
20	21	28	20	14	19	17
23	32	16	25	21	16	18
41	45	28	38	17	19	18
80	87	92	89	66	58	62
4	13	12	13	10	7	8
62	66	68	67	52	52	52
17	26	48	35	17	36	27
38	29	4	19	35	10	22
9	5	0	3	14	7	10
12	8	8	8	17	7	12
36	45	60	51	41	52	47
4	3	0	2	3	3	3
33	42	60	49	41	48	45
10	11	0	6	10	7	8
9	24	44	32	14	29	22
62	63	32	51	55	26	40
4	0	0	0	0	0	0
6	11	0	6	10	0	5
55	55	32	46	48	26	37
16	29	28	29	14	13	13
41	24	4	16	35	13	23

officials produced the profile that came closest to the relatively elite educational backgrounds of Carter amphibians. Twenty-three percent received their undergraduate diplomas at Ivy League schools and 41 percent obtained graduate degrees from these institutions.

The specific fields in which our respondents concentrated their studies suggested a number of different patterns between the five groups. Looking first at the Carter respondents, between 62 and 68 percent of all three groups majored in social science fields during their undergraduate years. This leaves us with fairly small proportions for all groups who majored in the classics or humanities, science or engineering, or business. Only among Carter amphibians and politicos who studied the classics or humanities, and career officials who took business degrees, did the figure exceed 10 percent. The bulk of social science graduates in all three groups majored either in political science or economics. Politicos strongly favored the former major.[b] Career officials preferred the latter.[b] Amphibians split almost evenly between the two fields.

The same tendencies sustained themselves among Reagan amphibians and politicos. The former reported science and engineering, or business majors somewhat more than did their Carter counterparts. Yet, social science majors comprised the largest proportions in both Reagan groups. Consistent with the Carter findings, Reagan politicos disproportionately majored in political science. Amphibians centered their work more on economics.[c]

Beyond their initial degrees, the Carter groups seemed to have taken two separate tracks. Sixty percent of politicos went on to professional schools, while only 45 percent of amphibians and 30 percent of career officials did so. On the other hand, 62 and 63 percent, respectively, of career officials and amphibians earned graduate degrees in nonprofessional programs.[c] Among the fields that drew the largest proportions of respondents, law claimed the most politicos[a] and economics the most career officials.[b] As a group, career officials hedged with 24 percent taking postgraduate degrees in law, 29 percent in political science, and 24 percent in economics. Although the differences are less pronounced, Reagan politicos also favored law while amphibians preferred economics.[c] Reagan appointees proved less likely than Carterites to take graduate degrees in political science.

Social Backgrounds

Neither comparisons between the Carter groups, nor between Carter and Reagan amphibians and politicos suggest strongly different recruiting biases. For instance, the figures fail to indicate unequivocally that career officials claimed simpler origins than did Carter amphibians or politicos. Further, Reagan appointees do not live up to any expectation that, as Republicans, they would hail from more advantaged segments of society. (See table 13.)

Beginning with the Carter groups, politicos were exceptionally young—40 percent were under thirty-five.[a] As we might expect for permanent civil servants, career officials were more likely to be between forty-five and fifty-four[a] or over fifty-five. Meanwhile, Reagan appointees constituted an older cohort than their Carter counterparts. For instance, only sixteen of Reagan politicos were under thirty-five.[c] As well, 41 percent of Reagan amphibians were between forty-five and fifty-four.[b]

With respect to female respondents, the 21 percent of Carter amphibians who were women dwarfed the 3 percent comparable figure under Reagan. Among politicos, the proportions were almost reversed, with 13 percent under Reagan and only 4 percent under Carter being women. Such figures point up the extent to which top government posts still remain relatively inaccessible to women. Only 6 percent of the career officials were females.

A number of biases appeared in respondents' reports of the cities and regions in which they grew up. Fewer than a quarter of all Carter groups hailed from rural areas, while 37 percent of Carter amphibians and 28 percent of Carter politicos—as against only 10 percent of career officials—came from major metropolises.[b] On the other hand, fully 41 percent of Reagan amphibians declared rural roots. As well, considerably fewer Reagan amphibians (17 versus 37 percent) grew up in a major metropolis.

Looking at regions, both career officials and amphibians interviewed during the Carter administration came disproportionately from the Mid-Atlantic states.[c] Predictably, southerners showed up much more frequently among politicos than in the other Carter groups.[b] Reagan amphibians favored no region strongly. However, 21 percent hailed from border states while 17 percent came from the mid-Atlantic, the east north-central area, and the Pacific coast, each. Surprisingly, the east north-central region provides the largest proportion of Reagan politicos (26 versus 4 percent under Carter).[c] The Reagan politicos who came from the Pacific coast— which, of course, takes in the president's home state—exceeded the proportion of amphibians from the same region by only 5 percentage points.

Table 13

Respondents' Sociodemographic Backgrounds (in percent)	
	Age
	Under 35
	35–44
	45–54
	55 or older
	Female sex
	Area of birth and upbringing
	Rural area
	Major metropolis
	Major metropolis and/or Washington, D.C.
	Geographical region
	New England
	Mid-Atlantic states
	East north-central region
	West north-central region
	South
	Border states
	Mountain states
	Pacific and external areas
	Southwest
	Father's occupation
	Professional/technical work
	Management/administration
	White-collar work (other than the above)
	Blue-collar work (includes farm work)
	Farming

Judging from the Carter groups, the fathers of central agents worked in relatively high-status occupations. Just over three-quarters of politicos' fathers held occupations in the professions or management and administration, as did 63 percent of amphibians' fathers. Career officials' fathers held positions lower down the oc-

Career N=69	Carter			Reagan		
	Amphibians N=38	Politicos N=25	All Appointees N=63	Amphibians N=29	Politicos N=31	All Appointees N=60
4	24	40	30	3	16	10
41	53	56	54	38	45	42
38	13	4	9	41	32	37
17	11	0	6	17	7	12
6	21	4	14	3	13	8
19	13	24	17	41	19	30
10	37	28	33	17	23	20
16	37	32	35	21	23	22
17	5	20	11	0	7	3
23	37	8	25	17	13	15
19	21	4	14	17	26	22
7	5	8	6	3	3	3
7	5	24	13	14	16	15
12	0	12	5	21	3	12
3	0	0	0	0	0	0
3	13	20	16	17	23	20
0	0	4	2	3	3	3
26	34	32	33	38	23	30
22	29	44	35	17	45	32
10	13	8	11	10	7	9
29	18	12	16	28	19	23
7	5	0	3	3	0	2

(Table continues on following pages)

cupational scale. Only 48 percent belonged to a profession, or held managerial or administrative positions. In fact, 29 percent of career officials identified their fathers as blue-collar workers.

The 44 percent of Carter politicos with fathers in management and administration exceeded the comparable figures for amphibians and career officials: 29 percent and 22 percent, respectively. Similar lineages whereby politicos came disproportionately from homes headed by managers/administrators surfaced again between the Reagan groups. Forty-five percent of politicos as against 17 percent of amphibians said that their fathers had worked in management or administration.[c]

The emergence of the same bias across two administrations in

Table 13 *(continued)*

Respondents' Sociodemographic Backgrounds (in percent)	
	Father's education
	Graduate degree
	Undergraduate degree
	Some postsecondary work
	Secondary degree
	Some secondary schooling
	Some primary schooling
	Religious preference
	Catholic
	Protestant
	Jewish
	None
	Atheist, agnostic
	Practicing Catholic, Protestant, or Jew
	Ethnic origin
	Noncaucasian
	Jewish
	English (includes "WASP")
	Irish
	Scottish
	Welsh
	European

politicos' origins perhaps indicates parental transmission of aptitudes to their offspring. Managers and administrators rely more heavily upon entrepreneurial and organizational skills than on formally acquired professional credentials. Their sons and daughters, likewise, find their way more readily into appointive posts calling upon a native ability for political operations than those requiring subject-matter expertise.

Contrary to the conventional image of Republicans, the fathers of Reagan appointees worked in less prestigious occupations than did those of Carter appointees. Only 68 and 55 percent, respectively, of Reagan politicos and amphibians reported that their fathers were either professional workers, managers, or administra-

Career N=69	Carter			Reagan		
	Amphibians N=38	Politicos N=25	All Appointees N=63	Amphibians N=29	Politicos N=31	All Appointees N=60
20	32	32	32	21	16	18
10	13	16	14	21	19	20
23	29	24	27	35	39	37
22	24	28	25	21	16	18
36	34	32	33	35	26	30
15	3	4	3	3	13	8
30	16	16	16	24	26	25
45	37	48	41	52	61	57
16	34	20	29	10	10	10
9	13	12	13	7	0	3
1	0	0	0	3	0	2
35	21	16	20	55	61	58
4	8	8	8	7	7	7
15	24	24	24	7	3	5
33	32	40	35	55	32	43
38	18	28	22	21	29	25
25	8	8	8	17	19	18
1	0	0	0	3	3	3
51	61	48	54	48	42	45

tors. As well, the proportions of each group saying that their fathers had blue-collar jobs exceeded the comparable figures for Carter politicos and amphibians by, respectively, 7 and 10 percentage points.

Even though comparable data were not collected during the Carter interviews, it is instructive to examine the occupational backgrounds of the mothers of Reagan appointees.[27] Over three-quarters of politicos described their mother's occupation as "housewife," while just over half of amphibians did so.[c] In addition, several amphibians made the point that their mother either was the sole breadwinner or held the highest-status occupation in their household. Three times as many amphibians as politicos (21 versus 7 percent) said that their mother belonged to a professional occupational group. In many cases, this was teaching or nursing. This suggests that, in regard to transmission of career aptitudes and aspirations, mothers might have played very substantial roles both in amphibians' upward mobility and in their esteem for professional expertise.

The educational backgrounds of fathers reflect the relatively high standing of their occupations. Almost a third of both Carter amphibian and politicos said that their fathers completed graduate or professional degrees beyond their undergraduate training. Only 30 percent of career officials' fathers took college or university degrees at all. As well, 15 percent of the permanent civil servants recalled that their fathers had not gone beyond primary education.

Turning to the Reagan groups, politicos said half as often as did their Carter opposites that their fathers had completed graduate or professional degrees. As well, amphibians fell 11 percentage points short of their Carter equivalents in attributing graduate or professional degrees to their fathers. Both Reagan groups together mustered only one respondent whose mother had finished a graduate or professional degree. However, amphibians' mothers went farther in school than did those of politicos. Forty-one percent of the former, as compared to 29 percent of the latter, actually finished university degrees.

Turning to religious backgrounds, our career group took in slightly more Catholics (30 percent) and Jews (16 percent) than is found in the general population. Comprising only 16 percent of both amphibians and politicos, Catholics were under-represented among Carter appointees. Meanwhile, the Jewish community did relatively well among Carter amphibians, with fully 34 percent of respondents in this group. Under the Reagan administration, Catholic representation among both amphibians and politicos crept up to the neighborhood of 25 percent, while the Jewish contingent shrank drastically to exactly 10 percent for amphibians[c] and politicos. Most strikingly, the Reagan appointees reported much more frequently than did their Carter equivalents that they still practiced their religion. For amphibians, the gap is 55–21 percent;[b] for politicos, 61–16 percent.[a]

With respect to ethnic background, four of the five groups shatter any perception that individuals with English heritage gain access to high-level public service positions more readily than those with other European roots. Only the percentage of Reagan amphibians claiming some continental European lineage fails to constitute the largest proportion within a group. Even in this instance, 48 percent of respondents pointed to a continental European heritage.

Conclusion

At the outset of this chapter, I underscored the difficulty of achieving a satisfactory blend of career officials and appointees in any administration. I then undertook a detailed examination of the role orientations, work worlds, views of public service, and backgrounds of respondents under Carter and Reagan. These findings take us beyond simply identifying the vagaries of career officials and appointees in their responses. As well, the analysis points to some structural effects. These features range from administration-bound emphases to deeply ingrained systemic factors. Reagan's utilization of cabinet councils serves as an instance of the former; the relatively narrow career experiences of permanent civil servants provide an example of the latter.

When it comes to policy roles and maneuvering within the salient networks, our career respondents showed themselves to be unlikely to wilt in the presence of heat. That is, they readily associated themselves with relevant central-agency core functions, admitted to roles within the policy process per se, and placed their bureaucratic organization within the mainstream of executive-branch coordination and control. As well, insofar as conditions dictated or permitted, they involved themselves in policy networks. For example, the spokes-in-a-wheel approach adopted by the Carter administration worked such an effect. It resulted in almost as large a proportion of career officials reporting direct interactions with the president as emerged among amphibians under Reagan.

The distinctive nature of the permanent civil service career revealed itself in relatively subtle ways. As against Carter amphibians and politicos, the assessments of career officials of their agency's sway gave less weight than did the appointees to authority stemming from the president and more emphasis to neutral competence. In relations on Capitol Hill, they appeared to be more comfortable interacting with staff than with congressmen and senators. Finally, they proved somewhat loath to maintain contacts with outside groups and interests not comprised of business people, academics, and other professionals.

The apparent convergence between amphibians and career officials under Carter perhaps constitutes the most striking finding of this chapter. With respect to core functions, the two groups gravitated toward economic and fiscal policymaking and the allocation and management of resources. They also tended more than politicos to style their policy roles in relatively modest terms. Most important, they shared a common esteem for expertise. This became clear in the value that amphibians and career officials placed on consultations with academics and other professionals.

As administrations increasingly stress expertise as the basis for selection of appointees, we might expect further signs of convergence between career officials and amphibians. However, comparisons between Carter and Reagan amphibians suggested considerable unevenness in the process. In fact, we found some evidence of a widening distance between amphibians and career officials under Reagan. For instance, Reagan amphibians proved more involved than their Carter equivalents with policymaking and facilitating policy rather than simply advising. They ascribed less significance to both experience and expertise in determining access to inner circles. With respect to outsiders, we found evidence that Reagan amphibians' expansive views of their policy roles might have fostered a superbureaucratic aloofness from outsiders. Indeed, their responses to questions about consultation of groups and interests proved less inclusive than did those of career officials under Carter.

At the beginning of this chapter, I stressed the fact that political appointees help a president in two ways. Ideally, they provide a cadre of loyal lieutenants who will identify with the president's priorities and work unstintingly for his legislative program. They also hopefully provide a core group with sufficient bureaucratic and political acuity to seize the state apparatus and make it yield the desired outcomes on schedule. This is not to say that loyalty and acuity always go hand in hand. In fact, severe disjunctions can appear. Certainly, this was the case with Carter appointees. In policy-oriented shops, Carter appointees proved to be too much policy professionals by half. That is, they worked too much from their own sectoral agendas. Many also demonstrated astounding naivete about how Washington actually runs. In more political positions in the White House, Carter's gaggle of Georgians left no doubt about loyalty to the president. Yet, they generally proved themselves woefully inept at political operations in a "governor's mansion" far beyond Georgian scale.

The central structural motifs of the Reagan administration have been the imposition of severe loyalty tests for appointees, enshrinement of broad strategic objectives, and fostering of policy networks. The Carter administration demonstrated to the entire world at what point disloyalty, fuzzy agendas, and policymaking by cottage industries will paralyze an administration. The results of our analysis permit us to assess whether Reagan appointees have pressed loyalty, simplification of agendas, and centralized policymaking to equally dysfunctional extremes.

The broad-stroke approach of the Reagan administration manifested itself clearly in the emphasis of the two appointive groups on overarching strategy and priorities over detailed policy reviews. Similarly, the Reagan respondents rendered heightened perceptions of themselves as policymakers and facilitators. They also registered relative ambivalence toward communication with outsiders.

Such responses reinforced the impression of solidarity and isolation from outside influences that emerges when a group of appointees share strikingly similar world views. However, the Reagan administration's strong networking ethos seemed—at least during the first term—to have mitigated the possible dysfunctions caused by ideological insularity, and macro approaches to policymaking. Reagan amphibians fell notably short in the value they placed on maintaining links with groups and interests outside government. However, politicos gave especially high recognition to the importance of facilitating communication within government. Both Reagan groups failed to mention Congress in describing the objects of their accountability. Yet they distributed authority much more widely than did the Carter appointees through the various parts of the executive branch itself. In all likelihood, Reagan respondents' relatively frequent exposure to cabinet-level committees encouraged their adoption of collective notions of the administration's decision making. For instance, very substantial proportions described their own agency's and competing organizations' roles with explicit reference to facilitating interagency dynamics. Such findings contrasted starkly with the fact that not a single Carter appointee chose to dwell on agency roles specifically associated with collective processes.

In 1985, the Reagan administration scaled down its cabinet committee system. In addition to the National Security Council, only Economic Policy and Domestic Policy councils now operate at the cabinet level. This move will sharply reduce the institutionalization and leverage of more specialized policy networks. Perhaps an administration that does not have to worry about a further outing at the polls can run certain risks connected with such centralization and streamlining. Within limited ranges, Reagan's round-tabling norm restrained administration ideologues during the first term. It also brought on more fine-tuning than macromanagers such as the Treasury Department's supply-siders or OMB's director would have preferred.

We might have found ourselves predicting, at this point in Reagan's second term, the rise of an imperious White House feigning control of willfully strident "Reaganauts" in the departments and agencies. Yet, Congress's newfound spine should limit idiosyncratic executive-branch behavior—both of the White-House and garden varieties. As well, sufficient numbers of Reagan appointees who want their party to do well in 1986 and win in 1988 have remained with the administration.

So far, we have dwelt on differences between our respondents' views of their roles and work worlds that seemed to stem from structural factors. In turn, we have seen that such effects often take root in the stylistic and procedural preferences of an administration or the enduring folkways of career officials. However, they might also find their origins in "cultural" differences across respondent groups and between administrations. For the purposes of this chapter, these have included respondents' views of accountability, career orientations and paths, and educational and social backgrounds. Many substantial differences appeared between our groups with respect to these factors. Many of these relate to three themes that have already emerged in this concluding section. First, we can make some further observations about the unique character of career civil servants within the central-agency milieu. Second, we can probe once more the amount of convergence between career officials and amphibians. Finally, we can assess the degree to which the Carter and Reagan appointive complements constituted variants of amphibian/politico cultures.

Even allowing for the partial affinity between career and amphibian respondents, it becomes clear that the former group comprises a distinct bureaucratic culture. On several items, the Carter groups divided ordinally. That is, politicos and career officials yielded either the lowest or highest percentages, and amphibians occupied the middle ground. With respect to accountability, career officials provided the highest proportions citing as salient factors obligations toward superiors short of agency heads, and their professional standards. In describing their career orientations, the permanent officials stressed the opportunities presented by public service to their personal advancement more than appointees did.

All three Carter groups admitted to having decided upon public service relatively late. Among these, career officials tended more than others to have made their decision as early as the time they completed university or military service. Once in government, career respondents passed through only slightly more positions than amphibians did. This finding underscored the narrowness of their work experience even within departments. The relative upward mobility of permanent officials was indicated by their educational and social backgrounds. Generally, their origins were more modest than those of other respondents. However, they brought to their careers specialized academic degrees along with links to Ivy League universities in numbers rivaled only by amphibians.

In several instances, characteristics of various groups tended to converge. In such cases, amphibians clustered so close to career officials that they effectively abandoned the middle ground. In describing the various authorities or standards to which they felt accountable, both Carter and Reagan amphibians joined career officials in focusing on superiors short of agency heads. The two amphibian groups were similar in having vocational motives in pursuing their careers and citing specific mandates and rules as underlying their views of accountability. Again, the amphibians shared these attitudes with career officials. First, Reagan amphibians, followed by Carter amphibians, include the highest proportions of Ph.D.s. Reagan amphibians joined career officials in stressing training in economics over other fields. Convergence, therefore, seemed to work its greatest effects in areas of overlap in the preparation and socialization of the permanent and amphibian groups. That is, requirements for work within career-based and policy-oriented shops and specialized and appointive positions dovetail in several ways.

Although Reagan appointees were often at variance with their Carter precursors on many items, these differences fail to point unambiguously to the conclusion that Reagan appointed officials enjoy stronger connections to the socioeconomic elite. No appointive cohort is a mirror image of the public at large. Yet, the Reaganites appeared to be more representative of the general populace than did the Carterites. Fewer went to Ivy League schools. A much higher proportion declared rural upbringings. They hailed relatively evenly from the various regions of the country. Their fathers stopped their education earlier and worked in lower-status occupations. The only hint of social backgrounds that might contribute to the Reaganites' conservatism emerged from the fact that they were more likely to be Catholics and/or to observe their religion more than Carterites.

The differences among the Carter and Reagan appointees' views of accountability and their career orientations and routes indicate a stronger influence of structural factors than conceivably could have stemmed from educational and social biases. Recalling the central motifs of the Reagan administration—loyalty, a broad-stroke agenda, and a commitment to networking—we discern echoes of these themes in the findings regarding the cultural factors of Reagan appointees. Their reluctance to cite a sense of accountability to the general public suggested their insularity. As well, their readiness to mention collective authority reflected the operation of the networking norm. Finally, their emphasis on obligations toward superiors short of agency heads revealed their relatively hierarchical discipline. In providing rationales for their selections of objects of accountability, the Reagan appointees demonstrated a much stronger awareness of the shared interests of their peers within the administration.

Finally, regarding career orientations, the Reagan appointees appeared better suited for the team approach to leadership. They stressed educational preparation over experience in the private sector and satisfaction with challenging and vital positions over personal, partisan, and political agendas. As well, they located their attraction to public service earlier than did Carter appointees and brought to their assignments greater actual experience in government.

8. The Future of the Institutional Presidency

At the outset, this book described executive leadership in this country as characterized by struggle. This centers on the conflict between the desire of individual presidents to leave their mark on history and the existing structures, folkways, and agendas of the institutional presidency. There are at least three rings in the complex of factors surrounding an incumbent's relationship to the presidency. Closest to home, they include the acceptable limits within which the president can staff and organize the White House and certain segments of the Executive Office of the President. Relatedly, they take in presidents' latitude in making political appointments to departments and agencies. This, in turn, can involve the "types" of people receiving such assignments as well as their number and level.

One step removed, the broad view of the institutional elements of presidency encompasses centers of neutral competence at the heart of the executive branch. This book, in fact, includes detailed examination of two agencies dedicated to central control and coordination, namely, the Office of Management and Budget and the Department of the Treasury. Both of these are overwhelmingly staffed by permanent civil servants. In yet another ring removed from the president, we find the various operational domains of the executive branch. Here frequently willful permanent officials run the specialized policy shops that actually develop and implement specific government programs. These units repeatedly frustrate the best-laid plans of presidents, White House aides, career central agents, and appointed departmental "masters" alike.

Running through the institutional dimensions of the presidency are the dynamics of executive-branch relations. The term "chief executive" implies some sort of synchronization within the federal government. However, presidents have used different combinations of means to guide departments toward their policy objectives. To begin, presidents might view the White House as the cockpit that sets the key coordinates for administration officials and monitors all of their initiatives and positions to assure that these harmonize with one another and with the center. In practice, presidents who view their roles in this way normally court disillusionment. When approached mechanistically, the federal government proves about as responsive as a jumbo jet that has lost much of its hydraulic system.

A control-oriented president might decide, on the other hand, to turn every operational agency's appointive complement into an administration nerve center. He can do this by carefully screening all departmental appointees to assure that they uphold every aspect of his program. Yet, this strategy inevitably runs up against three hard facts. The career bureaucracy is exceedingly large and intricate; its various offices have many friends in Congress and among interest groups; it has a way of winning over even the most devout presidential missionaries to native ways.

The known limits of White House–centered and appointive dynamics for guiding administrations have led some presidents to tap more neutral and facilitative means for steering the executive branch. Regarding the former tack, they can turn to central agencies staffed mainly by permanent officials. In so doing, they recognize that they must mix "big bang" approaches to directing the executive branch with conventional warfare. Of course, central agencies maintain the arsenals for the latter. Even Reagan's use of the budget to drive his policy priorities relied to a degree upon the institutional resources of the Office of Management and Budget. Here the big bangs were large decreases in spending for domestic programs and increases for national security. The conventional warfare was David Stockman's use of OMB figures to counter all pockets of resistance.

With respect to facilitative methods, presidents can use teamwork to augment neutral competence. As I have stressed throughout this book, incumbents inherit with the presidency a relatively underdeveloped system for cooperative coordination between elements of the executive branch. Notwithstanding some notable lapses, however, presidents have since World War II paid increasing attention to the potential utility of such dynamics.

This final chapter assesses just how well Jimmy Carter and Ronald Reagan came to grips with institutional presidency. Both did recognize the need to engage—even if selectively—the state apparatus. In this sense, they each aspired to policy competence. Thus, this final tally of their successes and failures goes beyond simply identifying a central element in the performance of two administrations. It also assesses where the Carter and Reagan experiences have left the presidency.

Maintaining Perspective

Any examination of a phenomenon as intricate as the institutional presidency requires very careful attention to its wider context. At various points this book has set out guideposts designed to orient our examination of the Carter and Reagan experiences in relation to the historical development of the presidency. More broadly, it has also pointed up several principles of institutionalization that seem to apply to executive leadership in any advanced liberal democracy.

Much of the growth and differentiation of the U.S. executive branch stems from the inherent complexity of governance. This has worked its effects just as surely in the emergence and operation of cabinet systems of government as it has on the presidency. In chapter 2, I focused especially on the British case. Even when monarchs effectively functioned as the chief executive, they found limits to the degree to which they could personalize and concentrate their actual exercise of authority. Thus, ebbs and flows—dependent upon historical epochs and idiosyncratic factors—have characterized the longitudinal plot even of the relative power of kings and their counselors.

Of course, Britain and other "Westminster" systems uphold collective authority as the centerpiece of their constitutions during our own democratic era.¹ These nations, however, have gone through discernible phases. At one extreme, the actual exercise of executive authority by political leaders has been concentrated excessively in the hands of prime ministers. At the other extreme, laissez-faire views of individual ministers' authority have allowed them to achieve baronial sway over their departments. In between, collegial interludes have achieved among cabinet members levels of coordination far beyond the ken and constitutional authority of U.S. agency heads.

Through various transitions, prime ministers and cabinets have built up and then scaled down the role of plenary cabinet sessions including all ministers. Likewise, they have expanded and then simplified committee structures. All the Westminster systems have experimented with different ways of enhancing the direct policy advice given prime ministers. In the process, they have employed various mixes of supporting staff. These have depended upon the levels of centralization, partisan input and neutral competence desirable in prime ministers' personal offices and cabinet secretariats.

American presidents, thus, are not the only ones struggling with the institutionalization of executive leadership. However, they often find themselves coming at problems from the opposite direction to those faced by prime ministers. Clearly, the U.S. Constitution allows presidents to operate under a bias which favors their personal exertion of executive authority. The Westminster ethos, on the other hand, requires that prime ministers always give obeisance to the rubrics of collective decision making. Especially through the expansion of appointive positions in departments, the U.S. presidents have flexed their muscles demonstratively against the willfulness of permanent officials. In Westminster, nostrums about the need for the state apparatus to serve alternating masters make such approaches "nonstarters." British conventional thinking on executive leadership simply will not entertain explicitly partisan politicization of the bureaucracy.

British prime ministers feel more at home with the knights of neutral competence than U.S. presidents ever would. After all, the former have usually headed several departments. Once they reach No. 10 Downing Street, they rely heavily upon career officials in the Prime Minister's Office and the Cabinet Office. Yet, the preservation of neutral competence—right up to and including the deputy heads of departments—affords a sense of cohesion among Whitehall's permanent leadership that could never be achieved by the U.S. bureaucracy. Thus, the pursuit of policy competence often proves no easier for prime ministers than it does for presidents. Prime ministers inherit resources weaker than those of U.S. presidents for combating an intractable bureaucracy, yet are more able to tap well-considered advice. However, this scarcely facilitates executive leadership.

The State of the Institutionalized Presidency

Notwithstanding the generalized nature of the difficulties stemming from the institutionalization of executive leadership in advanced liberal democracies, four factors have had special salience with respect to the modern presidency. The first of these makes the United States unique in the postwar period. The presidency survived in the 1970s two blows that would have torn apart a less stable constitutional system. These, of course, were the severe public disillusionment with executive leadership connected with the U.S. defeat and withdrawal from Vietnam, and the Watergate scandal. Since the Nixon administration, incumbents have wrestled with the rehabilitation of the presidency. At least on the rhetorical level, they have had to acclaim the end of overly centralized executive leadership. As well, they have had to take pains to avoid even the appearance of a Nixon-style White House.

On a less sensational level, three organizational principles are coming to play increasingly important roles in the United States. First, presidents who view their department heads as team members will strive to enhance interactions between them by regularizing meetings of the entire cabinet and/or specialized committees. The operation of the Eisenhower, Ford, and Reagan administrations lends especially strong support for this assertion. Second, a gradual secular process has allowed for a heightened articulation of specialized cabinet-level bodies. To a degree, this trend has functioned independently of administration styles. It now appears, for instance, that continuation of the standing councils for economic policy and domestic policy—in addition to the statutory National Security Council—will present itself as a serious option to future presidents.

Third, stress factors appear to impose limitations on hierarchies within the White House. These constraints inhibit any efforts toward centralization of administration decision making. Two additional propositions derive from these structural considerations. An excessively hierarchical White House will collapse under its own weight due to overload. That is, it does not allow sufficiently for the type of brokerage of special claims within the executive branch by presidential advisers and departmental appointees that makes the presidency manageable. A total lack of structure in the White House, on the other hand, gives too much latitude to the entrepreneurship throughout an administration.

Many of the above observations stem from phenomena embedded in the current state of the institutional presidency. Any assessment of the actual experiences of incumbents since World War II also drives home the fact that personalities play a huge role in how administrations actually function. In several places in this book, I acknowledge that not all presidents take the same approach to their office. In this regard, the distinction between priorities and planning, broker politics, administrative politics, and survival politics has provided useful bearings. It has turned our attention to the ways in which presidents resolve pressures toward centralized policymaking and the encouragement of countervailing views among advisory units.

Nixon's and Carter's notably unhappy encounters with the presidency underscore a crucial psychological premise concerning a president's performance. Namely, whatever style he prefers, a president must avoid becoming a drudge. On the other hand, the illusion of a nonchalance, such as that projected by Reagan, who, at least in the first term, enacted most of his program, can be too seductive. Admittedly, incumbents with strong public support, ample bonhomie and broad-stroke agendas will find the going fairly smooth. Yet, some presidents have actually carved out intricate and unpopular agendas and delivered them while enjoying themselves along the way. As for drudges, they seem never to realize that no relationship between an incumbent and the institutional presidency will succeed if the former expects total responsiveness. In the United States, successful chief executives have truly "presidential" senses of humor.

Engaging the Apparatus Beyond the White House

Presidents tend to give disproportionate attention to devising administration strategies and assuring that departments adhere to policy priorities. Yet, the processes whereby incumbents leave their mark through economic and fiscal policies, and the allocation and management of resources substantially affect the success of their administrations.

With respect to developing and integrating economic policy, we have found that this vital area of executive-branch activity is severely fragmented. At the heart of the problem rests the fact that the Department of the Treasury remains an unwieldy conglomerate. As such, it finds it difficult enough to coordinate its own affairs, let alone take the lead in integrating an administration's economic policy. Presidents have frequently created or enhanced executive office units in an effort to improve the handling of segments of economic policy in areas where Treasury has clearly failed. In more cases than not, such steps have simply exacerbated fragmentation. Currently, three executive office units play substantial statute-based roles in relation to economic policy. These are OMB, the Council of Economic Advisers, and the Office of the U.S. Trade Representative. In addition, special economic units in the National Security Council staff and the White House have gained entry to economic issues. They have done this largely through asserting presidential prerogatives for meshing and deciding all key administration positions.

Circumstances have made the relationships between the various economic agencies and units extremely volatile. The record under Carter and Reagan, however, supports five general assertions. First, the strength of participants' mandates provides a base line for their roles. Here players fulfilling statutory functions cannot readily be put on waivers. For instance, Ronald Reagan found early in 1985 that he could not abolish the Council of Economic Advisers by executive order. It retained functions that only Congress could revoke. Second, some agencies and units suffer while others gain in light of the approaches and policy agendas of an administration. For instance, the fact that CEA fared reasonably well under Carter was largely due to his administration's relatively serious approach to economic forecasting according to rigorous analysis. Third, personalities frequently make or break agencies' performance. Under Carter, Stuart Eizenstat whipped his Domestic Policy Staff into a nemesis for the Treasury. In the process, he so undermined Michael Blumenthal's authority that the treasury secretary's counterparts in other Western nations soon saw that he lacked the power to deliver agreements.

Two remaining observations concerning economic policymaking center on integrative machinery. The first addresses further the Treasury Department's poor internal coordination. To compensate, administrations can take two approaches. They can engage various parts of the Treasury selectively, according to what they seek to accomplish; and they can devise dynamics whereby political appointees in the department can cordon themselves off from permanent bureaucrats in order to improve the prospects for agreement on a broad-gauged strategy. Second, the record of the Ford and

Reagan administrations argues for the utility of one senior cabinet-level committee responsible for coordination of economic policies. Although no panacea, such a body could alleviate intra-administration tensions by settling disputes before, or even without, referral of policy divisions to the president. An irony emerges from the two propositions concerning coordination. Although usually more internally cohesive, Republican administrations have exploited these means for resolving their conflicts more than have the Democratic ones. Perhaps the strength of an administration's ideological ardor must reach a specific level before integrative mechanisms can be effectively deployed.

A separate set of institutional factors appears to operate regarding the president's role in the allocation and management of resources. Here discussion of developments quite naturally centers upon OMB's decline. One school of thought, best represented by Aaron Wildavsky, proposes that OMB's lower profile derives partly from the sheer magnitude of bugeting in the era of big government. That is, the size of the expenditure pie has reached a point where budgeting on the basis of detailed analysis leads to diminishing returns. As well, stringency-minded administrations during the past decade have overloaded OMB through calls for radical cuts in government expenditure. The combination of big government's complexity and intensified pressures for frugality have worked toward the deinstitutionalization of OMB. Thus, the agency increasingly uses blunt instruments to the detriment of fuller use of its analytic capability.

Some scholars, lead by Allen Schick, agree entirely with Wildavsky and others that OMB has lost stature. However, their assessments highlight presidents' conscious efforts to politicize the agency. The layering of political appointees between career officials and the director usually assumes the role of principal villain in such accounts. As well, the politicization theories promote the view that presidents since Eisenhower have worked to deroutinize OMB's budget reviews.

Both of these perspectives on OMB's lot have overstated somewhat the demise of its executive-bureaucratic clout and analytic salience. I have offered two caveats for any attempt to locate the OMB's institutional relationship to the presidency. First, the extended period of stagflation beginning in the early 1970s has led to a state of fiscal siege among advanced democracies. Even during the recovery beginning in 1982, an economics-of-decline mentality continued to dominate budgeting. These developments have put detailed policy analysis on hold in virtually every system. We do not know when major Western economies will kick back into more cyclical economic performances. Before they do, they might encounter a major depression. Regardless, pressure for an activist government will be revitalized somewhere along the line. By then, agencies such as OMB may have become seriously atrophied. Yet they will be called upon. They will remain custodians of the principle that policy competence includes an ability to give due regard to the analytic dimension of issues. OMB has declined, but its raison d'être remains. It is irrevocably linked to executive leadership.

The second caution concerning OMB's decline stems from the variability of presidential styles. Quite simply, the insertion of political associate directors (PADs) between the head of OMB and the career staff has not consistently constricted the analytic integrity of the latter. If anything, the Carter administration accorded permanent OMB officials too much access to the president. It also adhered religiously to a routinzed budget cycle. Even under Reagan, elements of OMB have thrived. For instance, the budget review division strengthened its ringmaster role regarding aggregate budget figures. It therefore provided David Stockman with just the type of scorekeeping capacity necessary for hour-by-hour tallies of his struggles with Congress. At the outset of the Reagan administration, Stockman also relied substantially on budget examiners' acumen when identifying and justifying prospective cuts in domestic programs.

The experiences of Carter and Reagan thus point up an institutional adaptability in OMB that makes its presence felt more or less vigorously, depending on the style of an administration. The budget agency's analytic presence will be more apt to loom large when presidents interest themselves in program details than when they do not. As well, presidential attention to OMB's traditional concerns can become excessive—as happened under Carter. If the president reaches the point where he spends hours receiving briefings from career officials in OMB, he will almost certainly fail to hold the line against appeals from operational departments.

One fatalistic note seems to emerge from any study of the institutional presidency as associated with the allocation and management of resources. Management policy, it appears, will always remain a weak sister to budgeting. Even the effort under Nixon to make the "M" side a full-blown partner—as reflected by BOB's name change to OMB—failed to obtain for management more than second-class citizenship. Today it functions as an entirely subsidiary activity to budget analysis. The restoration of conventional economic cycles would, however, do more than simply retrigger analytic budgeting. Periods of rapid growth followed by doubts about expansion would put the spotlight again on programmatic efficiency and effectiveness. This, in turn, would foster closer attention to management issues. In fact, precisely this chain of events has unfolded in the one area of expenditure in which the Reagan administration has allowed unfettered expansion—namely, national defense.

Administrations' Styles and Policy Competence

As we have seen, numerous factors constrain the institutional development of the presidency. However, individual incumbents enjoy considerable latitude for maneuver—even experimentation. Figure 5 summarizes the various options open to presidents. It does so by locating the four possible presidential styles spatially within the "policy competence" quadrant of figure 1. We assume, then, that virtually all presidents seek some mix of responsiveness and institutional competence. This will enable them to leave their mark without compromising the long-term national interest.

The priorities and planning style attempts to stretch the outer thresholds of the tension between partisan responsiveness and the institutionalized presidency. It allows a multiplicity of advisory agencies at the center of government and permits competition among these units. It also encourages regularized countervailing views by exposing agency and department initiatives to the scrutiny of standing cabinet-level bodies. It seeks, thus, to optimize an administration's creativity while giving due recognition to various institutional forces associated with contrasting perspectives on the long-term national interest.

In Figure 5, broker politics appears as a tempered form of priorities and planning. It therefore is a more realistic style for U.S. presidents. Conditions endemic to the American political system usually dictate that even the most optimistic and expansive incumbents can aspire only to a fairly limited mix between partisan responsiveness and regard for institutional considerations. Unlike perhaps any other chief executive in advanced liberal democracies, the U.S. president faces built-in limits to introducing institutionalized and competitive countervailing views into the center of government. These stem largely from the fragmented and noncollective nature of the U.S. executive branch. Survival and administrative politics, on the other hand, represent styles which seek to tip the scales to one or the other side of the perpetual tension between the responsive and institutional presidency. Survival politics starts with the assumption that incumbents must largely override the existing legacy of the presidency in order to deliver their policy program. Administrative politics works from the premise that an effective administration should take pains to utilize the counsel of the permanent bureaucracy.

Figure 5 portrays a harsh reality connected with presidents' actual follow-through on their styles. Most administrations fail to achieve the highest level of policy competence that might conceivably result from their chosen mix of responsiveness and the use of institutional resources. In those rare occasions when it is attained, a priorities-

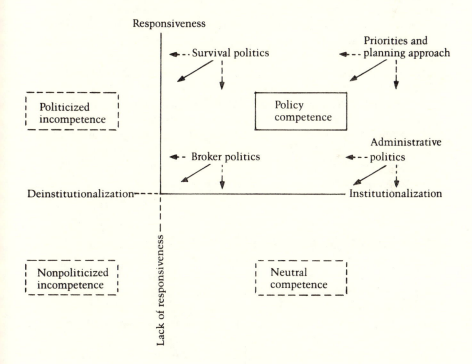

Figure 5. The Presidency, Partisan Responsiveness, and Presidential Styles

and-planning approach tends soon to slip into broker politics. How-ever, a threat of serious losses in electoral support could swing it into survival politics. Likewise, a president's inability to elicit creative countervailing views while maintaining his administration's internal harmony could shatter confidence in his executive leadership. The implicit decision on the part of its top appointive personnel to "ride this one out" could, in turn, plunge an administration into an excessive deference to neutral competence.

Broker politics is probably the best assurance that an administration will optimize its preferred style. Since they take a moderate stance toward both responsiveness and institutional resources, administrations that adopt broker politics tend to pare their agendas the farther they go into a term. As well, their centrist partisan approaches often mitigate adverse reactions to their legislative programs among the public. Barring exogenous factors that make the electorate highly volative, broker-politics administrations' support levels should remain relatively stable. Their moderation, in fact, tends to balance any adjustments made by broker-politics administrations toward greater emphasis on responsiveness or institutional resources. In addition, election years usually jolt them out of agenda paring before they face any danger of falling into the nether region of "nonpoliticized incompetence."

Adherence to survival or administrative politics thus poses the clearest danger of administrations drifting beyond the grasp of policy competence. The former so neglects the apparatus of state that it systemically courts partisan incompetence. The latter becomes so enamored of the status quo that it succumbs to the spell of neutral competence.

Achieving Viable Blends of Bureaucratic Cultures

With the above observations centered on style, we can now turn to a final assessment of how consistently and effectively Jimmy Carter and Ronald Reagan pursued their blends of advisory resources. The first fact that emerges here is that purity of form cannot be assumed in these matters. On the rhetorical level, Jimmy Carter stuck with one style—administrative politics—until summer 1979. Consistently with this choice, Carter tolerated exceptionally free-floating White House and cabinet systems. However, the depth and breadth of his personal engagement in matters of detail approximated that found only among chief executives energetically pursuing the priorities and planning motif. As a result, both Carter and his administrative-politics structure began to buckle from the overload. Interestingly, the post-summer-1979 Carter administration effectively migrated to survival politics. The fact that the president had subconsciously attached himself to priorities and planning all along made the transition all too easy.

During the first term, Ronald Reagan eschewed full commitment to one style. Both his use of anti-Washington rhetoric and imposition of loyalty tests on appointees bore strong shades of survival politics. In other respects, his administration followed broker politics in ways that tempered any tendency toward unadulterated messianism. The modified spokes-in-a-wheel format for the White House gave the "implementation" side a strong pragmatic voice in all key administration positions. As well, the cabinet council system introduced a "round-table" norm that made it difficult for cabinet ideologues to let the "Reagan" in them be "Reagan" all the time. Unlike Carter's experience, Reagan's approach—a mixture of survival and broker politics—achieved remarkable consistency and effectiveness in the delivery of the administration's central policy priorities.

Of course, any president must make astute use of appointees and career officials working in central agencies in order to assure that his chosen style actually works out. The findings presented in chapter 7 also suggest that the internal dynamics of administrations greatly affect central agents' role perceptions, their views of their work world, and their attitudes toward public service. If they correspond with the central nostrums of the president's approach, they reinforce the practical force of administration rhetoric. If they bear little resemblance to the avowed plan, they simply exacerbate the tendency for administrations to lose stylistic coherence during the course of a term. The resulting sense of drift can hobble appointees just as readily as it can confound career civil servants.

The current literature broadly acknowledges career officials' conscious involvement in executive-bureaucratic politics. However, administrations frequently seem at a loss as to how they might tap the acumen of permanent civil servants who work in the heart of the executive branch. For their part, the career officials among our respondents revealed no ambivalence about their own activities within the policy process and the location of their agencies at the hub of executive-branch coordination and control. However, the specialized career development of these officials revealed itself in several ways. They oriented themselves to relatively narrow segments of their agencies' mandates. In their characterizations of their accountability and efforts to garner advice and information, they emphasized neutral competence over responsiveness to political authority and to outside groups and interests. Their very career selection and advancement hinged primarily upon acquisition of specialized skills and adherence to professional standards.

Carried out in the third year of the Carter administration, our career interviews made one point clear. Permanent officials will insert themselves competently into whatever roles the chosen format of an administration gives them access to. Thus, several of our respondents even reported participating in lengthy briefing sessions with President Carter. Throughout central agencies, officials enjoyed near-collegial relations with their political masters. This included direct exposure to the principal committees and task forces in which political appointees worked out their differences. This fluidity of participation derived from the president's rhetoric in support of administrative politics. It drew further force from his personal involvement in a priorities and planning approach.

Of course, the amicable relations between his administration and career officials turned sour as Carter swung toward survival politics in summer 1979. And the Reagan administration subjected the entire permanent bureaucracy to hostile verbal attacks from their political masters. Under the current regime, career officials have found that they may be seen but not heard. The extent to which their political superiors minimized their grasp of administration plans certainly contributed to the dispatch with which the first term achieved its main objectives. Yet, even the fervent advocates of his various broad-stroke enterprises might come to their senses when the consequences of Reagan's pronounced reliance upon appointees come to light. Already, the Pentagon must regret the fact that an absence of central scrutiny enabled its profligacy to go unchecked. Certainly revelations of gross inefficiency and ineffectiveness have severely undermined public support for the defense buildup. As well, a megaton time bomb—the deficit—continues to tick away. When it explodes, no doubt will remain about the dangers of economic policymaking by the high priests of a primitive form of free-market wish fulfillment.

Over time, presidents have encouraged or permitted the intensification of career resources in central agencies. They have recognized that their administrations cannot respond effectively to partisan aspirations without a sense of history and hard-nosed realism. In a word, they acknowledge that any administration that underutilizes or engages only selectively the permanent officials in central agencies does so at considerable risk.

The attitudinal convergence between career officials and amphibians—the latter being appointees who won their positions mostly by virtue of their expertise—certainly amounts to one of the significant findings of this book. In part, it derives from the entrance requirements and prevailing ethos of a permanent bureaucratic culture that has developed at the center of government. Yet, administrations' increasing emphasis on expertise for appointments to policy-oriented positions would suggest that the common ground between career officials and amphibians will continue to expand. In this regard, Reagan has made as extensive use of amphibians as Carter did. In fact, Reagan amphibians—in addition to having as high an esteem for expertise as Carter amphibians—actually claimed a higher proportion of Ph.D.s.

The evidence from chapter 7 suggests the strong effects worked by Reagan's central stylistic motifs on his appointees' views of their work. This fact bears close attention by framers of future administrations. For instance, even Reagan's modest use of routinized cabinet-level committees inculcated a highly legitimized collective esprit among appointees. To be sure, the ideological homogeneity of Reagan's appointees and his administration's immediate enshrinement of its fundamental policy objectives facilitated such collective dynamics. Yet, the strength of Reagan appointees' explicit attachment to collegial decision making went far beyond mere ideological cohesiveness. This finding, thus, puts the case for the instrument utility of routinized cabinet-level bodies in a new light. The Reagan administration derived clear benefits from the approach even though its tendency to deal in broad strokes limited the necessity for the types of fine-tuning of major initiatives that really test the capacity of coordinative dynamics. That is, his routinized bodies maintained a sense of teamwork among cabinet secretaries that buttressed the administration's harmonious image. They also provided forums in which many medium-range isues could be amicably resolved without reaching the Oval Office.

In the future, the creative use of such mechanisms will present itself increasingly as the sine qua non of harmonious administrations. This will prove true especially under presidents seeking a policy competence that attempts to stretch the outer limits of partisan responsiveness and engagement of the state apparatus. Ironically, Ronald Reagan might well have achieved roughly his current level of performance with a Carter-style spokes-in-a-wheel cabinet system. On the other hand, Carter's only hope for executive harmony and policy competence might well have been adoption of routinized cabinet structures.

This book has attempted to redress an imbalance in the study of the presidency. While giving due regard to personalities, it has focused exceptionally strongly on organizational issues that transcend the stylistic preferences of specific incumbents. It has asked exactly how the presidency has changed institutionally in the past decade. And it has identified the threads of historical continuity in such developments. Along the way, it has resisted the temptation to declare that incumbents now can override the institutional presidency at will or vice versa. It even accepts the fact that presidents can maintain popular support and harmony among their appointees without fully engaging the state apparatus. Indeed, the case of Reagan demonstrates that ruthlessly selective and utilitarian employment of the state apparatus can—even if it does not provide genuine governance—greatly enhance an administration's image for *political* competence.

On the other hand, Jimmy Carter provides the instance of what will happen to future proactive presidents who approach the state apparatus ambivalently. No matter how they strive for *policy competence*, they must judge when and when not to engage in hand-to-hand combat with the permanent bureaucracy. They must also recognize at the outset that cabinet government simply cannot operate—even in a modest American-style instrumental mode—without regularized group dynamics.

Appendix Notes Index

Appendix 1

The research for this project was built upon my experience with interview studies of central agents beginning in 1976. In that year, George Szablowski and I developed an interview schedule which we employed with officials working in Canada's Prime Minister's Office, Privy Council Office, Federal-Provincial Relations Office, Finance Department and Treasury Board Secretariat. In devising this instrument, we drew heavily from those used by Allan Kornberg and William Mishler with legislators, and Robert Presthus and Ezra Suleiman with bureaucrats.[1] As well, we consulted with central agents to see how a prototype of the interview schedule might be adapted for use in bureaucratic organizations responsible for government wide coordination and control. With significant modification along the way, I have subsequently used the same instrument with British central agents as well with those in the Carter and Reagan administrations who participated in this study. The format of the U.S. version of the interview schedule is provided in Appendix 2.

Access

Unlike Canada and the United Kingdom, the United States presents no real problem for mature researchers who hope to interview U.S. central agents. To begin, I never found it necessary in Washington to seek the approval of agency heads for my project. Overwhelmingly, officials decided whether or not to see me without reference to superiors. This contrasted sharply with the situation in London and Ottawa where almost always officials must clear interviews with superiors.

Notwithstanding the relative cooperativeness of Washington officials, researchers can greatly improve their success at securing interviews by following a few rules of thumb. First, they should try to associate themselves with a recognized research center in Washington. In this regard, the Brookings Institution has proved to be an excellent base for me. However, the American Enterprise Institute or the Wilson Center at the Smithsonian Institution would serve most scholars' purposes as well. I hasten to add that I do not believe ideological orientation makes much difference as long as the center has a scholarly reputation. I say this simply because, as will become clear, I found it easier to obtain interviews from my Brookings base for the Reagan segment of my study than I did for the Carter portion. It is possible that officials find it difficult to pass up the opportunity to proselytize the other side?

Second, researchers should take special pains when approaching officials for interviews. They must avoid brushoffs from protective executive assistants and appointment secretaries. I found it best to request interviews in writing. Attached to a short cover letter, I provided a one-page statement of my research objectives and a one-page curriculum vitae. Within a few days, I called prospective respondents to set up appointments. Whether I spoke on the phone with an official or an assistant, I started the conversation by asking if they had received my letter. Normally, the letter was within reach. It therefore provided an important visual aid to my identity and my oral description of my project. If the letter was not available, this alerted me to the possibility that it might have been lost. And my call usually provoked a search. Bureaucracy is extremely paper-oriented. The researcher should take advantage of this fact to establish his or her persona.

Third, move cautiously. I generally started at the highest level at which I sought interviews. For instance, in the White House I first approached people rated as "assistants to the president." This way, no prospective respondent can say, "You've talked to all my people, I don't know what I could add." Above all, be conscious of the tendency for top officials to try to satisfy your request by arranging an appointment with a deputy. Stall a final *no* as long as possible. For instance, officials' assistants can become very cooperative if you register understanding of how busy their boss is. Thus, concessions such as, "I know you must be busy with the budget now; perhaps I should wait a few weeks" can do wonders. Often—after the decks have cleared, the office in question will call, out of the blue, with a specific time for an interview. An essential ingredient to caution is patience. A blitz will never work. I normally sent out only ten or fifteen interview requests per week. I would spread these around to prevent any agency or office from thinking that it was under siege by "this Canadian at Brookings."

Who Are the Respondents?

All of the officials interviewed for this project were either appointees or career civil servants who occupied senior positions. Regarding the latter, my cutoff point was GS-16. That is, I did not include respondents below GS-16 under the rating system in effect in 1979. Virtually all of my career officials qualified for membership in the Senior Executive Service when it was implemented shortly after completion of my interviews.

With respect to political appointees, I sought interviews with all such officials heading units in the White House, the Executive Office of the President, the Treasury Department and the Office of Personnel Management. If such units had more than one senior appointee, I would sample additional respondents according to the size of this complement. In each agency, I excluded senior appointees supervising units with largely technical or administrative—rather than policy—responsibilities. Regarding career officials, sheer numbers required that I selected two officials from each cluster of offices headed by a career civil servant. That is, I would try to interview the cluster head plus one head of a constituent unit whom I selected randomly. I made exceptions in cases where career units were especially large. For example, in the Office of Management and Budget I interviewed each deputy associate director responsible for budget examination in a policy sector. As well, I drew at least one branch chief under each sector. However, I interviewed more extensively in the national security division. Because of the size and the centrality of defense to the budget, I saw all but one of the division's branch chiefs.

As I have already suggested, I found it easier to secure interviews in the Reagan White House than I did in Carter's West Wing. The fact that I saw only three of eleven officials rated "assistant to the president" under Carter, while I saw eight of fourteen appointees at this level or above under Reagan, reflects the relative accessibility of the Reagan group. Under both administrations, I was able to substitute deputies in nearly every case where I failed to interview the head of a White House unit. Of the sixty-nine career officials interviewed during the Carter segment of the study, forty-two percent were from OMB, 10 percent from elsewhere in the Executive Office of the President, 36 percent from Treasury, and 12 percent from the Office of Personnel Management. Of the sixty-three Carter appointees, 27 percent were in the White House Office, 26 percent in OMB, 22 percent in the Executive Office of the President, 19 percent in the Treasury and 6 percent in OPM. Of all Carter respondents, 8 percent were assistants to the president, deputy heads of cabinet-level agencies or the heads of noncabinet agencies; 5 percent were deputy assistants to the president, undersecretaries or executive associate directors, 21 percent were special assistants to the president, assistant secretaries or associate directors; 34 percent were associate assistants to the president, deputy assistant secretaries, or assistant directors; 21 percent were office directors or branch chiefs; and 11 percent occupied senior positions below these levels.

As for the Reagan respondents, 25 percent came from the White House,

15 percent from OMB, 32 percent from elsewhere in the Executive Office of the President, 18 percent from Treasury and 10 percent from OPM. Regarding level, 22 percent were assistants to the president or above, cabinet agency deputies, or the heads of noncabinet agencies; 17 percent were deputy assistants to the president, undersecretaries, executive associate directors or deputy directors of noncabinet agencies; 39 percent were special assistants to the president, assistant secretaries or associate directors; and 22 percent were associate assistants to the president, deputy assistant secretaries or assistant directors.

The Interview Data

On average, the interviews took one and a half hours. As a rule, the very top political appointees expect such sessions to last about a half hour. A researcher can stretch this interval ten or fifteen minutes but no further. Lower level appointees normally expect you to take an hour. It is not difficult to stretch this to an hour and a half. Depending upon how talkative they are, career officials normally do not become fidgety until the interview has lasted one and a half to two hours. Thus researchers should pace themselves according to how pressured their respondent is likely to be.

All but four of the interviews were taped. In the case of each of these four exceptions, I dictated the interviews as faithfully as possible from detailed notes immediately after leaving the respondent's office. Verbatim transcriptions of the interviews were verified either by me, Gail Lyons, or Donald Naulls, two senior research assistants for this project.

In drawing upon the interview transcripts for quotations and background material, I tried to assure that the passages I used were genuinely representative of significant schools of thought among respondents. This process was greatly aided by the fact that I made detailed outlines of each transcript. Whenever I fastened upon a phrase or insight which seemed especially germane, I could assess fairly quickly where it fit in relation to the mainstream of thought on the topic at hand.

Of course, the transcripts proved invaluable for coding responses for computer analysis. During several long sessions, George Szablowski, Gail Lyons and I developed the original codebook while working together on the comparative central agency project. Donald Naulls and I made several modifications when we integrated the Reagan respondents into the U.S. data set. Research assistants did the actual coding. Every effort was made to assure that the codebook was modified each day to account for response types which we had not anticipated. Either Lyons or Naulls checked each coded interview for consistency and revisions necessitated by changes in the codebook.

Appendix 2

Interview Number _____

Comparative Central Agency Study: U.S. Segment

Interviewer _____
Date _____
Office _____

This questionnaire is part of a research project funded by Social Sciences and Humanities Research Council of Canada and York University in Toronto to study the roles of officials in the White House Office, OMB, the Department of the Treasury and the Office of Personnel Management. Your cooperation is necessary for its successful completion.

All answers to this questionnaire are absolutely confidential.

Any results will be presented in an anonymous or a statistical form.

Please tell me if you prefer not to answer a question and we will go on to the next item.

I would like to start with some questions about your present work in
_____.

1. What are your responsibilities here at _____?

2. How does what you do relate to the role of _____ as a central agency?

2-a. What other central agencies or departments are most involved in work directly related to what you do here at _____?

2-b. How would you characterize the roles played by each of these central agencies/departments in this area?

2-c. How do these roles compare with what you are trying to do here at _____?

2-d. With respect to each of these central agencies/departments, what level of person are you usually working directly with in this area of activity?

2-e. Taking into consideration your role and similar work being done elsewhere, please rank the roles played by people in other central agencies/departments and yourself in terms of influence in this sector of activity.

3. What in your view is the role of _____ in government?

3-a. Is this role being adequately performed? How so?

3-b. How might the performance of your department/agency be improved? Please elaborate? For example?

4. How do you view accountability in your position? Do you feel that you are accountable to your superior in this agency, to its head, to the president, to the cabinet, to Congress, to the people of the United States, to your conscience, or to some combination of these?

4-a. (If R says "some combination," ask him:) Specifically, to which of these do you feel accountable?

4-b. (For each to which R answers that he is accountable, ask:) In what sense are you accountable to _____?

4-c. (If R lists more than one, ask him:) To which of these do you feel most accountable? Why is that?

I have some questions about your usual interactions with others in government in the course of your work at _____.

5. With which of the following do you interact personally about some important matter during an average month?

Check off as mentioned	List A Frequency	Type of contact	Type of matter
( ) The president	_____	_____	_____
( ) The head of your department/agency	_____	_____	_____

( )   The heads of other
      agencies/departments   _____   _____   _____
( )   The deputy heads of
      other agencies/departments   _____   _____   _____
( )   Members of Congress   _____   _____   _____
( )   Senators   _____   _____   _____

5-a. How often in the average month would such interactions take place? (register
      above in times/month)

5-b. What is the usual form of these contacts; are they by telephone, personal
      visits, official meetings, in the hallway or restaurant, or at social occasions?
        1. telephone
        2. personal visits
        3. letters
        4. official meetings
        5. in the hallway or restaurant
        6. social occasions
        7. some combination of the above (ask R to specify which combination)
        8. other (specify)

5-c. Is the occasion for such contacts usually an administrative governmental mat-
      ter or government policy?
        1. usually an administrative matter
        2. usually a policy matter
        3. both
        4. neither (record)
        5. other (record)
      Please elaborate? May I have some examples?

6.   Let's turn now to interdepartmental committees of officials; which of these do
      you regularly attend?

6-a. Could you tell me, approximately, how often each of these met in the last
      year?

6-b. What percent of the meetings, approximately, did you actually attend?

6-c. How would you characterize your participation in these meetings? Are you
      simply an observer, do you speak only when called upon for advice, or do you
      actively involve yourself in the discussion?
        1. simply an observer
        2. speak only when called upon for advice
        3. actively involve self in discussion
        4. some combination of these (specify)
        5. other

6-d.   For each of these committees, could you tell me, approximately, the percent of meetings in which you actively participated in the discussion?

6-e.   Which of these assignments interest you the most?

6-f.   Why is this?

7.   What about cabinet-level meetings and councils: which of these do you regularly attend?

Committee   Meetings   Attendance   Kind of Participation   Frequency

7-a.   Could you tell me, approximately, how often each of these met in the last year?

7-b.   What percent of the meetings, approximately, did you actually attend?

7-c.   How would you characterize your participation in these meetings? Are you simply an observer, do you speak only when called upon for advice, or do you actively involve yourself in the discussion?
      1. simply an observer
      2. speak only when called upon for advice
      3. actively involve self in discussion
      4. some combination of these (specify)
      5. other

7-d.   For each of these committees, could you tell me, approximately, the percent of meetings in which you actively participated in the discussion?

7-e.   Which of these committees interest you the most?

7-f.   Why is that?

8.   No doubt you have seen the assertion, in popular literature or even in academic works, that an inner circle of members of the cabinet and/or senior officials decides all the important policy questions here in Washington. What do you think about this characterization of the policy process? If there is an inner circle, what seem to be the qualities required for membership? (If R names names, probe to see why he has mentioned each person.)

I would like to ask you about your interactions with people outside government.

9.   Which, if any, of the following do you normally consult if you want information about the public's views on an issue? (Hand respondent list B.)

9-a.   Which of these do you generally feel give you the most accurate and reliable information? (circle 1 or 2)

List B

	Consults	Most reliable source of information
Editorial opinions and letters to editors	1	2
Political party leaders and workers	1	2
Business leaders	1	2
Union leaders	1	2
Farm group leaders	1	2
Public officials in local governments	1	2
Public officials in state governments	1	2
Priests, ministers, or other religious group officials	1	2
Ethnic/racial group leaders	1	2
Personal friends and acquaintances	1	2
Citizens' groups which cut across economic, religious, and ethnic lines (specify)	1	2
Polls	1	2

Others (list)

9-b.   Depends on the issue. (Elaborate?)

How about interaction with organized subgroups and interests?

10.   On the basis of your own experience, how significant a role do you feel subgroups and interests generally play in helping you decide your recommendations on issues?
  1. highly significant
  2. moderately significant
  3. insignificant
  Please elaborate?

10-a. How often do you come into direct personal contact with representatives of organized subgroups and interests per month?

10-b. In your experience are you contacted most frequently by lobbyists who agree with you on a particular issue or by those who disagree?
  1. agree
  2. disagree
  Who usually initiates contact between yourself and interest group representatives?

  Why is this so?

I would like to end with some questions about your own career and background. First, regarding your career:

11.   Public officials in this country and in other Western democracies have given a variety of reasons to explain why they got into government initially. How about in your case? How did you get into government?

11-a. What year did you enter government service?

11-b. How long have you been in this agency?

11-c. How long have you held your present post?

11-d. What is your present public service category?

12.   What has been your career route in government, i.e., what positions have you held?

Title   Department   Date   Level

12-a. Have you held any positions outside of government, either before coming to government or inbetween jobs in the public service?

Title   Date   Firm/Organization

13.   Looking at your career in government, what are the most important things you have tried to accomplish?

14.   Is there a particular area of public affairs in which you feel you have become an expert?
       yes   1
       no   2
       n.a. 9

14-a. If "yes," record areas:

14-b. If "yes," how did you acquire your expertise in the(se) area(s)? (record)

15.   If you left government service, what would you miss about your work?

With respect to your background:

16.   What year were you born?

17.   What is your home town?

18.   Could you tell me your father's major occupation?
       Your mother's major occupation?

19.   Could you also tell me how much formal education your father received?
       How much your mother received?

20-a. What was the original ethnic background of your family on your father's side?

20-b. What was the original ethnic background of your family on your mother's side?

21. What is your religion preference?
    Catholic   1
    Protestant   2 (Denomination?) _____
    Jewish   3
    None   4
    Other   5

22. Could you tell me how much formal education you received?

23. (If R attended university:) What was your major field of study at university?

24. Do you have a graduate/professional degree? If so, in what field?
    1. no
    2. law
    3. economics
    4. politics
    5. public administration
    6. business administration
    7. engineering
    8. other (specify)

25. Which graduate or professional degrees have you received?

26. Where did you receive your education prior to university?

27. Where were your university degrees taken? (undergraduate and graduate)

28. Please name any professional and fraternal organizations to which you belong.

29. Could you also name any social clubs to which you belong?

That's all. Many thanks for your cooperation.

Notes

1. The Presidency, Executive Harmony, and the State Apparatus

1. Renate Mayntz, "Executive Leadership in Germany: Dispersion of Power or 'Kanzlerdemokratie,'" in *Presidents and Prime Ministers*, ed. Richard Rose and Ezra N. Suleiman (Washington, D.C.: American Enterprise Institute, 1980), p. 139; Johan P. Olsen, *Organized Democracy: Political Institutions in a Welfare State—The Case of Norway* (Irvington-on-Hudson, N.Y.: Columbia University Press, 1983), p. 79; Patrick Weller, *First Among Equals: Prime Ministers in Westminster Systems* (London: Allen & Unwin, 1985), pp. 105–07, 131–34; and Thomas T. Mackie and Brian W. Hogwood, "Decision-Making in Cabinet Government," in *Unlocking the Cabinet: Cabinet Structures in Comparative Perspective*, ed. Mackie and Hogwood (London: Sage, 1985), pp. 7–12.

2. Fred I. Greenstein, *The Hidden-Hand Presidency: Eisenhower as Leader* (New York: Basic Books, 1982), pp. 6, 238.

3. John Turner, *Lloyd George's Secretariat* (Cambridge: Cambridge University Press, 1980), pp. 78–82.

4. Anna Kasten Nelson, "National Security I: Inventing a Process (1945–60)," in *The Illusion of Presidential Government*, ed. Hugh Heclo and Lester M. Salamon (Boulder, Colo.: Westview, 1982), p. 231.

5. John Milton Cooper, Jr., *The Warrior and the Priest: Woodrow Wilson and Theodore Roosevelt* (Cambridge Mass.: Harvard University Press, 1983), ch. 20.

6. Richard E. Neustadt, *Presidential Power: The Politics of Leadership from FDR to Carter* (New York: Wiley, 1980), p. 116.

7. Stephen Hess, *Organizing the Presidency* (Washington, D.C.: Brookings, 1976), pp. 78–79.

8. Graham T. Allison, *The Essence of Decision: Explaining the Cuban Missile Crisis* (Boston: Little, Brown, 1971).

9. Colin Campbell, *Governments Under Stress: Political Executives and Key Bureaucrats in Washington, London and Ottawa* (Toronto: University of Toronto Press, 1983), ch. 1.

10. Woodrow Wilson, *Constitutional Government of the United States* (New York: Columbia University Press, 1908), pp. 70–71.

11. Walter Bagehot, *The English Constitution* (1867; rpt. Glasgow: Fontana, 1963), p. 70.

12. Theodore J. Lowi, *The End of Liberalism: Ideology, Policy, and the Crisis of Public Authority* (New York: Norton, 1969), pp. 180–86.

13. Ronald Reagan, "Address by the President to the Nation," Washington, D.C., January 29, 1984.

14. Campbell, *Governments Under Stress,* pp. 96–97.

15. Hugh Stephenson, *Mrs. Thatcher's First Year* (London: Jill Norman, 1980), pp. 40–42, 93; Campbell, *Governments Under Stress,* pp. 72–75; Peter Riddell, *The Thatcher Government* (Oxford: Martin Robertson, 1983), pp. 9, 52–56.

16. Falkland Islands: The Origins of a War," *Economist,* June 19, 1982, p. 38; "Falkland Islands Review, Report of a Committee of Privy Counsellors," *The Franks Report* (London: Her Majesty's Stationery Office, 1983).

17. "DuCann Advises Thatcher to Appoint Deputy," [London] *Times,* March 5, 1984.

18. Randall B. Ripley and Grace A. Franklin, *Congress, the Bureaucracy, and Public Policy* (Homewood, Ill.: Dorsey, 1980); Richard Rose, *Managing Presidential Objectives* (New York: Free Press, 1976), p. 161; and Anthony King, *The New American Political System* (Washington, D.C.: American Enterprise Institute, 1978), pp. 388–95. See as well Neustadt, *Presidential Power,* p. 212; Joel D. Aberbach, Robert D. Putnam, and Bert A. Rockman, *Bureaucrats and Politicians in Western Democracies* (Cambridge, Mass.: Harvard University Press, 1981), pp. 94–100; and Richard A. Watson and Norman C. Thomas, *The Politics of the Presidency* (New York: Wiley, 1983), pp. 292–94.

19. Robert A. Dahl, *Polyarchy: Participation and Opposition* (New Haven, Conn.: Yale University Press, 1971), pp. 26–29.

20. See, for example, Hess, *Organizing the Presidency,* pp. 212–16; Roger Porter, *Presidential Decision Making: The Economic Policy Board* (Cambridge: Cambridge University Press, 1980), pp. 214–21; Lester M. Salamon, "The Presidency and Domestic Policy Formulation," in *The Illusion of Presidential Government,* ed. Heclo and Salamon, pp. 193, 199.

21. Terry M. Moe, "The Politicized Presidency," *The New Direction in American Politics* (Washington D.C.: Brookings, 1985), p. 258.

22. Ibid., p. 239.

23. Ibid., pp. 244–45.

24. Thomas E. Cronin, *The State of the Presidency* (Boston: Little, Brown, 1980), pp. 224–25.

25. Ibid., p. 248.

26. Bert A. Rockman, *The Leadership Question: The Presidency and the American System* (New York: Praeger, 1984), pp. 194–97.

27. Ibid., p. 197.

28. Ibid., p. 195.

2. Presidents and Their Cabinets

1. Leon D. Epstein, "What Happened to the British Model?" *American Political Science Review* 74 (March 1980), 9–22; John E. Schwartz, "Exploring a New Role in

Policy Making: The British House of Commons in the 1970's," *American Political Science Review* 74 (March 1980), 23–27.

2. Hugh Heclo and Aaron Wildavsky, *The Private Government of Public Money: Community and Policy Inside British Politics* (Berkeley and Los Angeles: University of California Press, 1974), pp. 367–68.

3. John P. Mackintosh, *The British Cabinet*, 3d ed. (London: Stevens and Sons, 1977), p. 8.

4. Henry Barrett Learned, *The President's Cabinet: Studies in the Origin, Formation and Structure of an American Institution* (New Haven, Conn.: Yale University Press, 1912), pp. 11, 15, 39.

5. Mackintosh, *The British Cabinet*, pp. 40, 51, 146–47, 203, 275–78, 308–10, 378–79.

6. Ibid., p. 51.

7. John Turner, *Lloyd George's Secretariat* (Cambridge: Cambridge University Press, 1980).

8. Colin Campbell, *Governments Under Stress: Political Executives and Key Bureaucrats in Washington, London and Ottawa* (Toronto: University of Toronto Press, 1983), p. 19.

9. Learned, *The President's Cabinet*, pp. 66–74.

10. "A Presidency for the 1980's," a report on presidential management by a panel of the National Academy of Public Administration, November 1980, in *The Illusion of Presidential Government*, ed. Hugh Heclo and Lester M. Salamon (Boulder, Colo.: Westview, 1981), p. 308.

11. Fred I. Greenstein, *The Hidden-Hand Presidency: Eisenhower as Leader* (New York: Basic Books, 1982), p. 5.

12. Nelson W. Polsby, "Presidential Cabinet Making: Lessons for the Political System," in *The Presidency: Studies in Policy Making*, ed. Steven A. Shull and Lance T. LeLoup (Brunswick, Ohio: King's Court, 1979), p. 86.

13. Salamon, "Conclusion: Beyond the Presidential Illusion—Toward a Constitutional Presidency," in *The Illusion of Presidential Government*, ed. Helco and Salamon, pp. 288, 293.

14. Richard Rose, "The President: A Chief but Not an Executive," *Presidential Studies Quarterly* 7 (Winter 1977), p. 6.

15. Stephen Hess, *Organizing the Presidency* (Washington, D.C.: Brookings, 1976), p. 10.

16. Ibid., pp. 10, 146.

17. Larry Berman, *The Office of Management and Budget and the Presidency* (Princeton, N.J.: Princeton University Press, 1979), pp. 3–4.

18. Salamon, "The Presidency and Domestic Policy Formulation," in *The Illusion of Presidential Government*, ed. Heclo and Salamon, pp. 179–80.

19. Hess, *Organizing the Presidency*, p. 57.

20. Salamon, "The Presidency and Domestic Policy Formulation," p. 180.

21. Greenstein, *The Hidden-Hand Presidency*, pp. 5, 42, 80.

22. Salamon, "The Presidency and Domestic Policy Formulation," p. 181.

23. Heclo, "Introduction: The Presidential Illusion," in *The Illusion of Presidential Government*, ed. Heclo and Salamon, p. 12; Hess, *Organizing the Presidency*, p. 108; Salamon, "The Presidency and Domestic Policy Formulation," p. 181.

24. Richard P. Nathan, *The Plot That Failed: Nixon and the Administrative Presidency* (New York: Wiley, 1975); Heclo, "The Presidential Illusion," p. 12;

Hess, *Organizing the Presidency*, pp. 112, 125–26, 131–32; John H. Kessel, *The Domestic Presidency: Decision-Making in the White House* (North Scituate, Mass.: Doxbury Press, 1975), p. 112.

25. Richard F. Fenno, Jr., *The President's Cabinet: Analysis in the Period from Wilson to Eisenhower* (Cambridge, Mass.: Harvard University Press, 1959), p. 5; *A Presidency for the 1980's* p. 305; John Helmer, "The Presidential Office: Velvet Fist in an Iron Gate," in *The Illusion of Presidential Government*, ed. Heclo and Salamon, p. 51.

26. Norman C. Thomas, "An Inquiry into Presidential and Parliamentary Governments," in *Parliament, Policy and Representation*, ed. Harold D. Clarke et al. (Toronto: Methuen, 1980), p. 294.

27. Joel D. Aberbach and Bert A. Rockman, "The Overlapping Worlds of American Federal Executives and Congressmen," *British Journal of Political Science* 7 (January 1977), 23–27.

28. Roger B. Porter, *Presidential Decision-Making: The Economic Policy Board* (Cambridge: Cambridge University Press, 1980), p. 15. The author cites Eugene B. McGregor, Jr., "Politics and the Career Mobility of Bureaucrats," *American Political Science Review* 68 (March 1974), 22, 24.

29. Fenno, *The President's Cabinet*, p. 249. The author cites Pendleton Herring, "Executive-Leadership Responsibilities," *American Political Science Review* 38 (December 1944), 1160.

30. Fenno, *The President's Cabinet*, pp. 5, 9. See also Helmer, "The Presidential Office," p. 55; Hess, *Organizing the Presidency*, p. 208; Porter, *Presidential Decision-Making*, p. 15.

31. Learned, *The President's Cabinet*, pp. 47, 119.

32. Ibid., pp. 140–41.

33. Fenno, *The President's Cabinet*, p. 34.

34. Hess, *Organizing the Presidency*, p. 35.

35. Fenno, *The President's Cabinet*, p. 40.

36. Lawrence E. Lynn, Jr. and David deF. Whitman, *The President as Policymaker: Jimmy Carter and Welfare Reform* (Philadelphia: Temple University Press, 1981), p. 8.

37. Fenno, *The President's Cabinet*, p. 43.

38. Hess, *Organizing the Presidency*, p. 46.

39. Respectively: Fenno, *The President's Cabinet*, p. 35; Hess, *Organizing the Presidency*, p. 65; Greenstein, *The Hidden-Hand Presidency*, p. 108.

40. Greenstein, *The Hidden-Hand Presidency*, pp. 106, 108.

41. Berman, *The Office of Management and Budget*, p. 49.

42. Hess, *Organizing the Presidency*, p. 65; Greenstein, *The Hidden-Hand Presidency*, pp. 90–91.

43. Hess, *Organizing the Presidency*, p. 84.

44. Greenstein, *The Hidden-Hand Presidency*, p. 104; Lynn and Whitman, *The President as Policymaker*, p. 9.

45. Hess, *Organizing the Presidency*, p. 102.

46. Emmette S. Redford and Marlan Blissett, *Organizing the Executive Branch: The Johnson Presidency* (Chicago: University of Chicago Press, 1981), pp. 204, 214.

47. Porter, "The President and Economic Policy: Problems, Patterns and Alternatives," in *The Illusion of Presidential Government*, ed. Heclo and Salamon, p. 218.

48. Nathan, *The Plot That Failed*, p. 93.

49. Porter, *Presidential Decision-Making.*

50. Stephen J. Wayne, *The Legislative Presidency* (New York: Harper and Row, 1978), p. 201.

51. Campbell, *Governments Under Stress,* pp. 39–43.

52. Learned, *The President's Cabinet,* p. 127.

53. Fenno, *The President's Cabinet,* p. 92.

54. Ibid., p. 92; Hess, *Organizing the Presidency,* p. 46; Anna Kasten Nelson, "National Security I: Inventing a Process (1945–1960)," in *The Illusion of Presidential Government,* ed. Heclo and Salamon, p. 235.

55. Fenno, *The President's Cabinet,* p. 92; Greenstein, *The Hidden-Hand Presidency,* p. 113.

56. Hess, *Organizing the Presidency,* p. 78; I. M. Destler, "National Security II: The Rise of the Assistant (1961–1981)," in *The Illusion of Presidential Government,* ed. Heclo and Salamon, p. 267.

57. Hess, *Organizing the Presidency,* p. 106; Destler, "National Security II," p. 269.

58. Destler, "National Security II," pp. 270–71.

59. Wayne, *The Legislative Presidency,* p. 54.

60. Mackintosh, *The British Cabinet,* pp. 494, 497.

61. Nelson, "National Security I," p. 230. The author cites Alfred D. Sander, "Truman and the National Security Council: 1945–47," *Journal of American History* 59 (September 1972), 369. See also Nelson, "National Security I," pp. 231–33, 244.

62. Hess, *Organizing the Presidency,* p. 64; Greenstein, *The Hidden-Hand Presidency,* pp. 124–34; Porter, "The President and Economic Policy," p. 211.

63. Porter, "The President and Economic Policy," p. 212.

64. Ibid.; Salamon, "The Presidency and Domestic Policy Formation," p. 183.

65. Porter, *Presidential Decision Making,* especially pp. 15, 43, 54, 57, 69–70.

66. Rose, "The President," p. 14.

67. Hess, *Organizing the Presidency,* p. 3; Greenstein, *The Hidden-Hand Presidency,* p. 103; Wayne, *The Legislative Presidency,* p. 32.

68. Wayne, *The Legislative Presidency,* pp. 34, 135.

69. Hess, *Organizing the Presidency,* p. 3; Greenstein, *The Hidden-Hand Presidency,* p. 103.

70. Wayne, *The Legislative Presidency,* pp. 39–40; Hess, *Organizing the Presidency,* p. 99.

71. Hess, *Organizing the Presidency,* p. 126.

72. Porter, *Presidential Decision Making,* p. 90.

73. Destler, "National Security II," p. 273; Paul Charles Light, *The President's Agenda: Domestic Policy Choice from Kennedy to Carter* (Baltimore: John Hopkins University Press, 1982), p. 21; Campbell, *Governments Under Stress,* pp. 36–37.

74. Light, *The President's Agenda,* p. 136.

75. Hess, *Organizing the Presidency,* p. 57.

76. Greenstein, *The Hidden-Hand Presidency,* pp. 146–48.

77. Wayne, *The Legislative Presidency,* p. 221; Hess, *Organizing the Presidency,* p. 88.

78. Hess, *Organizing the Presidency,* pp. 93, 99.

79. Ibid., pp. 112, 124; Light, *The President's Agenda,* p. 101; Kessel, *The Domestic Presidency,* p. 114.

80. Berman, *The Office of Management and Budget*, p. 6. The author cites C. G. Dawes, *The First Year of the Budget of the United States* (New York: Harper and Brothers, 1923), preface.

81. Berman, *The Office of Management and Budget*, p. 20.

82. I. M. Destler, "National Security Advice to the President," in *The Presidency*, ed. Shull and LeLoup, p. 118; Nelson, "National Security I," pp. 235–36.

83. Hess, *Organizing the Presidency*, p. 57.

84. Greenstein, *The Hidden-Hand Presidency*, p. 118.

85. Ibid., p. 114; Fenno, *The President's Cabinet*, pp. 96, 105–06.

86. *The Hidden-Hand Presidency*, Greenstein, pp. 126–32; Nelson, "National Security I," pp. 246, 250, 254; Destler, "National Security II," p. 118.

87. Greenstein, *The Hidden-Hand Presidency*, p. 127.

88. Destler, "National Security Advice," p. 119; Destler, "National Security II," p. 264.

89. Berman, *The Office of Management and Budget*, pp. 67, 74.

90. Hess, *Organizing the Presidency*, pp. 103–04.

91. Berman, *The Office of Management and Budget*, pp. 74, 80–86, 97–98.

92. Ibid., pp. 105–07; Hess, *Organizing the Presidency*, p. 112; Nathan, *The Plot That Failed*, pp. 60–68.

93. Porter, *Presidential Decision-Making*, pp. 73, 78, 84, 99; Porter, "The President and Economic Policy," p. 216.

94. Light, *The President's Agenda*, p. 189.

95. Campbell, *Government Under Stress*, pp. 32–33, 36–43, 123.

3. Two Models for Cabinet Consultation: Carter and Reagan

1. Respondent 54 (1979), p. 12.

2. Quoted in Neal R. Peirce, "The View from the Top of the Carter Campaign," *National Journal*, July 17, 1976, pp. 993–94.

3. Respondent 110 (1979), p. 1 ff.

4. Respondent 56 (1979), pp. 3–6.

5. Respondent 56 (1979), pp. 5–6.

6. Dom Bonafede, "Carter Turns on the Drama—But Can He Lead?" *National Journal*, July 28, 1979, pp. 1237–38.

7. Respondent 3 (1982), p. 10.

8. Respondent 57 (1982), p. 6.

9. Respondent 47 (1979), p. 7.

10. Respondent 41 (1979), p. 12.

11. Respondent 147 (1982), pp. 6–8.

12. Richard F. Fenno, Jr., *The President's Cabinet: An Analysis in the Period From Wilson to Eisenhower* (Cambridge, Mass.: Harvard University Press, 1959), p. 42.

13. Respondent 53 (1979), p. 13.

14. Respondent 34 (1979), pp. 9–10.

15. Respondent 34 (1979), p. 10.

16. Respondent 23 (1979), p. 17.

17. Laurence E. Lynn, Jr., and David de F. Whitman, *The President as Policymaker: Jimmy Carter and Welfare Reform* (Philadelphia: Temple University Press, 1981), p. 191.

18. Ibid., p. 191.

19. Zbigniew Brzezinski, *Power and Principle: Memoirs of the National Security Adviser* (New York: Farrar, Straus, Giroux, 1983), esp. pp. 58–61; Respondent 40 (1979), pp. 6 ff; Respondent 52 (1979), pp. 8 ff.

20. Respondent 76 (1979), pp. 10–12.

21. Brzezinski, *Power and Principle*, p. 71.

22. Respondent 185 (1982), pp. 12–13.

23. Lou Cannon, *Reagan* (New York: Putnam, 1982).

24. Ibid., p. 45.

25. Ibid., p. 154.

26. G. Calvin Mackenzie, "Cabinet and Subcabinet Personnel Selection in Reagan's First Year: New Variations on Some Not-so-Old Themes," and Richard P. Nathan, "The President as a Manager," both papers presented at the annual meeting of the American Political Science Association, New York, September 2–5, 1981.

27. Respondent 198 (1982), p. 6.

28. Respondent 58 (1982), side 1, p. 15, side 2, p. 2.

29. Ibid., side 1, p. 15.

30. Laurence I. Barrett, *Gambling with History: Reagan in the White House* (Garden City, N.Y.: Doubleday, 1983), p. 176.

31. Cited in Colin Campbell, *Governments Under Stress: Political Executives and Key Bureaucrats in Washington, London and Ottawa* (Toronto: University of Toronto Press, 1983), pp. 174–75.

32. Respondent 63 (1982), pp. 15–16.

33. Respondent 152 (1982), pp. 17–18.

36. Respondent 160 (1982), pp. 10–11.

37. Respondent 133 (1982), p. 18.

38. Respondent 174 (1982), p. 2.

39. Respondent 192 (1982) pp. 6–7.

40. Respondent 142 (1982), pp. 13–14.

41. Respondent 185 (1982), p. 10.

42. Respondent 151 (1982), p. 15.

43. Respondent 171 (1982), p. 13.

44. Respondent 185 (1982), p. 13.

4. Mapping, Adhering to, and Changing Administrations' Strategies

1. Colin Campbell, *Governments Under Stress: Political Executives and Key Bureaucrats in Washington, London and Ottawa* (Toronto: University of Toronto Press, 1983), pp. 23–24.

2. Richard P. Nathan, *The Administrative Presidency* (New York: Wiley, 1983), p. 8.

3. Respondent 34 (1979), pp. 16–17.

4. Richard E. Neustadt, *Presidential Power: The Politics of Leadership from FDR to Carter* (New York: Wiley, 1980), p. 218; Stephen J. Wayne, *The Legislative Presidency* (New York: Holt, Rinehard and Winston, 1978), p. 216.

5. Paul Charles Light, *The President's Agenda: Domestic Policy Choice from Kennedy to Carter (with notes on Ronald Reagan)* (Baltimore: Johns Hopkins University Press, 1982), p. 21.

6. Zbigniew Brzezinski, *Power and Principle: Memoirs of the National Security Adviser* (New York: Farrar, Straus, Giroux, 1983), p. 67.

7. Respondent 48 (1979), pp. 12–13.

8. Respondent 47 (1979), pp. 13–14.

9. Respondent 31 (1979), p. 16.

10. For example, respondent 43 (1979), pp. 15–16.

11. Respondent 44 (1979), pp. 9–10.

12. I. M. Destler, "National Security II: The Rise of the Assistant (1961–1981)," in *The Illusion of Presidential Government*, ed. Hugh Heclo and Lester M. Salamon (Boulder, Colo.: Westview, 1981), p. 273.

13. Respondent 212 (1979), side 2, pp. 2–3.

14. Campbell, *Governments Under Stress*, pp. 108–10, 123.

15. Respondent 38 (1979), p. 17.

16. Respondent 140 (1982), pp. 12–13.

17. Dick Kirschten, "You Say You Want a Sub-Cabinet Post? Clear It with Marty, Dick, Lyn and Fred," *National Journal*, April 4, 1981, pp. 546–47.

18. Respondent 190 (1982), p. 2.

19. Ibid., pp. 9–10.

20. Respondent 192 (1982), p. 2.

21. Dick Kirschten, "Inner Circle Speaks with Many Voices, But Maybe That's How Reagan Wants It," *National Journal*, May 28, 1983, p. 1101.

22. Respondent 150 (1982), p. 15.

23. Respondent 173 (1982), pp. 11–12.

24. Ibid., p. 12.

25. Respondent 15 (1982), pp. 12–13.

26. Respondent 144 (1982), pp. 17–18.

27. Respondent 160 (1982), pp. 11–12.

28. Respondent 63 (1982), pp. 17–18.

29. Respondent 43 (1982), p. 10.

30. Respondent 181 (1982), p. 15.

31. Ibid, pp. 15–16.

32. Bernard Weinraub, "A Wall Street Wonder Comes to the White House," *New York Times*, January 18, 1985.

33. Bernard Weinraub, "How Donald Regan Runs the White House," *New York Times Magazine*, January 5, 1986.

5. Keeping Economic and Fiscal Policies Dancing in Step

1. Colin Campbell, *Governments Under Stress: Political Executives and Key Bureaucrats in Washington, London and Ottawa* (Toronto: University of Toronto Press, 1983), ch. 6.

2. Larry Berman, *The Office of Management and Budget and the Presidency* (Princeton, N.J.: Princeton University Press, 1979), pp. 3–4.

3. Ibid., p. 28.

4. Respondent 79 (1982), side 1, p. 20.

5. Respondent 14 (1982), side 1, pp. 15–16.

6. Respondent 177 (1982), pp. 4–8.

7. Campbell, *Governments Under Stress*, p. 111.

8. Respondent 62 (1982), side 1, p. 22.

9. Respondent 191 (1982), p. 7.

10. Respondent 32 (1982), p. 10.

11. Ibid., pp. 8–9.
12. Respondent 15 (1982), side 2, pp. 7, 9.
13. Respondent 60 (1982), side 1, p. 13.
14. Respondent 176 (1982), p. 4.
15. Respondent 137 (1982), p. 2.
16. Respondent 79 (1982), side 2, p. 2.
17. Respondent 189 (1982), side 2, p. 2.
18. Respondent 168 (1982), p. 4.
19. Respondent 36 (1982), side 2, p. 1.
20. Respondent 137 (1982), p. 6.
21. Respondent 14 (1982), side 1, p. 18.
22. Respondent 171 (1982), side 1, p. 10.
23. Respondent 5 (1982), side 1, p. 20.
24. Ibid., pp. 20–21.
25. Roger B. Porter, "The President and Economic Policy: Problems, Patterns and Alterations," *The Illusion of Presidential Government,* ed. Hugh Heclo and Lester M. Salamon (Boulder, Colo.: Westview, 1981), pp. 205–07.
26. Ibid., p. 222.
26. Ibid., p. 211.
28. Ibid., pp. 211–12.
29. Roger B. Porter, *Presidential Decision Making: The Economic Policy Board* (Cambridge: Cambridge University Press, 1980), p. 15.
30. Respondent 62 (1979), p. 15.
31. Respondent 37 (1979), p. 8.
32. Respondent 11 (1979), p. 7.
33. Respondent 147 (1982), pp. 19–21.
34. Ibid., p. 22.
35. Respondent 32 (1982), pp. 2–3.
36. Respondent 5 (1982), p. 15.
37. Respondent 191 (1982), p. 18.
38. Respondent 151 (1982), p. 13.
39. Respondent 136 (1982), pp. 7–8.
40. Respondent 166 (1982), p. 2.
41. Respondent 186 (1982), p. 10.
42. Respondent 20 (1982), side 1, p. 2.

6. Coping with Cyclical Forces Affecting the Budget and Management

1. Aaron Wildavsky, *The Politics of the Budgetary Process,* 2d ed. (Boston: Little, Brown, 1974), pp. xvii–xviii.
2. Ibid., p. xix.
3. Aaron Wildavsky, "From Chaos Comes Opportunity: The Movement Toward Spending Limits in American and Canadian Budgeting," *Canadian Public Administration* 26 (Summer 1983), 181.
4. Allen Schick, "The Problem of Presidential Budgeting," in *The Illusion of Presidential Government,* ed. Hugh Heclo and Lester M. Salamon (Boulder, Colo.: Westview, 1980), pp. 94–95.
5. Richard P. Nathan, *The Administrative Presidency* (New York: Wiley, 1983), p. 92.

6. Respondent 3 (1982), p. 3.

7. Larry Berman, *The Office of Management and Budget* (Princeton: Princeton University Press, 1979), pp. 3–4; Louis Fisher, *Presidential Spending Power* (Princeton, N.J.: Princeton University Press, 1975), pp. 27–33.

8. Frank J. Goodnow, *Politics and Administration* (New York: Macmillan, 1900).

9. Woodrow Wilson, "The Study of Administration," *Political Science Quarterly* 16 (December 1941), 481–506; Luther Gullick, "Science, Values and Public Administration," in *Papers on the Science of Administration,* ed. Luther Gullick and L. Urwick (New York: Institute of Public Administration, 1937), pp. 184–95.

10. Wilson, "The Study of Administration," p. 493.

11. Don Price, "General Dawes and Executive Staff Work," *Public Administration Review* 10 (Summer 1941), 169 as cited by Berman, *The Office of Management and Budget,* p. 6.

12. Berman, *The Office of Management and Budget,* p. 8; Schick, "The Problem of Presidential Budgeting," p. 88.

13. A. E. Buck, "Financial Control and Accountability," *Report with Special Studies,* President's Committee on Administrative Management (Washington, D.C.: Government Printing Office, 1937), p. 142, as cited by Schick, "The Problem of Presidential Budgeting," p. 88.

14. Berman, *The Office of Management and Budget,* pp. 18–23.

15. Ibid., p. 44.

16. William W. Kaufmann, "The McNamara Strategy," in *The Politics of Federal Bureaucracy,* ed. Alan A. Altshuler (New York: Dodd, Mead, 1968), p. 180.

17. Ibid., p. 181.

18. Emmette S. Redford and Marlan Blissett, *Organizing the Executive Branch: The Johnson Presidency* (Chicago: University of Chicago Press, 1981), pp. 204–09; Richard Rose, *Managing Presidential Objectives* (New York: Free Press, 1976), p. 46.

19. Rose, *Managing Presidential Objectives,* p. 63.

20. Respondent 47, side 1, p. 6.

21. Respondent 49, side 2, p. 1.

22. Richard E. Neustadt, "Presidency and Legislation: Planning the President's Program," *American Political Science Review* 49 (December 1955), 985; David C. Mowrey, Mark S. Kamlet, and John P. Crecine, "Presidential Management of Budgetary and Fiscal Policymaking," *Political Science Quarterly* 95 (Fall 1980), 405.

23. Respondent 47, side 1, p. 12.

24. Respondent 50, p. 5.

25. Rose, *Managing Presidential Objectives,* pp. 2, 68–69.

26. Colin Campbell, *Governments Under Stress: Political Executives and Key Bureaucrats in Washington, London and Ottawa* (Toronto: University of Toronto Press, 1983), pp. 206–07.

27. Respondent p. 8.

28. Berman, *The Office of Management and Budget,* p. 140.

29. Joseph A. Pechman, "The Federal Budget in Review," in *Setting National Priorities: The 1978 Budget,* ed. Pechman (Washington, D.C.: Brookings, 1977), pp. 43–46.

30. Graeme M. Taylor, "Introduction to Zero-Base Budgeting," in *Contemporary Approaches to Public Budgeting,* ed. Fred A. Kramer (Cambridge, Mass.: Winthrop, 1979), pp. 151–52.

31. Laurence E. Lynn, Jr. and David deF. Whitman, *The President as Policymaker: Jimmy Carter and Welfare Reform* (Philadelphia: Temple University Press, 1981), pp. 90–91, 193–96.

32. Ibid., pp. 191–208.

33. For example: respondent 1, side 1, p. 5; respondent 57 (1979), p. 10.

34. Respondent 1, side 1, pp. 5–6.

35. Respondent 47, side 1, pp. 7–8.

36. Respondent 63 (1982), p. 13.

37. Respondent 96 (1982), pp. 10–11.

38. Respondent 19 (1979), p. 6.

39. Respondent 33, side 1, p. 9.

40. Lynn and Whitman, *The President as Policymaker*, p. 98.

41. Respondent 59 (1982), p. 5.

42. Respondent 108, p. 20.

43. Peter Szanton, *Federal Reorganization: What Have We Learned?* (Chatham, N.J.: Chatham House, 1981).

44. Lester M. Salamon, "Federal Regulation: A New Arena for Presidential Power?" in *The Illusion of Presidential Government*, ed. Heclo and Salamon, pp. 147–76.

45. Respondent 10, p. 3.

46. Respondent 26 (1982), side 1, pp. 19–21.

47. Respondent 21, side 1, p. 4.

48. Respondent 92, pp. 7–8.

49. Joseph A. Pechman, "The Budget and the Economy," in *Setting National Priorities: The 1984 Budget*, ed. Pechman (Washington, D.C.: Brookings, 1983), pp. 16–17.

50. Paul Craig Roberts, *The Supply-Side Revolution: An Insider's Account of Policymaking in Washington* (Cambridge, Mass.: Harvard University Press, 1984), p. 96.

51. Respondent 43 (1982), p. 6.

52. Respondent 3 (1982), pp. 10–11.

53. Respondent 58 (1982), p. 3.

54. Respondent 80 (1982), pp. 5–6.

55. Respondent 180, p. 6.

56. Respondent 58 (1982), side 2, p. 2.

57. Respondent 163, p. 12.

58. Respondent 100 (1982), side 2, p. 4.

59. Respondent 180, p. 8.

60. Respondent 183, p. 6.

61. Respondent 58 (1982), side 2, p. 4.

62. Respondent 107 (1982), p. 3.

63. Respondent 96 (1982), side 2, pp. 11–12.

64. Campbell, *Governments Under Stress*, pp. 212, 216–21.

65. Peter Riddell, *The Thatcher Government* (Oxford: Martin Robertson, 1983), p. 122.

66. Respondent 148, p. 13.

67. Ibid., pp. 7–10.

68. Respondent 26 (1982), pp. 22–23.

69. Respondent 71 (1982), side 1, p. 20.

70. Respondent 135, side 2, pp. 1–2.

71. Hearings Before the Subcommittee on the Civil Service, House of Representatives, 98th Congress (Washington, D.C.: Government Printing Office, 1984). See especially testimony by the Comptroller General, pp. 1–75, Hugh Heclo, pp. 338–41, and Colin Campbell, pp. 442–51.

72. Respondent 155, p. 2.

73. Respondent 96 (1982), p. 8.

7. Structure and Two Different Mixes of Three Bureaucratic Cultures

1. Richard F. Fenno, Jr., The President's Cabinet: An Analysis in the Period from Wilson to Eisenhower (Cambridge, Mass.: Harvard University Press 1959), pp. 142–47.

2. Fred I. Greenstein, The Hidden-Hand Presidency: Eisenhower as Leader (New York: Basic Books, 1982), pp. 116, 120.

3. Fenno, The President's Cabinet, p. 142.

4. Lester M. Salamon, "The Presidency and Domestic Policy Formulation," The Illusion of Presidential Government, ed. Hugh Heclo and Lester M. Salamon (Boulder, Colo.: Westview, 1981), pp. 191–93.

5. "A Presidency for the 1980s," a report on presidential management by a panel of the National Academy of Public Administration, November 1980, in The Illusion of Presidential Government, ed. Heclo and Salamon, p. 319.

6. Roger B. Porter, "The President and Economic Policy: Problems, Patterns, and Alternatives," in ibid., p. 223; and I. M. Destler, "National Security II: The Rise of the Assistant (1961–1981)," in ibid., p. 279.

7. Joel D. Aberbach, Robert D. Putnam, and Bert A. Rockman, Bureaucrats and Politicians in Western Democracies (Cambridge, Mass.: Harvard University Press, 1981), Ch. 1.

8. Colin Campbell and George J. Szablowski, The Superbureaucrats: Structure and Behaviour in Central Agencies (Toronto: Macmillan, 1979).

9. Aberbach, Putnam, and Rockman, Bureaucrats and Politicians, p. 18.

10. See, for example, Hugh Heclo, A Government of Strangers: Executive Politics in Washington (Washington, D.C.: Brookings, 1977), pp. 236–40; Roger B. Porter, Presidential Decision Making: The Economic Policy Board (New York: Cambridge University Press, 1980), pp. 215–18; and Salamon, "The Presidency and Domestic Policy Formulation," pp. 191–93.

11. Colin Campbell and Donald Naulls, "Policy Makers and Facilitators: The Boundaries Between Two Bureaucratic Roles," International Yearbook for Studies of Leaders and Leadership 3 (1986), in press.

12. Chester Newland, "The Reagan Presidency: Limited Government and Political Administration," Public Administration 43 (January/February 1983), 2.

13. Ibid.

14. Aberbach, Putnam, and Rockman, Bureaucrats and Politicians, pp. 203–04, 224.

15. Colin Campbell, Governments Under Stress: Political Executives and Key Bureaucrats in Washington, London and Ottawa (Toronto: University of Toronto Press, 1983), pp. 279–80.

16. Richard Rose, Managing Presidential Objectives (New York: Free Press, 1976), p. 101; Hugh Heclo, "Issue Networks and the Executive Establishment," in

The New American Political System, ed. Anthony King (Washington, D.C.: American Enterprise Institute, 1978), pp. 102–05; Randall B. Ripley, *Congress the Bureaucracy and Public Policy* (Homewood, Ill.: Dorsey, 1980); Richard A. Watson and Norman C. Thomas, *The Politics of the Presidency* (New York: Wiley, 1983), pp. 292–94.

17. Kenneth Kernaghan, "Responsible Public Bureaucracy: A Rationale and a Framework for Analysis," *Canadian Public Administration* 16 (1973), 572, 598–99.

18. Campbell and Szablowski, *The Superbureaucrats,* pp. 11–12.

19. Aberbach, Putnam, and Rockman, *Bureaucrats and Politicians,* p. 40.

20. Max Weber in *From Max Weber: Essays in Sociology,* trans. and ed. H. H. Gerth and C. Wright Mills (New York: Oxford University Press, 1958), pp. 90–91; Robert D. Putnam, "Political Attitudes of Senior Civil Servants in Western Europe: A Preliminary Report," *British Journal of Political Science* 3 (July 1973), 268, 279; and Ezra N. Suleiman, *Politics, Power and Bureaucracy* (Princeton, N.J.: Princeton University Press, 1974), p. 117.

21. J. Chartrand and K. L. Pond, *A Study of Executive Career Paths in the Public Service of Canada* (Chicago: Public Personnel Association, 1970), pp. 48–49, 70; Nicole S. Morgan, *No where to Go?* (Montreal: Institute for Research on Public Policy, 1981); Colin Campbell, *Governments Under Stress,* pp. 310–19.

22. Hugh Heclo, "Issue Networks," pp. 100–03, 114–20.

23. Putnam, "Political Attitudes of Senior Civil Servants," pp. 268–69.

24. Suleiman, *Politics, Power, and Bureaucracy,* pp. 64, 68.

25. David T. Stanley, Dean E. Mann, and Jameson W. Doig, *Men Who Govern* (Washington, D.C.: Brookings, 1967), pp. 78–84.

26. Joel D. Aberbach and Bert A. Rockman, "The Overlapping Worlds of American Federal Executives and Congressmen," *British Journal of Political Science* 7 (January 1977), 26–28, 30–31.

27. Of amphibians' and politicos' mothers, 21 and 7 percent, respectively, were professionals; 11 and 7 percent, administrative personnel; 7 and 3 percent, white-collar workers; 7 and 9 percent, blue-collar workers; and 52 and 77 percent, housewives.[b]

8. The Future of the Institutional Presidency

1. Patrick Weller, *First Among Equals: Prime Ministers in Westminster Systems* (London: Allen and Unwin, 1985), pp. 200–12.

Appendix 1

1. Allan Kornberg and William Mishler, *Influence in Parliament* (Durham, N.C.: Duke University Press, 1976), pp. 342–64; Robert Presthus, *Elites in the Policy Process* (Cambridge: Cambridge University Press, 1974), pp. 481–511; and Ezra Suleiman, *Politics, Power and Bureaucracy in France: The Administrative Elite* (Princeton, N.J.: Princeton University Press, 1974), pp. 391–415.

Index

Pitt Series in Policy and Institutional Studies

Bert A. Rockman, Editor